AGAINST ALL ODDS

Compiled and Edited by
Adam Bushby & Rob MacDonald

HALCYON
PUBLISHING

PRAISE FOR
AGAINST ALL ODDS

"What a treasure trove this is, rich with gems of celebration
for that most excellent thing, the day when the minnow
humbles the shark. Excitement and comedy blend here with
rage and bewilderment in some fine and vivid writing.
We get the full picture — the when and the where, the how
and the why — with much sharp insight and a good
dose of sharp wit. Cracking stuff."

Pete Davies, Best-selling Author of
All Played Out: The Full Story of Italia '90

"Some of the greatest stories in the history of international
football, told with an eye for the beauty of detail.
Page after page of sheer delight."

**Patrick Barclay, Author of biographies of Sir Matt Busby,
Sir Alex Ferguson, Jose Mourinho and Herbert Chapman**

"Joe Gaetjens ... Pak Doo-ik ... Lakhdar Belloumi ... Gerry
Armstrong ... François Omam-Biyik ... Papa Bouba Diop
... you boys administered historic beatings. Glorious proof that
underdogs have their day, even in the World Cup."

Mike Calvin, Award-winning sportswriter

"Pure nostalgia for football lovers — this book serves as the
perfect reminder that nothing quite beats the euphoria of
a World Cup upset. A must-read for anyone who loves the
beautiful game."

Kelly Somers, Presenter and broadcaster

"The greatest football tournament in the world demands the greatest writers ... and here they are! If Qatar 2022 is even half as entertaining as this, we'll be very lucky people indeed."

Scott Murray, *The Guardian*

"Superb. A beautifully-crafted journey through the World Cup at its gloriously unpredictable best, lovingly told by some of football's most gifted storytellers."

Musa Okwonga, *The Ringer*

"Having been involved in football finance for many years, it is easy to forget why you fell in love with the game. This book is a reminder of those shared moments of unparalleled joy, despair and tension that are part of the makeup of all football fans. The quality of the writing, the recollection of individual moments of brilliance, and sometimes tragedy, serve as a testimony to this most universal of games."

Kieran Maguire, Best-selling Author of *The Price of Football*

"No one loves an Overdog! In fact, the word doesn't even exist. Great stories of snarling teeth and bite marks on prestigious bums."

Ned Boulting, Journalist and presenter

"A book about underdogs produced by a set of writers this talented may seem like a contradiction in terms, as if a group of Man City fatcats had been asked to write a report about scraping by on a budget. In practice, as these smart, funny, and wide-ranging essays demonstrate, the pairing produces an ideal combination of gifted storytellers and thrilling stories. A delightful excuse to revisit some of the greatest games ever played."

Brian Phillips, *The Ringer*

ABOUT THE AUTHORS

HARRY PEARSON

Harry Pearson is a columnist for *When Saturday Comes* and a regular on the magazine's podcast. His first book *The Far Corner – A Mazy Dribble through North-East Football* has been in print for over 25 years. He won the MCC/Cricket Society Book of the Year prize in 2011 and 2018. @camsell59

TIM VICKERY

Tim Vickery is a long-time contributor to *BBC Sport*, *ESPN* and *World Soccer*, and can be seen on-screen regularly in his country of residence, Brazil. @Tim_Vickery

ANDI THOMAS

Andi Thomas has been writing about football since 2010, and has written for *Eurosport*, *SB Nation*, *Football365*, *The Blizzard*, *ESPN* and various others. He used to blog at *Twisted Blood*. His first solo book, *Underground Overground: The fault lines of football clubs*, was published by Halcyon in 2021. He has also co-authored two Premier League season diaries, both available from Ockley Books. He lives in south London. @andi_thomas

TOBIAS JONES

Tobias Jones is the author of nine books, including the bestselling *The Dark Heart of Italy* and the Telegraph Football Book of the Year for 2020, *Ultra: the Underworld of Italian Football*. He appears regularly in the British and Italian press, and has written and presented documentaries for both the BBC and for RAI. His most recent book is *The Po: an Elegy for Italy's Longest River*. He lives in Parma. @Tobias_Italia

ADAM BUSHBY

Adam Bushby is one half of the (almost-defunct) football blog, *Magic Spongers*, and has written for *The Blizzard*, *When Saturday Comes*, *Football365* and *Nutmeg* among others. He co-edited, contributed to and compiled *From the Jaws of Victory*, an anthology about glorious defeat. This and other football books can be found at his publishing house, Halycon Publishing, which he co-owns with Rob MacDonald. @magicspongers & @HalcyonPublish1

DAVID WINNER

David Winner is a journalist and author based in London. His books on football and culture include *Brilliant Orange* (about the Netherlands), *Those Feet* (England) and *Around the World in 90 Minutes* (everywhere else). @dwinnera

RAPHAEL HONIGSTEIN

Raphael Honigstein is a London-based football journalist who originally hails from Munich, Germany. He writes for *The Athletic* and *Der Spiegel*, does TV stuff for *Sky Deutschland* and *BT Sport*, and is the author of *Bring the Noise*, *Das Reboot* and *BFG*. @honigstein

ROB BAGCHI

Rob Bagchi now writes about cricket and football for the *Telegraph* after 12 years in a similar role at the *Guardian*. He is the author of *The Biography of Leeds United*, co-author of *The Unforgiven* and the autobiographies of Frank McLintock, Norman Whiteside and Paul Merson. @unforgivenrb

SIMON HART

Simon Hart is the author of *World In Motion: The Inside Story of Italia '90* and *Here We Go: Everton in the 1980s*. He has written about football for 25 years — for newspapers and magazines in the UK as well as for UEFA's website and publications — and has reported on five World Cups in that time. @simon22ph

PAUL DOYLE

After peddling shillelaghs and inflatable sheep, Paul Doyle became a football writer for the *Irish Times* before moving to England and doing the same for the *Guardian* for 18 years. Now back in Dublin, he remains a writer with a particular interest in Irish, European and African football.

JAMES MONTAGUE

James Montague is an award-winning author and journalist from Chelmsford, Essex. He writes for the *New York Times*, the *Bleacher Report, Delayed Gratification* and *The Blizzard*, amongst others, and has reported from over 80 different countries and unrecognised territories. He is the author of four football books — *When Friday Comes: Football, War and Revolution in the Middle East, Thirty One Nil: On the Road With Football's Outsiders, The Billionaires Club: The Unstoppable Rise of Football's Super-Rich Owners* and *1312: Among the Ultras* — winning the Telegraph Football Book of the Year twice. @JamesPiotr

PHILIPPE AUCLAIR

Philippe Auclair is the author of *The Enchanted Kingdom of Tony Blair* (in French), *Cantona: the Rebel Who Would Be King*, which was named NSC Football Book of the Year, as well as Football Book of the Year in France in 2010, and a biography of Thierry Henry, *Lonely At The Top*. He writes for *France Football* and appears regularly on the *Guardian Football Weekly* podcast. @PhilippeAuclair

GUILLEM BALAGUE

Guillem Balague is an award-winning author, broadcaster and journalist. His biographies (on Rafael Benitez, Pep Guardiola, Lionel Messi (authorised), Cristiano Ronaldo, Mauricio Pochettino and Diego Maradona) are bestsellers in more than a dozen languages. His biography of Ronaldo won Telegraph Football Book of the Year in 2017 and his last five have been award-nominated. He has been the face of Spanish football in the Anglo-Saxon world for more than three decades through his punditry for *Sky Sports* and now *LaLiga TV*. He currently works for the BBC, CBS, ITV and Cope Radio. He is the host of the Pure Football podcast and Chairman of Biggleswade United. @GuillemBalague

Published by Halcyon Publishing

First published 2022

ISBN: 978-1-9196240-3-7

Front cover design by Steve Leard
Layout & design by Michael Kinlan, Rob MacDonald

Printed & bound by:
CMP (UK) Limited
G3 The Fulcrum
Vantage Way
Poole
Dorset
BH12 4NU

AGAINST
ALL ODDS

CONTENTS

FOREWORD

BARRY DAVIES

> I was lucky enough to be in a television commentary box for 10 World Cups from 1966 to 2002, and for five of the matches chosen by the writers in this fascinating book to qualify as 'Against All Odds', I had the microphone in hand.

In 1966, having come through a few tests, I was chosen as the youngest commentator on the ITV team and sent to the north-east to cover Russia, Chile, Italy and the barely-known players of North Korea, who played all their matches at Ayresome Park, Middlesbrough, and were adopted by the local fans. Their team would provide the upset of the tournament. The stadium has long since become a housing estate, but in one garden, just to the left of what was the penalty spot at the Holgate End, is a bronze cast of a boot commemorating the point from which Pak Doo-ik scored the goal that beat Italy on that memorable evening. In spite of politics, the connection between the fans and 'their team' remained strong for many years.

What I said about the match I have little idea, but I remember very clearly the words of Frank Bough, the BBC commentator that night, for their clarity, simplicity and the way they were expressed: "What is happening here, North Korea have beaten Italy!" The disbelief was palpable.

That the crowd played a big part in the victory of North Korea, there was no doubt. But this was the British supporting the underdog: it was not until what proved to be my last World Cup (2002) that I found the most enthusiastic home crowd, first when South Korea beat Italy and then even more so in the quarter-final against Spain. Their influence was incredible and according to the losers, affected the referees. They had an attractive team to watch and an interesting coach in Guus Hiddink. As the winning penalty left the foot of the team captain, Hong Myung-bo, the stadium in Gwangju erupted. This commentator remained silent. The pictures and the sound told the story.

In 1974, I took my seat in the Volksparkstadion in Hamburg for what promised to be the most politically-charged football match of all time — West Germany v East Germany. It was a clash of two political systems, of polar opposites. The Cold War may not have been as it was in the sixties, but I confess that my thoughts went back to those days I experienced in my National Service, driving through Checkpoint Charlie and seeing the greyness behind the wall. In those days, Berlin was still divided by barbed wire and concrete. It was a strange feeling and very quickly the approach of the two sides represented the character of their countries — the West expected to win, had their chances but didn't seem sure, the East had brought along part of their defensive wall.

The only goal came in the 78th minute when Jürgen Sparwasser chased a long ball, eluded the centre-half with a clever headed flick and fired the ball high into the net. His effort brought victory to the East and their 1,500 Stasi-cleared supporters in the stadium and palpitations to the West, with the ensuing arguments over selection and who was running the team lasting until their second match in the next round (a 4-2 victory over Sweden). However, losing the match never to be repeated put the West into the much weaker group. Defeats by Brazil and Holland would follow for the East, while the West ended up with the trophy in their hands.

The next upset in the series I witnessed first-hand was the opening match of Italia '90, which featured the holders, Argentina, and Cameroon, whose style of crude yet calculated tackles were a severe test for the referee and the speedy Argentinian, Claudio Caniggia, who was so often a victim. The referee, Michel Vautrot, from France, had the task of enacting Fifa's warning that officials would be severe on foul play, and he gave a red card to two Cameroonians. The first, just after the hour, was to

Kana-Biyik for a trip, which seemed a little harsh. The second came late on in the game with Cameroon hanging on to a lead given them by Omam-Biyik six minutes after his brother had been dismissed. The cross-field, running charge by Benjamin Massing, after two of his colleagues had failed in their illegal attempts to stop the speeding Caniggia, was worthy of an arrest for grievous bodily harm.

The victory over the holders was much welcomed by the crowd and the popularity of the African challengers grew as they made their way, in less aggressive style, past Romania to top their group and then, with their 37-year-old 'guiding star' Roger Milla coming from the bench to score twice, beat Colombia in the second round. They could, maybe should, have won the quarter-final against England, but after leading 2-1 and often looking the better side, they gave away two of the stupidest penalties I have ever seen. Fortunately for England, Gary Lineker held his nerve from the spot in extra time.

The fifth game in this compilation that I put my voice to live was at the aptly-named Giants Stadium, for this was a 'David against Goliath' clash. The Republic of Ireland against Italy at USA '94 saw two of New York's largest and certainly most vocal diasporas go toe to toe. The stadium was expected to be awash with Italian supporters, New Jersey being an Italian stronghold after all. However, on the day, it was as if it was completely decked out in Irish tricolours.

Improbably, after just 12 minutes, Ray Houghton's scuttle allowed him to find a yard of space and dink a chip past Gianluca Pagliuca to send the large and vocal Irish crowd into raptures — and the boys in green one up. And there the score would stay until the end. An English manager (Jack Charlton), a Scottish goal-scorer, a truly Irish tale.

I think the Americans did a good job hosting the World Cup finals of '94 and the crowd's knowledge of the game had improved a lot from the Olympic tournament eight years earlier … huge applause for a long clearance going nowhere but gaining distance was rarely heard. I had many interesting matches and enjoyed seeing more of this huge country. And, of course, I was pleased to be offered the commentary seat for the final with Trevor Brooking and Terry Venables. But the match played in high temperatures was hugely disappointing. That Roberto Baggio, who at times had carried Italy to the final, should have blazed the last penalty of the shoot-out high into the sky was very hard on him, but only Romário ever looked like a star in the match. Exhaustion stole the day.

On that occasion, and as this book beautifully illustrates, football rarely exists in a vacuum. There are always stories there for the telling which go far beyond 90 minutes and this phenomenal array of writers make sure that these 'tales of the underdog' are described in stunning detail. Upsets capture the imagination and many create legends which should be celebrated. There are 13 contenders here for sure.

Like most commentators, I imagine, I am often asked which was the best goal I commentated on. The answer, for all the fact that it knocked my home country out, is Diego Maradona's second in the quarter-final for Argentina against England in Mexico City in 1986. I said it was 'magnificent'. I hope you feel that word comes to mind when you finish reading this remarkable book.

INTRODUCTION

ADAM BUSHBY & ROB MACDONALD

The ground of a second-tier German football club might seem an odd place to begin a journey through sensational World Cup upsets, but it's a place that boasts a rich heritage.

This is the Fritz-Walter-Stadion in Kaiserslautern, south-west Germany, a characterful yet boxy, straight-lined stadium home to the city's 2. Bundesliga side since 1920.

Betze, as the stadium is also known given its location on the Betzenberg hill, was the recipient of a €76.5m upgrade in the lead-up to the 2006 World Cup, at which it hosted five matches. But beyond the increased seating capacity, a shiny new media centre and, if it's your thing, a new floodlight system, was an addition that looked to the past.

"The role of outsider", the inscription on Richard Henkel's sculpture reads, "is the key to the treasure chamber of great power which — if awoken and spurred on — releases energy which is energy that moves mountains".

Fritz Walter's likeness is included among the five men cast in bronze in front of the stadium they named after him. An illustrious goal-scorer, he racked up a scarcely credible 357 of them in 364 games for Kaiserslautern either side of the Second World War, and 33 in 61 for his country. What's more, Walter captained West Germany to their first World Cup final victory against the Mighty Magyars of Hungary in 1954 — the event this statue commemorates. The 'outsider' quote is attributed to Sepp Herberger, the team's manager.

As commemorative statements go, the statue is an unassuming one. As statements commemorating unexpected World Cup final victories go, it is barely perceptible. In that way, and in

Herberger's summation of the ingredients needed to 'move mountains', it is the perfect starting point: there may be plenty of ingrained disparities between sporting haves and have-nots, but occasionally, unexpectedly, they can be overcome.

In many ways, this is a book about levels. Levels and layers, actually. Levels being raised, levels being dropped. Layers being added, and layers being removed. You'll know the basic details of many of the matches included in this collection, but what we set out to do with this book is explore the contexts for these shocks, to tell the stories behind the disparities — and those that overcame them — that made them so surprising. To that end, we are helped by an astonishing collection of authors to whom we are indebted for their time, expertise and extraordinary writing. This is a level up for us, as well.

Along with the prestige of the tournament, and these writers, are the games themselves, which represent some of the most spectacular sporting accomplishments of their eras — staggering results on a global stage. Documenting these stories together is also to tell the historic journey of football as it appeared and then thrived on the global stage.

The biggest disparity of them all — between professional and amateur — was still in place in the World Cups of the 1950s; statistically, the USA's victory over England in 1950 is still the least likely outcome of any game ever played at the finals at just 9.5%, according to research reported by the BBC in 2018. Add to that Uruguay's shock triumph over Brazil and the-then-still amateur West German victory over a team who would only lose once — that game — in six years, and you already have a book's-worth of disbelief from just three tournaments. But there are, inevitably, many angles, many ways to cause an upset.

There was a shabby innocence to those competitions, but it was quickly expunged: you don't become the most popular sport in the world without people seeking to exploit your pulling power. Especially not when it can be broadcast to the masses. The politically-charged World Cups of the 1970s, not least in

Argentina in 1978, furnish us with different types of upsets, different types of shocks and a foreboding pre-cursor to the authorities' comfort with less-than-palatable human rights records and dictatorships.In turn, it shows the pronounced willingness of the latter to manipulate the sport and the tournament for political gain and legitimacy on the world stage.

That should inform, but not wholly detract from, the joy inherent to many of these games as isolated results, all of which can be filed in our favourite folder of the unheralded underdog sticking it to the man, whether by 'the man' we're talking about former colonial masters, the arrogant, the entitled or the ignorant — a feature of the tournament through time. See Middlesbrough's uncommon bond with a North Korean team that embarrassed the Italians in 1966, Algeria's glorious debut at the World Cup in 1982, Cameroon's dancing, convention-bending shock of Argentina in 1990, Ireland's sweaty, breathless victory over Italy in 1994, Senegal bloodying dysfunctional French noses and the explosion of emotion as South Korea rode a wave of national pride all the way to a semi-final in 2002.

It's noticeable, however, that our choices for genuine 'upsets' seemed to run out after the World Cup in Japan and South Korea. There are reasons for that, such as distances from the results themselves that can give them new colour, new meaning, new resonance. We — as is well-known — look at the tournaments of our youth and the storied figures from history largely through rose-tinted glasses; we called our publishing house 'Halcyon' for a reason. We have the benefit of half of these stories already being accepted folklore before we were born, with most of the more troubling socio-political contexts processed out in the re-telling. But increasingly — if we look at the last 20 years anyway — it feels to us like the game is different now from the cohort of stories told here.

(That's not to say that the upsets contained in this anthology were unique in somehow bringing about particularly meaningful change, whether sporting or otherwise — they didn't, not in the World Cups in which they occurred, and certainly not in the world at large. At a tournament level, the only upsets that directly altered the destination of the trophy were Uruguay and West Germany in the fifties — Walter and his team of course providing a profound exception by seeding a post-war sense of recovery and pride in a reeling nation. Upsets seem to disappear once the finals reach their knock-out stages: only eight of 79 teams to have been to the finals have ever won the trophy.)

Either way, the vast majority of these results feel as though they would be impossible now — things are increasingly weighted in favour of the haves, not the have-nots. Expanding tournaments, although it does give less-decorated nations more opportunities to qualify, also means the real superpowers have greater room for manoeuvre in the event of disastrous results. The advent of more substitutes favours Argentina not Azerbaijan, England not Eritrea. It is now a near-impossible hegemony to break.

Football's great power is increasingly employed without great responsibility. To suggest the sport holds up a mirror to society is to assign it too passive a role. To pretend that a tournament can take place without its social and political context is a myth. A World Cup in Qatar takes the contradiction we all have to live with at the heart of the sport — the joy we can take from its community, the comfort, the drama, the meaning we imbue it with vs. the naked profiteering and cover for all sorts of nefarious practices — to the *nth* degree, certainly at the elite level. With unfettered investment in clubs all over the world by nation states, sportswashing is now a completely brazen foreign policy and is colouring our cultural discourse more than ever, almost exclusively to its detriment. We should have been denouncing a World Cup in Russia. We very much denounce the 2022 edition.

All of which, we can admit, may make this a slightly hypocritical book to have created at this particular moment in time. Trust us, it doesn't sit even the slightest bit easily that many more people have died building the stadiums than will play in them, nor that a host nation of a supposedly globally inclusive tournament has draconian restrictions on the rights of various sections of its society firmly enshrined in law. But we love football, and we love the World Cup, and sincerely hope there is the appetite within the sport to ensure it lives up to its billing as a force for good.

For our part, we've tried to make these stories representative of the full spectrum of World Cup history (and Qatar will take its place in that history, for better or worse). And by giving context to their achievements we are celebrating the players and coaches that took part who, as you'll see from the vast array that have also given their voices to these chapters — found collective strength in each other, found a way to overcome the odds and offer joy, solace or succour to their supporters. The football world delighted in their unexpected triumphs and saluted their extraordinary efforts. We do too — they say far more about what will always remain football's saving grace than we ever could. Overall, it's these values that we hope speak through this book. The game, and the vast majority of the people in it, still have the power to move mountains.

BRAZIL 1950

USA
1

ENGLAND
0

USA	ENGLAND
1. Frank Borghi	1. Bert Williams
3. Harry Keuogh	2. Alf Ramsey
17. Joseph Maca	3. John Aston
14. Edward McIlvenny (c)	4. Billy Wright (c)
4. Charles Colombo	5. Lawrence Hughes
6. Walter Bahr	6. James Dickinson
7. Francis Wallace	7. Tom Finney
8. Virgino Pariani	8. Wilf Mannion
18. Joseph Gaetjens ⊕ (38')	9. Roy Bentley
10. John Souza-Benavides	10. Stan Mortensen
11. Edward Souza-Neto	11. James Mullen
Manager: William Jeffrey	Manager: Walter Winterbottom

Estádio
Independência

Belo Horizonte,
Minas Gerais, Brazil

ATTENDANCE
10,151

REFEREE
Generoso Dattilo (Italy)

HARRY PEARSON

> The arrival of Stanley Rous at the Football
> Association headquarters in London was a
> cause of no little consternation to the clerks and
> committee men who oversaw English football.

Rous' predecessor, the autocratic and stately Sir Frederick Wall
— who had run English football from 1895 until 1934 — came
to work in a morning suit with tails, a top hat, spats and shoes
burnished to a reflective sheen. By contrast, the FA's new secretary
dressed like a hooting denizen of Bertie Wooster's club. The sight
of his Prince of Wales check suit, a florid silk square billowing from
the chest pocket, caused lips to purse at 22 Lancaster Gate. When
Rous showed up one morning wearing a pair of houndstooth
plus-fours, eyebrows were raised so high they disappeared down
the backs of blazer collars. The FA Chairman, Charles Clegg,
was so appalled he sent Rous a letter of rebuke warning against
further sartorial outrages.

Clothes were not the worst of it, though. There were even
more worrying aspects of Stanley Rous. The man had that
most un-English of all things; ideas. A former international
referee, the dapper chap from Watford was a globalist and a
moderniser. He wanted to forge closer links with the rest of the
world. He demanded that England engage with foreigners. He had
— the horror! — married a Frenchwoman.

Sir Frederick would have been even more alarmed by these
developments than by Rous' polka-dot ties. The severe Victorian
had always kept "the continentals" at arms-length, refusing to
allow his England to play in international tournaments. Officially,
it was a dispute over the payment of compensation to amateur
players which led Wall to withdraw England from the world

game's governing body Fifa in 1924. Yet to many it seemed that preserving the Corinthian ideals of English amateurism was merely a pretext. Sir Frederick sensed that no good would come of English professionals rubbing shoulders with Italians, Uruguayans and the like. Who could tell what monstrous practices impressionable working-class men would learn from such encounters? England did play the occasional match against the nations of mainland Europe, of course. But these were more like those punitive expeditions carried out by the British Army against the unruly tribesmen of The Empire. They were swift, smartly organised and brief. A well-aimed punch to the chin — quite literally in the case of the notoriously violent match with Italy at Highbury in 1934 — to remind everybody who the masters were and then back home in time for tea.

This sensible policy had worked. England had preserved a reputation as the Kings of Football throughout the first half of the twentieth century with minimum risk. But when Sir Frederick died in 1944, his influence was interred with him. In 1946, thanks to Rous, England re-joined Fifa. That same year, the national team had embraced the continental trend and appointed a coach, Walter Winterbottom. A PE teacher who had played as an amateur for Manchester United, the pipe-smoking coach spoke in such a pedantic and long-winded style that by the time he got to the end of a sentence most players had forgotten how it started. Not yet content with his revolution, Rous went even further — apparently determined to hazard everything — he announced that he was sending England to play in the 1950 World Cup in Brazil.

Faced with radical change, the FA's bureaucrats did what all long-embedded civil servants do in such situations, they went along with things, up to a point. Coach Winterbottom was paid a meagre salary of £1,000 a year (his Brazilian counterpart, Juan Lopez Fontana earned that sum in a month) and he was not allowed actually to pick his own team. This duty generally fell to the FA's selection committee, but in Brazil would be handled by Arthur

Drewry, a Grimsby fish merchant who had become president of the Football League in 1949, more through his behind-the-scenes smoothness than through any great knowledge of the game.

Lancaster Gate's approach to the World Cup was equally half-hearted. Despite the fact that England had never played in South America, or, indeed, against any South American opponents, the FA did not feel it necessary to send an envoy to Brazil before the tournament to inspect accommodation and training facilities. Nor did attending the finals themselves seem much of a priority — only Rouse and Drewry actually bothered to travel to Rio de Janeiro, where, naturally, they selected more luxurious accommodation for themselves than for the team. Furthermore, the FA ordered England's greatest player, Stanley Matthews, to go on a goodwill tour of the USA and Canada shortly before the tournament started and allowed Manchester United players John Aston and Harry Cockburn to make a similar trip with their club. The three players would arrive later than the rest of the squad, giving them less time to train with the team and to acclimatise. Matthews would be delayed so long by his spurious diplomatic duties he wouldn't get to South America until after England's opening match with Chile. To the shrewd and ultra-professional Blackpool winger, the FA's attitude smacked of laziness and amateurism. Other nations complained that the English were arrogant. But a little arrogance is no bad thing in sport. The men who ran the English game were something far more damaging — they were complacent.

When the draw for the finals was made in the conference hall of the Itamaraty Palace on the afternoon of May 22, 1950, nobody from the FA was in attendance. England had been selected as one of four seeded teams, alongside hosts Brazil, holders Italy and previous winners Uruguay. They were allocated Pool 2. When the silver sphere holding the numbered balls representing the other 12 nations was spun, England found themselves paired with balls 2, 3 and 4: Chile, Spain and the USA. That they had avoided the Olympic Champions Sweden — who had beaten them 3-1 in

Stockholm the year before — might have been greeted with a sigh of relief in London, had anyone been paying attention. England, however, did not care who their opponents were. They may have been the only team in Brazil who had never appeared in a World Cup before, had limited experience of playing overseas and none whatsoever of the pressures of tournament football, but so what? They were England and the others weren't.

The USA did not much bother about the draw either, but for quite the opposite reason. Expectations in the United States were so low they could have crawled under a duck. Amongst the tiny minority of citizens who had any expectations, that is. As Walter Bahr, the Philadelphia Nationals half-back who was as near to being what the British press would have dubbed a "stalwart" as North American soccer possessed, observed: "A very, very small percentage of people in the States knew what the World Cup was about. I didn't know much about it either, other than that I knew some players who'd played in the 1930 and 1934 World Cups".

Though the USA had excelled in reaching the semi-finals in the first of those tournaments, since then soccer's popularity in the States had plummeted like a gannet spying sprats. The national team had taken such regular canings from European sides an observer might have suspected masochism. In 1934, they'd been thrashed 7-1 by Italy. At the 1948 Olympics, they'd been knocked out in the first round, whacked 9-0 by the Italian amateur team at Griffin Park, Brentford. Since that humiliating defeat they'd been battered 11-0 by Norway, 5-0 by Northern Ireland and 4-0 by Scotland. They were 500-1 outsiders to lift the trophy and even that seemed like the fever-dream of a crazed optimist.

In the USA, football was a niche interest, a game played largely by immigrants and their children. In the lead-up to the World Cup, the United States Soccer Federation placed adverts in newspapers that served Italian, Spanish and Portuguese-speaking communities, attempting to attract new players from the vast wave of arrivals escaping a Europe devastated by the Second World War. Trial matches were arranged for those who responded and, for a while at least, as Bahr observed drily, the horrors of the previous six years worked for the benefit of US football.

Unlike the stoutly homogenous English team, the US squad was an ethnic patchwork. Frank Borghi, Charlie Colombo, Gino Pariani and Frank "Pee Wee" Wallace (whose family had Anglicised their name from Valicenti) had grown up in an area of St Louis that in those racially charged times was known as "Dago Hill" and played for the city's outstanding team Simpkins-Ford (named in honour of its sponsor, a local car dealership). John and Ed Souza, who were not related to each other, were part of a close-knit Portuguese community in Fall River, Massachusetts, and played their football for Ponta Delgada, an amateur side of such high calibre they'd been picked en bloc to represent the USA at the North American Championships in Cuba in 1947 (they'd lost both matches, shipping 10 goals). Joe Maca was a Belgian who'd played as full-back for Brussels club La Forestoise; Ed McIlvenny and Jack Hynes were both Scottish; winger Adam Wolanin was a Pole who'd escaped for the USA after the Nazis invaded his homeland; Joe Gaetjens came from Haiti, though the British journalists in Brazil would, routinely and for no reason anyone can fathom, refer to him as Argentinean and quite often as Larry.

While a number of the Americans were paid by their clubs, none were full-time professionals. Most trained two nights a week and played on Sunday. Many played on cinder pitches. Bahr earned $50 a week as a Junior High School teacher and picked up $25 per game with the Nationals in the American Soccer League. Pariani worked in a canning factory, Borghi in a brickyard, pocketing extra cash driving the hearse for his uncle's funeral home; McIlvenny delivered eggs, Wallace drove a liquor truck, Harry Keough was a mailman. Gaetjens was earning a wage playing for Brookhattan in the ASL and also helped out as a washer up at club owner Rudy Diaz' restaurant. The latter detail was picked up by the US media and as time wore on Gaetjens would increasingly be portrayed as an Ellis Island immigrant, a member of the huddled masses, ignorant of modern American ways and with superstitious beliefs in omens and voodoo. In truth, he was from an influential Haitian family, privately educated, fluent in three languages and had come to New York to study accountancy at Columbia University. After the World Cup, Gaetjens would settle in Paris and play for the glamorous Racing Club. As plucky underdogs go, the Haitian forward was more pedigree labradoodle than rescue terrier, but that didn't quite fit with the future legend.

Despite their different backgrounds, the US players shared common traits. They were modest in both their attitudes and their habits (few of them drank), self-deprecating, tough and tenacious. Many of them had seen active service in the War. Wallace had been captured by the Germans shortly after D-Day and spent 16 months in a POW camp, Keough served on a destroyer in the Pacific, Borghi was an army medic in Europe, winning two purple hearts and two bronze stars for gallantry, Maca had been decorated for bravery fighting in the Belgian resistance, Hynes badly wounded in the Battle of the Bulge. They were used to discipline and hardship. The clean-living Bahr — who never swore on or off the field — described the team in typical down-to-earth fashion: "We had a pretty good set of players. There were no finger-pointers. The chemistry was right".

Though they had played fewer international matches than the English team, their experience of the sort of conditions they might expect to find in Brazil was far greater. While England had qualified without leaving the British Isles (they had finished top in the Home International Championships ahead of Northern Ireland, Wales and Scotland), the USA had travelled to Mexico City in September 1949 to compete in the North American Championships.The matches were played at high altitude, in sizzling temperatures and in front of raucous, capacity crowds. The hosts crushed the USA 6-0 and 6-2, but the Americans rallied to qualify in second place thanks to a 5-2 win over Cuba.

The US players had relished the hostile environment in Mexico, it had helped them bond as a team. Not that everyone in the

USA was working with the same common purpose. Football administrators seemed to have been put on the earth to irritate the people who actually played the game and the American versions were no exception. When selecting the US team, the USSF tended to favour the players from clubs who competed in the National Amateur Cup, rather than the semi-pros from the ASL. Bahr thought this nonsensical, since to his mind the ASL (In which he, Gaetjens, McIlvenny, Hynes and Maca played) was the highest standard of football in the country. He kept his thoughts to himself, however. Hynes was not so circumspect. The Scot complained loudly to a New York journalist about the situation shortly after helping the USA qualify for Brazil. His comments were published. The winger from Lochgelly never played for the USA again.

The lack of interest in, or even knowledge of, the World Cup amongst most Americans also created problems for the US players. When Philadelphia Nationals' Benny McLaughlin — one of the country's most potent strikers — approached his factory boss to ask for time off to go to Brazil, the reply was straightforward: "Go if you want, but there won't be a job for you when you get back". Fearing for his livelihood, McLaughlin opted to stay at home. The team might have lost inside forward Gino Pariani, too. His wedding was scheduled for a few days before the squad departed for South America. With his wife Janet's blessing, he agreed to fly down to Rio to join the team midway through his honeymoon in Mexico.

There was even greater disruption when it came to the coach. Budapest-born Erno Schwartz, who managed the New York Americans in the ASL, had led the team through qualifying, but a couple of weeks before the team were due to leave for South America, he announced that he wouldn't be travelling with them. There was a frantic scramble to find a replacement. The man chosen was William Jeffrey, 57-year-old coach of Pennsylvania State College. It was just the stroke of luck the USA needed.

Born and raised in Newhaven, a fishing village just north of Edinburgh, Jeffrey had arrived in Pennsylvania in 1920. A keen footballer, he quickly began to organise and play in the works teams that dominated soccer in the Quaker State. In 1926, he was acting as player-manager of the Altoona Railway team when his skills caught the eye of Penn State athletics director, Hugo Bezdek. Bezdek offered Jeffrey the chance to become Penn State's sixth coach in seven years with the added incentive of earning extra as a teacher in the industrial engineering department. The Scot accepted. Though he favoured the well-worn, traditional British WM formation, Jeffrey's other methods were less orthodox. A big, craggy man with a voice that could shake rust off steel, he inspired his players by reciting Robert Burns poetry to them before games in his broad accent, illustrated his tactical points with anecdotes form his own years as a player and encouraged his team to sing together on the team bus ('I belong to Glasgow' was a particular favourite). It worked.

Penn State won their first national championship in Jeffrey's first season. Two more followed in quick succession. With Jeffrey in charge, the college became one of the powerhouses of US soccer. (Such terms were relative, of course. When Jeffrey took his all-conquering side on a tour of Scotland they were gubbed 7-2 by Gala Fairydean.) Jeffrey, like the US players, was modest and humble. When asked the secret of his success, he replied simply, "my love of the game".

Thanks to bans, withdrawals and general lack of interest, Jeffrey was able to assemble a squad of only 18 players rather than the regular 22. They travelled to Brazil by steamer out of New York, stopping off in Cuba on the way. In Rio, they were based at an army camp at the foot of Sugarloaf Mountain. Conditions were Spartan but, as Bahr said, "we'd lived through the Depression and many of the team had served in the military. There were no complaints". The same would not be true of their future opponents.

England came to the tournaments as 3-1 favourites. This wasn't just a last kick of Empire. England had an impressive record in the post-War era: they'd played 30 matches and lost just four of them. In the run up to the World Cup, they'd beaten Wales, Scotland, Belgium and fellow finalists Switzerland. Yet there were people who complained about the make-up of the squad, or fretted that England might be undone by the heat and erratic foreign refereeing.

The team was also missing one of its best players. Stoke City's Neil Franklin was a ball-playing centre-half and one of the best defenders in world football. Like many of his team-mates, Franklin had become increasingly frustrated with his lot. Football League rules allowed players to be paid a maximum of £12 a week, a fraction of the wages pros in Spain and Italy earned, while a system known as retain-and-transfer made it impossible for them to leave a club without the express permission of its directors. It was iniquitous and unjust (Franklin's England colleague Wilf Mannion called it "a slave contract"). The situation left many top English players feeling bitter and aggrieved. Now a solution in the unlikely form of an unsanctioned "bandit" league in Colombia had presented itself. As the English season wound to a close it emerged that Franklin had negotiated a mind-boggling £170 a week contract for himself to play in Bogota. Fearing an exodus, the FA barred him from selection and banned him for life. England skipper Billy Wright — who thought Franklin "the lynchpin of the side" — confessed to understanding why his team-mate wanted the money, but criticised the timing and said he felt like "kicking him up the backside". Franklin's replacement was Liverpool's Laurie Hughes. Tall, fair and jug-eared, the Scouser's international career was destined to be brief and sacrificial.

Even without Franklin, England looked to the outside world like an unstoppable force. Insured for £250,000 — an extraordinary sum in an era when the world record transfer fee was the £26,500 Preston North End had paid Sheffield Wednesday for Eddie Quigley — the team was led by wing-half Wright, the Golden Boy of English football, whose crinkly blond hair, good manners, mild temper and singular lack of sex appeal made him the ideal hero for every

English child. In goal was Wright's Wolverhampton Wanderers' team-mate, Bert Williams, a brilliantly athletic keeper who flew around his area as if suspended on wires. England's right-back was Spurs' Alf Ramsey, dour, tough-tackling, technically gifted and tactically astute. On the left was Aston, who'd learned his football under the watchful eye of Matt Busby. Next to Wright in midfield was "Gentleman" Jimmy Dickinson, a gifted passer of the ball who'd helped Portsmouth win back-to-back league titles and would never be booked or sent off in a career that spanned 1,000 games. It was the forward line, however, that gave opponents night sweats. Preston North End's Tom Finney — probably the only man ever to turn down a fortune to play for Real Madrid so he could focus on his plumbing business — was at outside left with the fair-haired Mannion, the man Finney said played "like an angel sent down from heaven" at inside right. The rampaging Blackpool forward, Stan Mortensen was at inside left and operating as centre-forward was the swift and intelligent Roy "Gently" Bentley of Chelsea. Bizarrely, England's greatest player and arguably the most famous footballer in the world at that point, Stanley Matthews, never quite seemed to find a place. For though the English public loved the tricky Blackpool winger and clamoured for his inclusion, the FA men who picked the team were wary. Matthews was quiet and unassuming but something about his talent, pride and celebrity, the way he — the son of a Potteries barber — had managed his money so cleverly he'd become, despite the maximum wage, the wealthy owner of a string of hotels, unsettled the little men of Lancaster Gate. They omitted Matthews from the England team at every opportunity as if in an attempt to diminish him. The great man had not appeared in any of England's World Cup warm-up matches. His chosen replacement at present was Jimmy Mullen, a chirpy Geordie who played alongside Wright and Williams at Molineux.

The England team had flown to Rio in a four-prop Lockheed Constellation, stopping off in Paris, Lisbon, Dakar and Recife on the way. After the 31-hour journey, they checked into the Luxor

Hotel overlooking Copacabana Beach. Though food rationing was still in place in Britain, the players were soon grumbling about the local cooking. The hotel chefs had no idea how to prepare the bland, stodgy grub the team were used to, and the smell of garlic pervading the restaurant was — to Winterbottom's way of thinking — appalling. Goalkeeper Williams claimed he was served "a bowl of olive oil with a rasher of bacon on the top" at one meal, while Finney shuddered at the sight of fried eggs "swimming in grease" and North-Easterner Mortensen summarised like a music hall comedian, "even the dustbins had ulcers". That nobody from the FA had thought to inspect the hotel before booking it spoke volumes. Meanwhile, the coach and his two trainers, Bill Ridding and Jimmy Trotter, fretted about the debilitating effects of the infernal foreign sun and banned the team from going on the beach after 10am.

Soon the English players were complaining of "tummy troubles" and of gasping for breath in the hot air. Part of their problems were surely psychological. The pernicious nature of overseas weather and kitchens had been drummed into the British from birth. Little wonder they seemed to have far more dramatic effects on the English than it did on players from other northern European countries — such as Sweden — whose climates and diets were little different from those in the British Isles.

Whether the problems were real or imagined, disquiet filled the England camp. Training sessions were lethargic and lackadaisical with many players preferring to play cricket rather than go through the drills Winterbottom had organised. The Brazilians, mindful that England were the greatest threat to the hosts, let off firecrackers throughout the night and jeered the English players on the rare occasions they were let out. There were rumours of Machiavellian scheming to strip Wright of the captaincy; agents from Bogota infiltrated the training ground and tried to tempt Mortensen, Aston and Cockburn to join Franklin in Colombia. Money remained a fractious issue. The England players in Brazil were paid £2 a day as a living allowance and £20 per game. Even those who featured in all three matches received just £120 for the trip. Those who never made the starting XI (and there were no substitutes except for injuries) cleared less than 60 quid. The USA's part-timers were on $100 a week — the unheralded amateurs earning more than the Kings of Football.

England's World Cup debut came against Chile in a 3 o'clock kick-off in the cavernous Maracana, where workmen were still hammering away at the finishing touches to the 200,000 capacity venue. The team performed listlessly, the 30,000 crowd booing their every touch. They won thanks to goals either side of half-time from Mortensen, heading home a Mullen cross, and Mannion, who slotted in a centre from Finney. It was fitful, yet the great Charlie Buchan saw enough to conclude that England were justifiable favourites to lift the Jules Rimet trophy. The England players were less convinced. The astute Bentley felt Winterbottom had "no tactics or game plan at all". As the team sat in the dressing room after the game with oxygen masks over their faces, the coach told them they could play much better. "What he didn't say," Bentley remarked bitterly years later, "was that we could also play far worse".

The USA's opening match was against Spain later that day, over 500 miles south at the Estadio Brito in Curitiba. Jeffrey handed Keough the captaincy. The Simpkins-Ford right-back was of Scottish descent, but he spoke Spanish and the coach thought that might come in handy. Keough and his team mates were battered from the opening whistle by a Spain side who passed and moved with the speed and precision of pistons. Yet somehow they held out and then, in the 17th minute, with what amounted to their only attack of the entire match they went 1-0 up, Pariani firing in a low cross shot from 25 yards. For the next hour, the USA, marshalled by Bahr, a strapping man with legs that, like Popeye's arms, appeared improbably wider at the bottom than the top, defended wholeheartedly and courageously as the Spanish pin-balled passes around the pitch. It seemed like the Americans might hold out, but then with fewer than 10 minutes remaining, centre-half

Charlie Colombo stopped in his pursuit of a ball he believed had gone out for a goal kick. The linesman disagreed and a Spaniard took advantage to whip in a cross. It was met by Silvestre Igoa of Valencia who levelled the score. With the Americans winded, Barcelona's Estanislau Basora gave his side the lead two minutes later. There were seconds remaining when Athletic Bilbao's Telmo Zarra added a third. It might have been a demoralising defeat but the US players shrugged it off. "We thought we'd lose by eight or nine," Borghi said, claiming the defeat as a moral victory.

A couple of days after the win over Chile, England flew up to Belo Horizonte on Dakota transport planes. They were relieved to get out of Rio. Their new base was Morro Velho, a thousand feet up in the hills above the city. It belonged to the British St John d'El Rey Mining Company, which owned one of the largest gold and silver mines on the planet. Morro Velho boasted a full-size football pitch with turf Winterbottom considered "the equal of that at the Maracana". There was a swimming pool, tennis and squash courts, table tennis and snooker tables. It was run by the British and much more to the team's liking than the garlic-tainted Hotel Luxor.

The mood of the squad seemed to lift. In the cooler air, they trained twice a day and according to reports in British newspapers "worked up a greater pace than ever before". They looked impressive and "their demeanour has been perfect".

The game against the USA was to be played at Estadio Independencia. Built for the World Cup the concrete oval with its uncovered stands had a capacity of 30,000. It had already hosted Yugoslavia's 3-0 win over Switzerland. Observers said that the pitch was small and the surface as hard and lumpy as a flophouse mattress. England were offered the opportunity to train on it, but preferred to stay in the hills where the players strolled around under the trees and organised a nightly snooker tournament, invariably won by Mannion.

There was talk that Bentley — who liked to roam around and drop deep — might be replaced with the more orthodox Jackie

Milburn, but the Newcastle United centre-forward injured his back after a collision in training and was ruled out of contention. The arrival of Stanley Matthews after a 28-hour flight from Canada also caused a clamour. Rous in particular was keen to see the right-winger included. Winterbottom thought it might be wise to rest four or five of the men who'd played against Chile, so they'd be fresh for the greater challenge of the clash with Spain. The FA secretary and the England coach made their cases to Arthur Drewery. The Grimsby fishmonger listened politely and shook his head. It was, he told them with a note of condescension, never done in football to change a winning team. Later, it would become a well-known "proof" of England's over-confidence that Matthews had been omitted. The truth was very different — the Wizard of Dribble hadn't actually played for his national side for over a year, his last start in a 1-3 defeat to Scotland in April 1949. For better or worse, the England team that faced the USA was at full strength.

Not that England weren't confident, at least in the newspapers. Letter-writers to the press back home who had watched the US team training for the London Olympics reckoned they would "struggle to beat a third division side", while the *Daily Express*, then as now a bastion of brainless jingoism, chortled that it would only be fair to give the USA "a three-goal start".

The US players seemed to share the assessment. Jeffrey told the press that his players were going "like lambs to the slaughter", while both Borghi and Bahr confessed that they would be delighted if they kept England's margin of victory down to a couple of goals. "They didn't dream we could beat them," Keough would say later, "and neither did we".

On the day of the game, both teams travelled to the stadium already in their kit. Winterbottom, in a predictably late acknowledgment that local conditions were a little different from those in Britain, had ordered sets of canvas boots to be flown out from Liverpool, but the rubber-soled, lightweight footwear had yet to arrive. One thing that was new were the England shirts. Mindful that the

USA would be playing in white with a red sash, the FA had opted for dark blue. It was the first time England had ever played in that colour. It would turn out to be the last.

The USA made just one change to the side that had fought so gamely against Spain, Ed Sousa replacing Wolanin. It was the winger's first start for the national team for two years. This time, Jeffrey gave the job of captaining the side to fellow Scot Ed McIlvenny, a former Clydeside shipyard worker who'd played as a pro for Morton and Wrexham before moving to the USA in 1949 to join his sister. Jeffrey later said he'd given the wing-half the job because he "was British"; others would conclude that he reckoned McIlvenny's ferocious dislike of the Auld Enemy would be embraced by his team-mates.

When the game kicked off, it appeared as if the scoffing of the *Daily Express* might have been accurate, after all. England had six shots in the first 12 minutes. Roy Bentley hit the post and then "I got above the keeper and really met a cross. I thought, "that's a goal". But I got too much on it, so it didn't drop." Instead the number nine's powerful header cannoned back off the crossbar.

In the US goal, Borghi flew around as if fired from a catapult, saving brilliantly a Bentley long-range shot. The Italian-American had grown up fixated on baseball. A good enough player to make the St Louis Cardinals Double A team as third baseman, he'd taken up football to keep fit in the winter, becoming a goalie only because his outfield skills were moderate to the point of non-existence. "I've got big hands, but no ball skills or passing ability", he'd explain. He disliked kicking the ball and preferred to throw it out. His goalkeeping style was similarly unorthodox — he caught the ball like a baseball fielder rather than getting his body behind it. In Mexico, the home fans had reacted to his antics with howls of derisive laughter and called him "the clown". For the England full-back Alf Ramsey, this may have been an eerie foretaste of humiliations to come. Twenty-three years later, another keeper who'd been similarly derided, Jan

Tomaszewski of Poland, would produce an equally acrobatic display between the sticks and effectively bring down the curtain on Ramsey's reign as England manager.

Encouraged, the Englishmen continued to press, dominating possession so completely that Keough felt "like we were just standing watching them play". The Americans took until the 25th minute to get a shot at the England goal, but then the Kings of Football struck back. Mortensen twice smacked the woodwork, Borghi tipped over a Finney header that was destined for the top corner, Mannion scooped over from 12 yards. Afraid that all these missed opportunities might come to count against them, the English ex-pats in the crowd became anxious. "Wake up, England!" one of them shouted.

The call went unheeded. In the 37th minute, the unimaginable happened. Bahr collected McIlvenny's throw-in and dribbled the ball forward a few paces before blasting a shot goalwards from 20 yards out. "It was going to the far post," Bahr recalled, "the goalkeeper had to move to his right to get the ball and somehow Joe Gaetjens came in from the side and deflected it with his head". Bahr considered the centre-forward's intervention "accidental", a fluky ricochet. Keough disagreed: "Joe dove and made that goal". Opinions among the England players were similarly divided. The wrong-footed Williams thought it had cannoned off the Haitian accidentally, but defender Hughes believed it was a deliberate deflection designed to send the keeper sprawling. However the goal had come about, Gaetjens wheeled away in gleeful celebration, his smile flashing in the afternoon sun.

Unlike many of his US colleagues, the centre-forward was a party animal who liked to relax by going out to nightclubs on the eve of big matches. According to Keough, he was often so "relaxed" on match day he had to be lifted out of bed by his team-mates. Languid and skilful, he drifted in and out of games, his style on the pitch as much at odds with the gritty, blue collar nature of the team as his playboy antics were off it.

Stung by the goal, England hit back. They worked the ball rapidly, creating chance after chance. The woodwork of the US goal rattled and thrummed like a railway track. Mannion missed another sitter. Mortensen might have scored 10. Borghi flung himself around and occasionally tugged and nudged his opponents. Bahr, Maca, Keough, McIlvenny and Colombo scurried around demonically, occasionally finding relief through inside forward John "Clarkie" Sousa, the best player in the US team and the only one able to retain possession long enough to give his team-mates a moment to collect their breath.

At half-time, Winterbottom switched his wingers round and ordered his full-backs to advance up the pitch. With substitutions only allowed for injuries, there was little else he could do. England's territorial dominance continued after the interval with Jeffrey's 10 outfield players dropping so deep Williams would later claim he couldn't see the opposition goal for them.

This wasn't a tactic, Bahr would point out. "Bunkering [defending in depth to protect a lead] was not really part of the game back then. If you had one goal, you went for two and if you had two, you went for three. If you plugged the goalmouth it was because the other team pushed you back. You didn't do it by design."

And England did push them back. Shots pelted in. The defending got more ragged. Colombo was the toughest player in the US team. He always wore leather gloves and carried himself like an MMF fighter. Sometimes, he played football like one too. As Keough recalled, "Charlie was a guy who really wanted to win any game he was playing. If his mother got in his way, he'd kick her out of it". Now, as Mortensen bustled menacingly towards the US penalty area, Colombo launched himself at him from behind in a tackle any NFL line-backer would have been proud of, diving head first and hitting the Blackpool forward behind the knees. The force was sufficient to bulldoze the Geordie almost to the penalty spot. "Mortensen was mad as hell," Keough said, "as anybody would have been." The referee ran over.

Generoso Dattilo was Italian. Baby-faced with the hooded eyes of a Roaring Twenties lounge lizard and the patent-leather hair to match, he'd taken charge of close to 300 Serie A games. Amongst Italian supporters, Datillo was infamous for refusing to give penalties unless the infraction was as obvious as a gorilla in a fruit bowl. Colombo's foul evidently did not meet that criteria. To the astonishment of the England players, the Italian simply cried, "Bueno! Bueno!" and waved play on.

Further controversy was to follow minutes later when Mullen headed goalwards from Ramsey's cross only for Borghi to dive and scoop the ball away as it flew into the net. The England forwards signalled that it was a goal. Mortensen was livid again, chasing Datillo across the field. Ramsey dismissed the idea that the ball had crossed the line. "It couldn't have done. It was as if there was some magical impenetrable barrier on the goal line. Even when we had an open goal we couldn't put the ball in the net".

Similar fatalism was infecting the other England players. "We couldn't have scored if we'd played till midnight," Mannion said later, "it was one of those days …" After Mullen's chance, something broke in England. Everything seemed to be conspiring against them. The Americans were dogged, the heat was stifling and Lady Luck was laughing so hard in their faces they could see her tonsils. They ran out of energy and heart.

By now, the crowd had been swelled by locals who had heard the score on the radio and flocked to the ground in the hope of witnessing an historic upset. They waved white handkerchiefs as a sign of England's surrender, set light to newspapers — the soft pale ashes blowing across the pitch like a snowstorm — and chanted, "Mais um! Mais um!" ("One more! One more!"). They almost got their wish too when winger "Pee Wee" Wallace broke away at the half-way line, advanced to the edge of the box and struck a low shot past Williams, only to see Ramsey slide in at the last minute and clear off the line.

When Datillo blew the full-time whistle, the Brazilian crowd stormed onto the field and carried the two heroes, Borghi and

Gaetjens, shoulder high on a lap of honour. "Those Brazilians literally went wild when we licked the English," Jeffrey told a reporter from the *Pittsburgh Press* when he'd returned to Penn State. "They set off giant firecrackers when we scored, then broke through the police cordon to carry our boys off the field after the game. It was the noisiest demonstration I had ever experienced."

Typically, in this moment of triumph, Keough was concerned about the opposition, turning to Bahr he indicated the blue-shirted Englishmen trooping disconsolately off the field and gave a rueful smile. "Boy, I feel sorry for those bastards. How are they ever going to live this down?"

Watching from the stands, the man who had travelled from Canada only to be omitted breathed a sigh of relief. Stanley Matthews had been aggrieved not to be selected but, "come the final whistle, I thanked the lucky stars I hadn't been part of it".

In the England dressing room there was a sense of horror and disbelief. "Our lads were dejected and humiliated. We could barely believe what had happened, the shock of it ..." Mannion recalled. Bentley shook his head in despair and wonder: "It was as if Babe Ruth had turned up at Lord's and hit a century with a baseball bat".

Inevitably, the finger-pointing soon began. Winterbottom blamed the officials. "The refereeing was a farce. If Fifa had wanted to, they could have suspended the referee for a lifetime". Rous blamed Drewry for not selecting Matthews "the ideal man to undermine a team like them", Billy Wright complained about the pitch, before remembering his manners and concluding "but it was the same for both teams".

Though Finney would later deride the USA as "a rubbish side, really" the England players were generally gracious. Borghi recalled that the team, "were cordial and very nice to us". "They handled their loss better than most would," Bahr would recall. The usually pugnacious Ramsey was magnanimous: "Fair play to them, they won".

In the years that followed the defeat, an urban legend arose that English newspaper editors saw the 0-1 scoreline on the wires, and, filled with Imperial hauteur, assumed it was missing the obvious digit and printed the score as England 10 USA 1. There seems to be no truth in that whatsoever. The regional and local evening press that gave the first accounts of the match all led with stunned, or doom-laden headlines. "England get Soccer shock: USA Win" read the one in the *Newcastle Journal*; "Black Day for English Sport" grimaced the *Birmingham Daily Gazette*.

The *Nottingham Evening Post* concluded, "yesterday's team gave probably the worst display ever by an England side, and not a single player should be proud of his showing". More scathing criticism came in the nationals. Bentley and Mortensen were singled out for their wastefulness in front of goal, while poor Laurie Hughes — the man who wasn't Franklin — found his England career brusquely terminated.

After England's ignominious departure from the tournament was confirmed by a 0-1 defeat to Spain (Matthews selected but ineffective), Winterbottom and Drewry returned straightaway to England with the squad. The idea that they might learn something from watching the rest of the tournament barely seems to have crossed their minds. The England players could see what the FA chose to ignore — that the rest of the world was moving forward without them. Instead of taking the opportunity to study their rivals, Matthews would write bitterly, "we all went home and buried our heads in the sand".

Jeffrey was hailed as a hero in Brazil. One American Embassy official in South America later told the press that he and his side had done more to promote US-Brazil relations than anything else in years. Reaction in the USA was far more muted. The only American pressman who was present in Belo Horizonte was Dent McSkimming of the *St Louis Post-Despatch*. A veteran reporter entering his fourth decade of service with the paper, McSkimming was the foremost writer on soccer in the USA. Yet despite that and the fact there were five players from St Louis in the US squad, his newspaper had refused to pay him to travel to Brazil. Understandably miffed, McSkimming funded his trip with winnings from the office Kentucky Derby sweepstake. Despite the tales that came to surround him, McSkimming didn't send any reports back from South America — and since he wasn't getting paid, who can blame him? The *St Louis Post-Despatch* thought the momentous events in Belo Horizonte worth just a single paragraph, wedged down the sports page between reports on men's and women's baseball.

A 5-2 defeat by Chile ended the Americans' World Cup campaign at the group stage. Jeffrey predicted that his team's victory over England would elevate football's standing in the country. It was false optimism. On their return home, the US players found the scene was much the same as it had been when they left, the reception party made up of family and friends, the media noticeable only by their absence. Decades later, the USA's win in Belo Horizonte would be heralded as "The Miracle on Grass" and Gaetjen's deflected header as "The Goal Heard Around the World". Such hyperbole lay 50 years in the future, however. For now, as Bahr put it, "the victory remained a well-kept secret amongst the US soccer community".

By the time most Americans came to celebrate what was perhaps the greatest upset in World Cup history, many of the men who'd orchestrated it, including coach Bill Jeffrey and skipper Ed McIlvenny, would be dead. Goal-scorer Joe Gaetjens left the USA shortly after the World Cup. He played professionally in France before returning to settle in Haiti, where he turned out for the national team. In July 1964, he was dragged from his home by Tonton Macoute thugs acting under orders from the newly-declared Haitian President for Life, Francois "Papa Doc" Duvalier. He was never seen again.

BRAZIL 1950

16 JULY
WORLD CUP FINAL

URUGUAY
2

BRAZIL
1

URUGUAY	BRAZIL
1. Roque Máspoli	1. Moacir Barbosa
2. Matias González	2. Augusto (c)
3. Eusebio Tereja	3. Juvenal
4. Schúbert Gambetta	4. Bauer
5. Obdulio Varela (c)	5. Danilo
6. Victor Rodriguez Andrade	9. Bigode
7. Alcides Ghiggia ⊗ (79′)	**6. Friaça ⊗ (47′)**
8. Julio Pérez	11. Zizinho
9. Óscar Míguez	8. Ademir de Menezes
10. Juan Alberto Schiaffino ⊗ (66′)	10. Jair
11. Rubén Morán	20. Chico

Manager: Juan López Fontana Manager: Flávio Costa

Maracana
Stadium

Rio de Janeiro,
Brazil

ATTENDANCE
172,772 (officially)

REFEREE
George Reader (England)

TIM VICKERY

> In the late nineties I was doing some work at the *Jornal dos Sports*, Rio de Janeiro's late, lamented, pink-covered sports daily.

The archive was run by Sr. Osmar, a sweet little old man who kept me going with endless cups of even sweeter coffee. As I searched through back copies, he gave me a piece of living history. As a young man he had been in the Maracana for the final game of the 1950 World Cup, when Brazil went down 2-1 to Uruguay. And he had found the experience so traumatic that he never went back.

Has a game of football ever mattered more? Brazil's defeat was dubbed "our Hiroshima" by Nelson Rodrigues, the country's leading playwright and probably its most influential football columnist. Even from today's perspective, so many decades after the Second World War, the comparison comes across as insane. Back then, with memories and consequences of the conflict still fresh and abundant, it must surely have been seen as grotesque by anyone with a balanced mind. But, lunacy or not, we can probably relate to it — all of us who at some stage have temporarily fooled ourselves into thinking that for 90 minutes nothing else is as important as the outcome of a football match. It might make us wish that we had a time machine, that we could fly back to the ultra-packed, newly-built Maracana stadium, joining the record official crowd of 172,772 — the real number was higher — to taste the atmosphere of a game with so much at stake.

But that might be to miss the point. Besides, in a sense, it has already been done — curiously enough, on the Brazilian side, grimly searching for self-flagellation. Books have been written poring over every minute of the match. And what tends to get lost is that vital word, context.

Because it is well worth asking an inconvenient question. Does this game even belong in this collection of essays? Can it really be seen as an upset?

From two perspectives, there is no doubt that it does, and it can.

One is that of subsequent events. As might be expected from the respective size of the countries, the footballing paths of Brazil and Uruguay diverged. With its continental dimensions, Brazil soon afterwards emerged as a global powerhouse of the game, winning three of the four World Cups held between 1958 and 1970, and doing it with a style and a swagger that has forever seen them associated with the 'beautiful' game. They have since added two more triumphs and are among the favourites at every World Cup.

Uruguay, meanwhile, sunk back so far that they became accustomed to mediocrity, failing even to reach three World Cups in four between 1994 and 2006. They have since staged a rally, but for a country of such a small note they are clearly punching well above their weight.

Everything that has happened afterwards makes 16 July, 1950 look like an upset — and the same applies to our second perspective: the events of the preceding seven days.

The final stage of this World Cup was not played on a knockout basis. Instead, there was a pool of the four group winners — a typical South American system of the time, guaranteeing more games and more revenue to offset the costs of travel and construction. In front of an exuberant Maracana, Brazil thrashed Sweden 7-1 and followed it up with a 6-1 drubbing of Spain. Over in Sao Paulo, meanwhile, Uruguay had problems against the same opponents, coming from behind to draw 2-2 with Spain, and needing a late goal to beat Sweden 3-2. Brazil, then, only needed a draw on 16 July to become champions. Based on these results, it looked like a mismatch, and the Brazilian press appeared justified in proclaiming their team winners on the eve of the final match.

Through every other prism, though, the warning lights were flashing for the hosts. In the pre-game euphoria, it was generally forgotten that just 72 days before the big game, Uruguay had beaten Brazil 4-3 in a warm-up match — and that was a Uruguay side that at the time did not even have a coach.

Uruguay were also the undefeated first kings of the global game. They had won the South American title eight times to Brazil's three. They also considered themselves world champions three times over — which was more than an idle boast.

The modern version of the game can be traced to the Paris Olympics of 1924. Unknown and unheralded, Uruguay arrived and breezed their way to the gold medal, playing a brand of football that left the Europeans open-mouthed in astonishment. Influential French writer Gabriel Hanot could hardly get over their "beautiful football, elegant but at the same time varied, rapid, powerful and effective ... they have pushed to perfection the art of the feint and the swerve of the dodge." Hanot saw them as "Arab thoroughbreds," capable of making the English professionals look like "farm horses." A competition, open to amateurs and professionals alike, was clearly necessary — a point re-enforced four years later when Uruguay successfully defended their Olympic title in Amsterdam. And so the World Cup came into being in 1930 — hosted by Uruguay, and won by them, too. The Uruguayans gave equal weight to all three titles — and after not entering 1934 and '38, they had never been knocked off their perch. On the eve of the journey to Brazil for the 1950 World Cup, the squad had a barbecue with the old champions from the past, sending them off to conquer with the magic touch. Other countries had their history, it was already beginning to be said, and Uruguay had its football.

The speed of this process is remarkable. In, say, the 1890s, the idea that South America would so soon be synonymous with football would have seemed ludicrously far-fetched. As late as 1922, Graciliano Ramos, one of Brazil's great writers, was arguing that this football thing was an unnecessary foreign quirk that would never catch on.

Ramos, though, was writing from a small town in the remote North East. Down in the Southern Cone, immigrants were pouring into Buenos Aires, Montevideo, Rio de Janeiro and São Paulo, coming from all across Europe, especially Italy, and the Middle East. These cities were expanding rapidly, and as they grew, so did football. The immigrants were hungry for novelty, and the new sport of football provided it. The game was inclusive, open to all shapes and sizes — but ideal for those with a low centre of gravity, the build of many in South America. It offered a means of integration into a new society — on the players' terms, since the game was sufficiently flexible to be interpreted in many ways. It was easy to learn and cheap to play — and that explains why Uruguay were so good, so early.

Down the years, Uruguay has often been an innovative, progressive society. At the start of the twentieth century, the country became a pioneer of the welfare state. Football was a beneficiary of such inclusive values. The game had been brought to South America by the British. It was born full of First World prestige, and the local elites fought to keep it to themselves. In Uruguay, this was always going to be a losing battle. The game — and selection policies — quickly permeated all levels of society. When Uruguay won the inaugural Copa America in 1916, the star player was winger Isbalino Gradin, a poor black man. One of the outstanding members of the all-conquering team of the twenties was José Leandro Andrade — one of the first black players that European crowds had seen (and whose nephew, Victor Rodriguez Andrade, was part of the 1950 team).

This would have been unthinkable in Brazil at the time. In the early twenties, it is even argued that Brazil's president intervened to request the non-selection of black players and, therefore, avoid what would be perceived as national disgrace. In semi-feudal Brazil, where slavery had only been abolished in 1888, the obstacles to mass inclusion were far higher. But the dynamic of competition would help bring them down.

One of the most significant matches in Brazil's history came in December 1932, when they visited Uruguay. At this point, there was no doubt about it. Up against the world champions in their own stadium, Brazil were the underdogs — especially as they were fielding an experimental side. But Brazil won 2-1. The best players were two young black stars who were to have glorious careers — elegant defender Domingos da Guia and elastic striker Leônidas da Silva. They were snapped up afterwards by Nacional and Peñarol, respectively — the two Uruguayan giants in a country where professionalism was just being introduced. In Brazil, there was great resistance to professionalism. Losing these two players was an important external shock which helped win the battle, open up careers to talent and produce the likes of Pelé — and before that, his idol Zizinho and the rest of the 1950 team. Back in 1932, when the Brazil team went back home there was a victory parade through the streets of Rio, noted with interest by Getúlio Vargas, the country's president. If football was important in Uruguay, in Brazil, it was about to become an affair of state.

Vargas came to power in 1930, one of a wave of regime changes in Latin America in the wake of the Wall Street crash. The export market for raw materials had collapsed. Brazil could no longer function like a giant farm. It now had to do what its elites had feared and industrialise. As both elected politician and dictator, Vargas was to dominate Brazil for two and a half decades, at the head of a conservative project of industrialisation — develop the country without changing its essential social structure.

His rule became increasingly authoritarian — in 1937, he proclaimed his *Estado Novo* (New State) in which his dictatorship was dubbed 'functional democracy.' It was a relatively benign, non-militaristic version of tropical fascism. Benito Mussolini was a huge influence. Vargas did not have a political party and had none of the strutting braggadocio of *Il Duce*. An avuncular figure, he was adept at playing people off against each other. But there were similarities, especially in the focus on nationalism. A biography of Mussolini was one of his favourite books, and some Brazilian law was a direct copy of Italy's. His government controlled the vital new medium of radio, which became important in the thirties. Samba — its lyrics strictly censored — became the national soundtrack. Carnival — its content also censored — grew under state patronage. The idea of a happy, all-singing, all-dancing people, bereft of racial discrimination — this was all part of the regime's message. And sport, forging the physical fitness of the new Brazilian citizen, was a big part of the mix — with the power of football quickly making itself apparent to the political class.

The head of the important Department of Propaganda was a far-right-winger called Lourival Fontes, who back in 1934 had been the head of Brazil's World Cup delegation in Italy, and had seen first-hand how Mussolini had made political use of the tournament — and how these efforts were all the more effective because the home side won the cup.

In France four years later, Brazil made their first serious impression on the World Cup. With Leônidas starring up front and Domingos at the back they came third. Vargas was keen to take advantage. His daughter Alzira was appointed the team's godmother.

When the Spanish Civil War broke out, Vargas was quick to side with General Franco. Then came World War. Given his ideological sympathies, few could imagine him sending his country to take up arms against Nazi Germany and fascist Italy. But geography trumped ideology. The USA wanted the strategically important port of Natal, on Brazil's north-east coast, as a naval base. They made it clear that they would invade if Brazil did not cooperate. Ever the pragmatist, Vargas negotiated concessions with the USA, and Brazil came into the war on the side of the Allies.

Before long, it became apparent that there was an inherent contradiction in the *Estado Novo* fighting a war for democracy. Vargas was forced to step down and elections were held. He was not done, though, and would return to power through the ballot box in the elections at the end of 1950 — elections which would have an influence on the build-up to 16 July.

As a prize for its wartime role, in 1946 Brazil was awarded the right to host the next World Cup, originally scheduled for three years later. But there was something distinctly pre-war about the first post-war tournament. The dominant attitude was straight out of the height of the Mussolini-inspired *Estado Novo*. Brazil gave itself a two-pronged challenge — build the biggest stadium in the world, and then become champions in this sparkling new arena. Both were necessary if this giant country were to fulfil its destiny — and drown out its own insecurities.

Putting the World Cup back a year to 1950 was undoubtedly a sensible move. It gave Brazil extra months to prepare, and the time was well spent. Brazil hosted — and won — a Copa America in 1949. The bulk of the matches were staged in Rio, with some in São Paulo. One game was timidly taken to Santos, the port an hour away from São Paulo, and one was taken to a tiny stadium in Belo Horizonte. The entire tournament, then, was restricted to the south east. A year later, things were very different. The 1950 World Cup took place on a genuinely nationwide basis. It has very seldom been mentioned, but from the perspective of spreading the game the tournament, whatever the outcome, was a success. The cup went to Porto Alegre and Curitiba in the south, and to Recife in the north east. And in the traditional heartland there was São Paulo, a new stadium in Belo Horizonte and, of course, the Maracana in Rio.

There were arguments and endless commissions set up to study the Maracana before the location and the design were chosen and work could begin, and, like some giant spaceship, the stadium could be parked to the north of the city centre.

The capacity had to be bigger than Glasgow's Hampden Park. There was a pharaonic touch to the whole project which did not inspire confidence. Historian Luis Antônio Simas catches the mood, and its inner insecurities. "The optimists," he writes, "were sure that the stadium would not be ready for the first game of the World Cup. The pessimists agreed, and also thought that the stadium would collapse, with apocalyptic consequences."

In truth, the Maracana was not entirely completed until 1965. But it was close enough to open its doors for the inaugural game, when Brazil met Mexico on 24 June. This was a huge relief to the Rio Mayor, General Ângelo Mendes de Morais. He had worked hard and spent plenty of political capital associating himself with the stadium. There was a bust of himself in the hallway and during the tournament the ground was referred to as the Estadio Mendes de Morais. After the defeat to Uruguay, the bust was thrown into the local river and the stadium was looking for a new name — but he got what he deserved. As the players lined up for that opening game, Mendes de Morais made a speech. "Players of Brazil," he said, "the effort to organise this cup is made up of two parts. The first, building this immense stadium. The second, winning the title of champion. The State has carried out the first part. Now it's up to you to carry out the second."

Nearly half a century later, this was still the cause of deep resentment among the players. The great Zizinho could still recall the speech, word for word. Alongside him, Jair Rosa Pinto, his inside forward colleague, shook his head sadly and said "you don't win like that".

But until the last few days — as we will see — the Brazil team could have few complaints about its preparation. They started early, even before they knew they would be hosting the competition. Flávio Costa was appointed coach in 1944, with a mandate to construct a young side. His side played three versions of the Copa America. In Chile in 1945, they came a creditable second to Argentina — who hosted and won the following year's tournament, where Brazil were once again runners up. There was a brutal game between the two powers which soured relations between them, and was one of several reasons for Argentina boycotting the 1950 World Cup. The sides would not meet again for a decade. And in 1949, Brazil won the Copa on home soil.

Time and resources were made available. Brazil held training camps, and money was found to send Costa to Europe in April 1950, where he watched Portugal against Spain and then headed for Glasgow to catch Scotland against England. In ration-hit Britain, he was delighted to be given chocolate — and he came away imagining that England would be a serious threat in June and July.

Costa was a charismatic, autocratic figure who was most associated with Rio's Flamengo club, where he was player, coach and also assistant to Dori Kürschner, one of a breed of nomadic Jewish Hungarian coaches who helped implant the WM system in Brazil. Through the second half of the forties, though, Flávio Costa was in charge of Vasco da Gama, Flamengo's main rivals, whose victorious team supplied the spine of the national side. Five of the line up against Uruguay were Vasco players — plus winger Friaça, who had only just left the club, and Jair, whose spell with Vasco ended in 1947.

Jair was included in the strongest part of the team — the attacking three through the middle. He was a wiry little figure whose left foot generated enormous power. A few years later, Jair was the wise old head in the Santos side who helped bed in the teenage Pelé. The idol of the young Pelé, though, was Zizinho, the other inside forward. Full of sinuous talent, Zizinho made a deep impression on the European press in 1950. Italy's *Gazzetta dello Sport* compared him to Leonardo da Vinci, transforming the Maracana into a canvas with the beauty of his play. And Zizinho was all the more effective because he had a special relationship with centre forward Ademir. "The guy playing in midfield," recalled Zizinho, "to set up things really needs the guy up front. You can't give him the ball if he doesn't move to receive it. You die with the ball at your feet. You need to be on the same wavelength. And Ademir was my brother. We were very connected. He knew what I was going to do. And when he got in sight of goal, he was terrifying. He loved goals." Ademir was fast and uncomplicated, good in the air and with two excellent feet. Zizinho and Jair kept him supplied, and he kept scoring.

The problem in the Brazil team was always at the other end. Flávio Costa searched for the right blend. In the build up to the tournament, he made it clear that the most likely partner for captain Augusto in defence was Mauro Ramos — who would be the immaculate captain as Brazil won the World Cup in Chile 12 years later. But as a result of that 4-3 warm up defeat to Uruguay, Mauro was left out, and in came Juvenal — a decision the coach would spend half a century regretting.

While Brazil's coach fretted about some of the components of his team, Uruguay were in a very different situation. They had no coach — but they had a team.

This was the consequence of the work of another nomadic Jewish Hungarian coach, Emérico Hirschl, who built a side with Peñarol which in 1949 brought to an end years of domination by their local rivals, Nacional. Hirschl developed a group of young strikers who fired together, and who went to the World Cup as unknowns outside their own country — unknown especially to Brazil's problematic defence.

There was centre forward Óscar Miguez, a goal-scorer with a rich technical repertoire. There was inside forward Juan Schiaffino, sleek and intelligent, who would go on to be considered one of the all-time best imports to Italy's Serie A. And there was right winger Alcides Ghiggia, bullet fast and, rarely for a wide man of the time, carrying a consistent goal threat. All these players flourished under Hirschl. Five of the team that won the title came from Peñarol — it would have been six, but left winger Ernesto Vidal picked up an injury and after playing in all the other games, he was not ready to take on Brazil.

Hirschl was an obvious choice to take charge of the national team. But there was a problem. Then, as now, Uruguayan football was characterised by squabbles between Peñarol and Nacional. So often, it is very hard to reach a consensus. Peñarol pushed for Hirschl, Nacional pushed against — and were aided by the coach's supposed involvement in a bribery scandal. A compromise was reached, and a month before the competition,

Juan López of little Central was appointed. He had coached the national team before, in the Copa America of 1947. But most of his time with Uruguay, before and after, was as the assistant. In marked contrast with Flávio Costa, López was a low-profile figure, with the wisdom to handle a group that had such experience and strength of character in its defensive unit that it was almost capable of self-administration.

There were fires to put out, though. One of them came as the consequence of a players' strike in Argentina in 1948 that also spread to Uruguay. In the case of Argentina, many of its leading talents were lured north to Colombia's 'pirate' league — another strong reason to stay away from the 1950 World Cup. In Uruguay, the 235-day strike came to an end in early May 1949. The Copa America had been played in Brazil the previous month. The team sent by Uruguay was viewed as a collection of scabs by the players union — but it had included young defender Matías González, seen as an important part of the side. What to do with him? The Uruguay side sat down and decided that they needed him — some recalled González throwing himself in front of a Brazilian to block a shot on the ground with his head. This type of commitment would be important. But right-back Schúbert Gambetta was not impressed. Now 30, Gambetta was both respected for his ability to work the entire flank, and feared for the force of his opinions. In the 1945 Copa, he attacked a referee after Uruguay had a goal disallowed, and picked up a two-year suspension. He was refusing to share a room with his strike-breaking colleague. New coach López had to get Gambetta and González singing from the same song sheet, and his ally was team captain Obdulio Varela.

If Gambetta was a man not to be messed with, the same applied a hundred times over to Varela. Some 60 years later Diego Lugano, one of his successors as Uruguay captain, simply referred to Varela as "God." A simple man of firm convictions, Varela encapsulates the force of character and rebellious spirit that are so important to the Uruguayan game, a human incarnation of the mouse that keeps on roaring. Seen as one of the leaders of the strike, Varela went back to his previous profession of stonemason while the players were out. With a face that looked as it had been carved out of rock, Varela was 'El Negro Jefe' — the black boss. He was never the greatest player, but from the old centre-half position, he imposed his will on proceedings. While the row about Hirschl was raging, Odbulio Varela was the decision maker, and it is both to his credit and that of López that things went so smoothly once the coach was appointed. In the Maracana dressing room soon after Uruguay had won the World Cup, López dissected the relationship with the press. "We've had long conversations," he said. "This very morning, I spoke with Varela and, as is usual, we disagreed on some points and argued a bit. In such arguments, solutions arise, and we ended up agreeing." At the last moment, and almost by accident, Uruguay got their structure right.

And so, fortified by their barbecue with the champions of old, Uruguay set off in search of the title. Their first hurdle was getting out of a very strange group.

With some of the qualifiers running deep into April, Fifa conducted the draw for the World Cup before it was known which countries would be taking part. And then, one by one, nations started dropping out; India, for example, in protest at not being able to play barefoot. Argentina were joined on the South American sidelines by Ecuador and Peru. And from Europe, both Turkey and Scotland won a place but declined to travel. This left 13 teams. Two of the groups had the full complement of four teams. One had three. And the other, Uruguay's group, had only two. France and Portugal were invited. Both ending up declining. The French case is most surprising, given that Jules Rimet was the Fifa president. But they were unhappy with a schedule that obliged them to travel from Porto Alegre in the south to Recife in the north east. And so the entire group consisted of one game — Uruguay against Bolivia.

Why not have a redraw and level things up? Because at least Brazil had their full number of games — three in the group phase, followed, if they came out on top, by three more in the final phase. This was good news for the box office, the overwhelming source of revenue in a pre-TV age, and so group four was settled in a single afternoon in Belo Horizonte.

Three days earlier, the new Independência stadium had played host to the historic USA win over England. But there was no upset this time. Uruguay beat Bolivia 8-0, and the beaten coach, Argentina's Mario Pretto, was impressed. He described Míguez as "extraordinary", and said that Ghiggia "would cause a sensation in any stadium in the world. I believe," he concluded, "that Uruguay are once again candidates to be champions of the world." There were two weeks to go until the final game, and at this point, no one would have seen the events of 16 July as an upset.

Going into the tournament, visiting journalists were struck by the pessimism in Brazil, which the group phase did little to dissipate. The hosts began with a routine 4-0 win over Mexico, and then came a trip to São Paulo — their only game away from the Maracana — to face Switzerland. Trying to curry favour with the local fans, Flávio Costa made sweeping changes, bringing in São Paulo-based players. It did not work. Brazil tried to sit on a lead and were punished in the end, having to settle for a 2-2 draw. The pressure was on then, for the third game against Yugoslavia, who had won both of their matches. With only the group winners going through to the final phase, Brazil had to win. Thankfully, Zizinho was fit for the first time in the competition, and played superbly in a 2-0 win — even scoring the same goal twice after his first effort was ruled out for a dubious offside. Everything was ready, then, for Europe versus South America in the final phase, with Brazil and Uruguay, Spain and Sweden. Emerging from the three-team group, the Swedes had not looked like potential champions, but Spain had won all three games and conceded just a single goal. At this point, then, it looked like a three-way battle for the title, with no clear favourite.

This was confirmed on 9 July, the first day of the final pool. In Rio, Brazil brushed aside Sweden 7-1, while in Sao Paulo, Uruguay had to dig deep to force a 2-2 draw with Spain. They had been the better side, and took the lead through Ghiggia. But Spain took advantage of defensive lapses to lead 2-1, and in torrential second half rain, it took a long-range special from Varela — imposing his personality on the game when it was most needed — to earn a point.

It was the events of 13 July, then, that shouted out a message that the title was going to Brazil. On a cold afternoon in São Paulo, Uruguay produced their worst performance of the tournament in front of a small crowd against Sweden. They trailed for much of the game, and only hit their stride in the last 20 minutes, when two moments of opportunism from Míguez gave them a 3-2 win.

Meanwhile, in the Maracana, Brazil were producing one of their all-time great displays. Nearly half a century later, Zizinho described it as "an accident," and Flávio Costa recalled "the most beautiful game that I've ever seen in my life, because the crowd was singing and dancing, and the players came up with such beautiful football." Spain took the field as one of the candidates for the title and were blown away. Three down after half an hour and six down at the mid-point of the second half, they were thrashed 6-1. The crowd waved their handkerchiefs and sang a recent Carnival song about bullfights in Madrid. It was one of those games when everything went right — and Flávio Costa told me many years later that "in a team where he sees no weaknesses, the coach pats the players on the back and hardly has anything to do".

But something was about to go wrong in the Brazil camp. They had been based in the then-remote neighbourhood of Joa, a tranquil paradise. "If Rio is the most beautiful city in the world," wrote a Uruguayan journalist, "then Joa, the base of the Brazil team, must be the most beautiful place in Rio." The players had enjoyed the calm. But now they moved to São Januário, the stadium of Vasco da Gama, the other side of a park from the Maracana. They were near the centre of town — and, in an election year, that brought plenty of unwanted attention.

Zizinho recalled that São Januário became "the headquarters of national politics. Our space was invaded by all those who wanted a bit of publicity." There was great bitterness in the ranks. "We became puppets of political propaganda," said keeper Barbosa. "There were candidates for president, deputies, councillors. We paid the price for all of this. It robbed us of the peace that we were enjoying." Ademir complained that normal routines for meals could not be followed, and that the players were on their feet for hours listening to speeches. Flávio Costa could hardly complain. He was running for office as a councillor.

Uruguay, meanwhile, were relaxing in their hotel in the Flamengo district — and probably enjoying the absence of their directors, who were in Copacabana — where midfielder Julio Pérez nearly drowned when he was caught in strong waves. Indignation was rising, though, at the way that their chances were being written off. In the streets, in the papers, there were banners and headlines declaring Brazil world champions. The doubts and pessimism of previous weeks had given way to certainty of triumph.

That was the overwhelming feeling of the giant crowd which assembled early on Sunday afternoon, and which, with Rio well established on the tourist circuit, included such celebrities as North American businessman Nelson Rockefeller and some French luminaries — actors Yves Montand and Simone Signoret, and writer André Maurois.

It was certainly the feeling of Mayor Mendes de Morais — him again — who made another speech in which he directed himself to the home team and said "you Brazilians, who I consider to be winners of the World Cup ... you, who in a few minutes will be acclaimed champions by millions of your compatriots ... you, who have no rivals in the hemisphere ... you, who outperform any other competitor ... you, who I already salute as winners!"

The gods of football may not have liked it. The Uruguayans certainly did not. As the two teams posed, most of the photographers swarmed over the Brazil side. Uruguay defender Eusebio Tejera, normally a man of few words, let out a bellow. "Hey," he shouted. "Don't be idiots. Come and take a photo of the world champions."

There are reports — unconfirmed — that in the dressing room, Obdulio Varela had collected newspapers proclaiming Brazil as champions, laid them on the floor and urinated all over them. What is in no doubt is that Uruguay had thought long and hard about their approach to the game, and had decided that one thing was certain. They would not be humiliated, brushed aside with the contemptuous ease with which Brazil had treated Sweden and Spain. And in this, their confidence was thoroughly justified.

"Journalists were hugely impressed by Brazil's big wins," recalled Julio Pérez, "but they didn't factor in that their opponents felt diminished. And no wonder. The huge stadium, the massive crowd, the fireworks and all these things weighed heavily against the Swedes and the Spanish, paving the way for Brazil to thrash them. But it wasn't going to work with us."

Just as South American football got a kick-start during the First World War, inventing the Copa America while European youth were slaughtering each other, so the 1940s was another golden age for the continent, with great players, tactical development, huge crowds and the development of the stadium atmospheres for which South America is famous. Sweden and Spain had never seen anything like the Maracana in the 1950 World Cup. "We looked at a Spanish player and he was blue, or white with fear," recalled Jair in 1997. "They were terrified." The Uruguayan team, on the other hand, were not going to be intimidated. They knew that they would have to hang in there, that their experienced defensive unit would have to hold firm, draw the sting of the Brazilians and provide a platform for their young strikers to win the game — a necessity, since Brazil would be champions with a draw.

So Uruguay, in their sky blue shirts, black shorts and socks, lined up in their WM formation with two changes from the side that had beaten Sweden. Roque Máspoli had recovered from a hand injury to play in goal; Matías González and Eusebio Tejera were the defenders; the half-back line — which would spend most of the time defending — was made up of Schubert Gambetta on the right, Obdulio Varela in the middle and Victor Rodríguez

Andrade on the left; the inside forward pair were the deep-lying Julio Pérez and the more adventurous Juan Schiaffino; Alcides Ghiggia was on the right wing, Óscar Míguez at centre forward, and with Vidal injured, 19-year-old Rubén Morán came in for his first game on the left wing.

In the white shirts they had worn since beating Exeter City in 1914, white shorts and socks, Brazil, also playing WM, named an unchanged team for the first time in the tournament. Barbosa played in goal, with Augusto and Juvenal in front of him; the half back line had Bauer on the right, moving infield to use his range of passing, Danilo — 'the prince' — making the play from the middle, and the mainly defensive Bigode on the left; Zizinho and Jair were the inside forwards, with Friaça on the right wing, Ademir through the middle and Chico on the left wing.

And so, at five to three on a sunny Rio afternoon, English referee George Reader blew his whistle and the game began — with Brazil immediately looking to take up where they left off against Spain three days earlier. They came straight out of the blocks, with that Zizinho-Ademir combination launching a dangerous attack which ended in a corner.

Uruguay's defence had slipped up in both previous games. This was different. Facing Spain and Sweden in a half-full stadium in Sao Paulo had seemed small, provincial. Now they were in the Colosseum, in front of the baying masses. The situation demanded total focus, especially in the first half hour, when Brazil kept up a hallucinating rhythm, attacking in waves.

The Uruguayans sought to counter the threat through the middle by marking man for man. Varela took Jair. But Tejera was unable to get a grip on Zizinho, who was beating him at will and slipping through passes for Ademir. Keeper Máspoli had to be alert, quick off his line and sharp with his reflexes. There was one spectacular save from a point-blank Ademir header. But this was not to be Ademir's afternoon. The tournament top scorer could not get shots on target when it mattered — and much of this had to do with the unsung hero of the afternoon, Matías

González, who picked up Brazil's centre-forward and spent the match getting in his blocks and tackles, and forcing Ademir into inferior shooting positions.

Uruguay knew that their main task was to keep Brazil at bay. A remarkably well-balanced *Rádio Nacional* transmission in Brazil was not impressed by the time they were taking over goal kicks — "it's as if they are winning the game" — or with Varela's tendency to argue about everything. But Uruguay were doing more than weathering the storm. They were extremely confident as they went in for half time, feeling that they could — and maybe should — have been in the lead. As Brazil's intensity began to drop off, Uruguay had enjoyed the clearest chances. Ghiggia crossed for Schiaffino to head wide with keeper Barbosa lost — at which point, *Rádio Nacional* described this as Brazil's toughest game of the tournament. Schiaffino set up Morán one on one with the keeper. Overcome by nerves, the young winger shot wide. And a Míguez snap-shot from outside the area rattled the Brazil bar. Humiliation was not only being avoided, but victory was a possibility.

However, Uruguay were soon reminded of the size of their task. Brazil were out early for the second half — with captain Augusto nagging the referee about Uruguay being late. And Brazil came with a fury. Within two minutes, they had forced one chance, and then taken the lead. The move came down the right, with Zizinho and Ademir combining to slip Friaça behind Rodríguez Andrade, and the right-winger scored with a cool cross-shot. The Maracana exploded. Fireworks went off and the handkerchiefs came out.

Gambetta kicked the ball towards the halfway line, where Varela tucked it under his arm and went to argue with the linesman. He was claiming offside. Perhaps he was genuine. More likely is that he was seeking to slow down the rhythm and give his side time to recover and regroup.

Zizinho was convinced that Brazil lost the game when they took the lead. "It seemed that we had a collective drop in pressure," he said. "When we scored, our team stopped playing. It was as if we had carried out our duty in the game. Our responsibility had ended there, when we opened the scoring. It was a collective drop of pressure when we made it 1-0."

It seems entirely plausible. All of the nervous energy was expended with the euphoria of the goal, and maybe those hours spent standing up listening to speech after speech also took their toll. Perhaps the energy level of the crowd dropped as well, drained by the tension of the occasion, by having to get to the ground early and by the overcrowding in the stands.

There seems little doubt that the team lost focus. Left winger Chico, a temperamental figure, confessed afterwards that at this point he could imagine Uruguay turning the tables, and proposed taking Varela out of the action with a bad foul.

The Uruguayans still fancied their chances, and felt the tide turning as Brazil dropped off. Augusto was forced into a saving tackle on Morán, as was Danilo on Schiaffino. The key, though, was Ghiggia on the right wing. At half time, he had asked for a change of service. "The problem," he told coach López, "is that Julio Pérez is hitting long balls, and I get past Bigode, but before I reach the ball, Juvenal is coming across to cut it out. Tell him to play it shorter, to come closer and give it to my feet. Then we can play one-twos round Bigode, because I can outrun him." López called over Pérez and Varela, made the tactical change — and won the title.

For the equaliser, half-way through the second half, Varela and Gambetta combined down the right, played into Pérez who fed Ghiggia to his feet for a run past Bigode. Ghiggia pulled back for Schiaffino to plant past the keeper. Schiaffino later admitted that it was a mishit. His intention had been to shoot across to the far corner, but he caught the ball slightly wrong and it flew in to Barbosa's left.

"There was a silence," recalled Flávio Costa nearly half a century later, "and this is important — a silence in the Maracanã which terrorised our players. They felt responsible for this.

They didn't react. Uruguay felt this, and kept attacking."
The crowd kept supporting the team. But their worry was palpable,
and was being transmitted to the pitch.

There were more moments of panic in the Brazil defence
and, with 11 minutes to go, Ghiggia undressed them once
more. Again, it came from an exchange of passes with Pérez,
and again Ghiggia outpaced Bigode. In the centre, Míguez was
calling for the ball, and, anticipating a cross, Barbosa edged off
his line. In full flight, the hunch-shouldered winger sensed his
opportunity and — just as he had done against Spain a week
earlier — he swerved his shot in at the near post. Schiaffino
had not followed the attack, and from the halfway line had the
impression that the ball had gone into the side netting. Then
he saw Ghiggia pump his arms in celebration, and he realised
that Uruguay were just a few minutes away from winning the
World Cup.

Flávio Costa was watching from the sidelines, helpless. Uruguay
had found the hole in his defence — and there was nothing he
could do about it. "Juvenal was not giving the necessary cover
to Bigode," he explained many years later. "Perhaps he was
worried by the crowd. He hid from the game in the middle of
the others. There were no substitutions. If I could have changed
things, I would have. One defender who didn't perform caused
great harm to my team, because Bigode was having problems
marking Ghiggia, who did the same thing four or five times,
beating him in midfield and having a free run."

Brazil were roused into a reaction. They could not rediscover
the fluency of the first half hour, but they had chances. Jair shot
wide. Ademir also shot wide and was then robbed at a vital
moment by Matías González. And with a corner taken and still
bouncing dangerously around the Uruguayan goalmouth, Mr
Reader blew his whistle and it was all over.

Jules Rimet had made a long and slow walk down to pitchside
for the presentation. He started when it was 1-1. By the time
he reached the field, he was astonished to see Uruguay in the

lead. There was chaos at the whistle. The presentation plans were scrapped. Rimet appeared perturbed by the confusion. In the midst of the melee, he handed the trophy to Varela, who passed it straight on to the Uruguayan ambassador and headed for the dressing rooms, where the players held their own celebrations — which, no doubt, drowned out the river of tears coming from the Brazil side.

With the presence of Pedro Cea, a hero from the triumphs of 1924, '28 and '30, the Uruguayan players let the feelings of euphoria wash all over them before heading back to their hotel some four hours after the final whistle. It was Sunday night, and there was no food available, so although they had been warned about keeping their heads down, several of them took to the streets. When recognised, they were astonished at how well the Brazilians treated them. Obdulio Varela spent the whole night drinking and riding the trams with new friends who, however deep their disappointment, showed him not the slightest anger.

But there was a flipside. If the Brazilians did not turn on the victors, it was because they were saving their ire for their own team. It took a while. Initially, the dominant emotion was sadness, as Zizinho recalled from meeting fans on his walk home. But, with time and probably stoked by the press, villains were appointed. And the fragility of Brazil's 'racial democracy' was quickly exposed. President Vargas had spoken of the country as being "a racial and linguistic unit, a national spirit." The 'racial unit' was clearly nonsense, an attempt to disguise the power imbalance between the until recently enslaved and the former slave owners. And that imbalance became clear as the black players took the brunt. Barbosa was never allowed to forget the way he had been beaten at his near post. Ghiggia's strike gave rise to decades of prejudice against black goalkeepers in Brazilian football. Many years later, Barbosa even staged a ceremonial burning of the Maracana goalposts in a vain attempt to put the past behind him.

Left-back Bigode found himself at the centre of a myth. In the first half, he had committed a bad foul on Julio Pérez. Characteristically, Varela came over to him to protest. According to legend, Varela had either slapped him or spat at him and Bigode had not reacted! He had allowed the Uruguayan captain to bully him in this way on his own pitch! It was clear proof of Brazil's lack of moral fibre, of the inherent weakness of its mongrel breed! Two problems. One, it was not true. Two, Varela was also black, so no racial conclusions could be drawn from the mad story anyway.

It was harder to blame Zizinho, Brazil's outstanding player on the day. But his bitterness ran deep. In the mid eighties, he published a book. On the first page he wrote that "even today, parents stop me in the street and say to their children, 'this is Zizinho, who played in the 1950 World Cup.' I played for 19 years, I have some titles to my name, but together with the other players of that campaign, I'm remembered as a loser." Twelve years later, sitting alongside Zizinho, Jair was even more emphatic. "In other countries you can lose — and it's not that you lie down and accept it, but you don't fight about it. Here, no. Here, for God's sake! A guy meets you in the street and he's well capable of coming at you with a knife because you lost."

By the time of the next World Cup, Brazil had symbolically abandoned their white shirts. They now played in yellow. But the Bigode-Varela story still held enormous weight. If they were to be beaten in Switzerland 1954, it would not be for lack of machismo! They doubled down on the nationalism. Before taking the field for their quarter final against the great Hungarians, they staged a bizarre ceremony in the dressing room, with all the players kissing the flag and swearing to avenge the deaths that Brazil had suffered in the Second World War at Monte Cassino. What ensued went down in history as The Battle of Bern, with an out-of-control side kicking the Hungarians all over the place on its way to elimination.

By Sweden 1958, sanity had prevailed. New FA boss João Havelange was a shrewd organiser. Their level of preparation was extraordinary, with a full battery of physical trainers, doctors, a dentist and even a sports psychologist. And on the field, they had come up with a solution to the problem of 1950 — lack of defensive cover. Brazil pioneered the back four, and with Mário Zagallo working back from the left wing to make the extra man in midfield, they found the right balance between attack and defence. They won their first World Cup in magnificent style — and did not concede a goal until the semi-finals.

Uruguay, meanwhile, did not even make it to that World Cup — a melancholic signal that such a small country could not be kings of the global game forever. And they surely should have made more of their time at the top of the hill. On the Tuesday after the final, a big national holiday in Uruguay, the players flew home and had the chance to be acclaimed by their own public in the Centenario stadium. But it would be almost three years before the national team would play there, when England came for a visit in May 1953. A year later, the sides met again in Switzerland. After humbling Scotland 7-0 in the group phase, the quarter-final against England remains a bittersweet occasion; Uruguay's 4-2 win is the last game of their long unbeaten World Cup run. In the semi-final, it was their turn to meet the Hungarians, and they went down 4-2 after extra time. Six years later, when *World Soccer* magazine was launched, the first edition carried a double-page spread devoted to this match, described as the greatest ever played in the history of football.

It is a game which now seems to have been forgotten. And Uruguay surely forgot some of the lessons of their golden years. Yes, force of personality had been a big part of their 1950 success. But there was also plenty of football. The statistics of 16 July, 1950 show that Brazil committed many more fouls than Uruguay. In the desperation of defeat, Uruguay subsequently were too inclined to reach for the more violent parts of their tool kit, as if the whole footballing nation had become an ugly caricature of Obdulio Varela. This was one thing that coach Óscar Washington Tabárez, in his long reign as Uruguay coach that brought them back to the top table, was anxious to stress, and he was proud of picking up fair play awards.

But there is a lesson even more important than this which is taught by the epic game in the Maracana. Two sets of players had been in the Colosseum together. Only they knew that it was like to play in that atmosphere, with that much at stake, running the risk of being weighed down and found wanting in the eyes (and the ears, given the importance of radio) of their compatriots. It forged a bond between them, one of shared experience and of mutual respect. The Uruguayans realised that they had overcome a great team, who, on another day, would have come out on top. The Brazilians were left shaking their heads, but acknowledged that they had been beaten fair and square. Some of the players of both sides held frequent reunions. Friendships were forged which lasted for half a century, and that, amid all the hysteria of 16 July 1950, is surely one of the most important messages that football can send out to the world.

SWITZERLAND 1954

W.GERMANY

HUNGARY

3

2

W. Germany	Hungary
1. Toni Turek	1. Gyula Grosics
7. Josef Posipal	2. Jenő Buzánszky
10. Werner Liebrich	3. Gyula Lóránt
3. Werner Kohlmeyer	4. Mihály Lantos
6. Horst Eckel	5. József Bozsik
8. Kari Mai	9. Nándor Hidegkuti
12. Helmut Rahn ⊗ ⊗ (18', 84')	6. József Zakariás
13. Max Morlock ⊗ (10')	**11. Zoltán Czibor ⊗ (8')**
15. Ottmar Walter	8. Sándor Kocsis
16. Fritz Walter (c)	**10. Ferenc Puskás (c) ⊗ (6')**
20. Hans Schäfer	20. Mihály Tóth
Manager: Sepp Herberger	Manager: Gusztáv Sebes

Wankdorf
Stadium

Bern,
Switzerland

ATTENDANCE
62,500

REFEREE
William Ling (England)

ANDI THOMAS

SO WHAT HAPPENED?

On the fourth of July, 1954, the World Cup final was held at the Wankdorf Stadium in Bern, Switzerland. Hungary were expected to win, because Hungary were the best team in the world. West Germany weren't because they weren't. And then the wrong team won.

The bare facts are these. The two sides had met earlier in the competition, and Hungary had stuck eight past Germany's squad players. In the final, Hungary took the lead after six minutes, then added another goal in the eighth. West Germany scored their first goal in the 10th minute, equalised in the 18th, and then over an hour later they took the lead. Hungary scored to make it 3-3, only for the linesman's flag to wave it back off the board. And that, with the exception of one final chance, well saved by German keeper Toni Turek, was that.

What is a miracle? Perhaps we might think along the lines of a disruption in the orderly progress of things. There is a way things should go and then — miracle! — they veer off in some other exciting direction. Lazarus should have continued down the unmapped paths to the undiscovered country. The five thousand should have gone home: lovely man, terrible catering. St. Patrick should have been bitten by a snake. And in 1954 Hungary should have beaten West Germany in the World Cup final, but they didn't, and that was hailed as a miracle as well. "The Miracle of Bern". History is named by the winners, though it has to be lived by the losers as well. Perhaps there was a story in Pharaoh's family, told that night and all the nights that followed, of the coming back together of the Red Sea.

▌ FIRST GOAL

Hungary's place in football's folk memory is defined by their failure to win this game: brilliance unrewarded, medals unreceived. But this is all sharpened by their reputation for the beautiful. They weren't just moving football on, they were taking it to wonderful places and treating it to wonderful times. They were doing things, so the stories go, that other teams couldn't imagine, let alone counter. That's the motor of the tragedy. Defensive football doesn't generate doomed romance.

Anyway, here is how one of football's greatest attacking sides scored the opening goal, after six minutes. From just outside the area, Sándor Kocsis kicked the ball very hard towards the West German goal. It hit a defender square in the backside and pinged across the box, where Ferenc Puskás was arriving. You'd assume "keep an eye on Puskás" featured quite heavily in West Germany's pre-game thinking, so perhaps there was some off-camera brilliance: the great man disappeared up his own sleeve and then reappeared a few yards away. Or perhaps it was just some good old-fashioned poor defending. Either way, Hungary had the lead, and it was crude, and it was easy.

And the fact that Germany had made a couple of decent half-chances before this goal arrived? An oddity, a detail, a splash of colour for the retrospectives. Nothing to worry about.

▌ PLACE YOUR HANDS

Many miracles are healing things. Somebody gets better. There are seven signs of Jesus's divinity laid out in the second part of the gospel according to John, and four of them are acts of healing: the royal official's son, the paralytic at Bethesda, the blind man, and Lazarus. And we can probably claim a fifth, the changing of water into wine. Please, my wedding, it's very sober.

Bern's miracle was a miracle of words. The final of the 1954 World Cup was the first broadcast for live television, but television sets were luxury items in post-war Europe. So a nation turned to the radio, and to the voice of journalist Herbert Zimmerman. Here's the winning goal: "Kopfball ... abgewehrt ...". Then "Aus dem Hintergrund müsste Rahn schiessen ... Rahn schiesst!" Then "Tor! Tor! Tor! Tor!" A pause, one of the great pauses; nearly ten whole seconds. "Tor für Deutschland!" And finally, "Drei zu zwei führt Deutschland. Halten Sie mich für verrückt, halten Sie mich für übergeschnappt!"

That's: "Header ... saved ... Rahm should shoot from deep ... Rahm shoots! Goal! Goal! Goal! Goal!" After the pause comes, "Goal for Germany!" And the real abracadabra comes in right at the end: "Germany leads 3-2! Call me mad, call me crazy!"

Uli Hesse — whose history of German football is called, simply, *Tor!* — claims that in Germany "every true football fan beyond school age can still recite the words as if they were a poem." But it rang out beyond football. The commentary was released as a record and sold in the millions. The win over Hungary has been identified by politicians, writers and thinkers as the moment that transformed post-war West Germany into the nation it became; this commentary, then, was the means by which that transformative power was delivered. It was a magic spell. It healed a nation, so the story goes, and what is a miracle if not a story applied to a wound.

SECOND GOAL

First was easy, second was peasy. If you subscribe to the "Hungary got the lead and then got cocky" theory, here is your smoking gun. Werner Kohlmeyer tries to pass the ball back to his goalkeeper; unfortunately, Turek is advancing towards him, and the pass nearly becomes a smart finish. Turek manages to make the save, but, caught in that awful place where panic runs into physics, he ends up scooping the ball back under himself. It's not entirely clear how, but he does. Out of his grasp it rolls and there's Zoltán Czibor and it's 2-0, and the game has gone from foregone conclusion to over already in just a few minutes.

In a couple of the highlight reels available on YouTube, footage of this goal cuts directly to the face of a man in the crowd, presumably a West Germany supporter. He is wearing a battered cloth cap and an expression of vacant and totalising horror, as he realises that his team, who had been playing quite well for eight whole minutes, are not just outmatched but totally overwhelmed. He is a Neanderthal caught by the beautiful workmanship of the arrow that is sticking from his stomach. He is the first Roman scout to see Hannibal's elephants descending from the Alps. He is a Japanese fisherman watching Godzilla emerge from the boiling ocean. Hungary aren't just better; they are other. West Germany aren't bad, but they are melting away. They have turned up to a gunfight with a child's drawing of a knife that is actually a child's drawing of a banana, and not a particularly good one at that.

This is not the ideal scenario in which to find yourself in a football match, let alone a World Cup final, but it's fertile ground for a miracle.

▍ WHAT HAPPENED?!

Miracles demand explanations, and then miracles reject them all. In his autobiography, Ferenc Puskás points to the obvious wrongness of what actually happened — "I call to witness the experts of the whole world who saw the match. Is it likely that Hungary, playing harmoniously at the top of their form, and already leading 2-0, could possibly lose against a team whom they had beaten a few days before, and playing only with 10 men, by eight goals to three?" — and then attempts an explanation. Many explanations. Too many explanations.

It was the officiating. There was a foul in the build-up to Germany's third, and Puskás' late equaliser was incorrectly flagged offside. It was the strain of the earlier rounds, the battle against Brazil and the thrilling exhibition against Uruguay. Hungary were "near to a state of nervous exhaustion"; "man is not a machine". It was Hungary's attacking play. Perhaps their normal modes of attack had "gone astray", or perhaps they were making chances as they always did, just missing them as they never did. It was the hotel. There was music through the night, and the Hungarians didn't sleep until five in the morning, and also it was the very same hotel at which Napoleon had stayed before the battle of Borodino. (A full 15 years before the battle of Borodino, which suggests some deep magic at work here.)

Other explanations offered by other people, then and since: Puskás was still injured. No, Puskás was lucky to be playing, for he had been deliberately targeted by the West Germans in their earlier game as part of a broader plot to ensure that no communist nation would ever win the World Cup. Nándor Hidegkuti was unusually slow. The rain came down, soaking the actual playing field and levelling the metaphorical one. West Germany were fitter. Hungary were tired. West Germany were stronger. Hungary were disjointed. West Germany analysed the Hungarian playing patterns. Hungary did not return the courtesy. They took the lead too early, and then relaxed. A 2-0 lead is the most dangerous lead in football, so they say; perhaps here is where they got the idea. And then, at 2-2, Hungary panicked. They left their comeback too late. They began to argue among themselves. Puskás was angry with everybody around him. Puskás was embittered by his injury. Puskás was not offside. József Boszik had a poor game. Czibor had a poor game. It was a mistake to drop László Budai. It was a mistake to pick Mihály Tóth. And Turek, in goal for the other lot, had a great game. West Germany passed the ball sweetly, they were faster on the break, they had been isolated from the intellectual development of football after the war and so had been forced to develop new methods that caught the Hungarians by surprise. We'll come back to the syringes in the West German dressing room later on. We'll come back to their studs as well.

That list is incomplete — it could be twice as long again — and it is riddled with contradictions. The Hungarians were poor and over-confident, but they missed lots of chances and West

Germany's goalkeeper had a great game. They panicked at 2-2 and started bickering among themselves, but they also mounted a siege, drew yet more saves from Turek, scored a goal that was incorrectly ruled out and only conceded the third after a German foul went unpunished. Hungary simultaneously failed to turn up, turned up without their finishing boots, and turned up just fine, thank you very much, only to find themselves robbed by referee and linesman.

These contradictions are partly down to the fact that football matches are very complicated things with lots of moving parts. A result can be more-or-less explained by the progress of ideas across a continent or by a shift in the weather from good to bad, and it can also be explained by a single striker wasting a single chance.

But this orgy of evidence refuses to resolve into a satisfactory who- or what- or whydunnit. Every reason sounds like an excuse, and every excuse sounds like a guess, and every guess comes with an intimated shrug and the implication: you don't like this reason? I have others. No one particular explanation does the job on its own, but take them all together and it feels so wildly overdetermined that it collapses into parody. How could any one team be so variously and excitingly cursed, so incompetent and unlucky, so deserving of victory while also destined for defeat? All of the reasons are good and none of them are good enough.

▌ THIRD GOAL

This is the moment, really. The moment things stop being silly and start being weird. The moment this game begins its slow uncoupling from the sensible. Hungary taking a two-goal lead was not unexpected, after all, nor the fact that it should prove straightforward. Getting it done in eight minutes was a little startling, but hey, genius moves to its own timetables.

And yet two minutes later, the game which was off became suddenly on again. West Germany advanced down their left, some neat passing opening up a little pocket of space for Helmut Rahn. He sends in a cross or a shot with his left foot and it is, if we're being honest, a poor cross or a worse shot. It scoots along the floor to the feet of the nearest Hungarian defender, before — a miracle! magic! a total loss of concentration from a player already wondering where he'll keep his medal! — passing through his legs.

Now the ball is in the box. Now the players are turning. Now another Hungarian defender, covering for his colleague, is throwing out a leg, stretching for the ball. He's a couple of feet from the penalty spot, facing his own goal. Football hadn't yet stolen the phrase "corridor of uncertainty" from cricket, but that didn't make it any less real.

Had the defender missed the ball, he might have got away with it. It looks on replay as if Max Morlock, lurking behind him, might have overrun the cross. At the very least, the finish would have been trickier: off-balance, cutting back across the ball, one of those that can easily fly up and away. But the defender just gets something on it, both too much and not enough. The barest scraping of his studs sends the ball rolling gently into the six yard box. Morlock dives, Morlock sprawls, Morlock gets there just before the keeper. Our miracle is up and running.

THE MIRACLE OF THE METAL TEETH

Tor! begins with Fritz Walter standing on a hotel balcony looking out over Lake Thun, less than an hour's drive south of the Wankdorf, waiting for clouds to appear in the summer sky. He waits through sunrise, he waits through breakfast, he waits until noon — and then, as he's having his lunch, he hears the good news from a smiling team-mate. It's raining. "Ugly, fat raindrops are falling from what is now a grey mass above Lake Thun, driving tourists away from the beach. They promise wind and cold and mud." And so Walter concludes: "Now nothing can go wrong."

Walter, unable to bear too much humidity since a wartime brush with malaria, was no doubt delighted with the promise of wind and cold, but this was more than personal. The whole West German team was hoping for mud. The weather falls under 'act of God', but the German response to it was an act of modular design supplied by Adi Dassler. Removable, replaceable studs.

Seven months or so before the final in Bern, Hungary were at Wembley to take on England. As the teams walked out, England captain Billy Wright looked down at his opponents' feet and saw what he later called "strange, lightweight boots, cut away like slippers under the ankle bone." He then turned to Stan Mortensen and provided as neat a sketch of English football in the 20th century as anybody could ask for. "We should be alright here, Stan, they haven't got the proper kit." And out clattered the English to a 3-6 humiliation, clodhoppers on their way back from the wrong cobbler.

What goes around comes around. Off came the short studs and in went the long ones, down came the rain and up came the mud, up stayed the West Germans and down fell the Hungarians. You'd probably call it marginal gains these days, although equally you'd be surprised if any modern World Cup final ended up being affected by something as old-fashioned and quotidian and kids-up-the-rec as mud. Advances in pitch preparation and drainage mean that most high-level professional football matches are played on decent surfaces, whatever the weather. This makes the games better, for a given value of better. This makes the games more predictable. And it makes the arguments farcically small, marginalia pains. Who turned off those sprinklers? This grass is a millimetre too long! These days God can act all He likes — the ground no longer listens.

▌ FOURTH GOAL

We pause now to consider the strange sadness of the flapping goalkeeper. Out they come for the cross, windmilling through the empty air, and there goes the ball, wholly unbothered. There are certainly worse mistakes that a keeper can make, and there are plenty funnier, but there can't be many less dignified. We gave you the use of your hands! And this is how you choose to employ them?

The corner comes in from the German left, looping up and then descending into the six-yard box. Hungary have a man on each post, as was the tradition, and Gyula Grosics moves out to meet the ball. But he's hesitant, he's got no momentum. And by the time he makes it to where he's supposed to be, there's already an attacker there. Grosics jumps, a weak, flat-footed jump. His head doesn't make it above the attacker's shoulder, and the arm of his opponent comes down across his body, and he brings his own arm up but he's already falling, falling away from the arc of the ball, falling back down to the mud.

Rahn meets the ball close to the ground, a bobbling volley that looks suspiciously like a heavy touch. Perhaps that confuses the defenders on the line: one stands still, one falls over. 2-2.

Grosics played 86 times for Hungary and tends to get just as much credit for the overall magic as Puskás, Hidegkuti and all the rest. He is sometimes described as the first sweeper-keeper. (He was also, apparently, nervous to the point of vomiting before the final.) And that means this moment — this flail, this flap, this failure — could be the origin of one of football's most celebrated traditions. The first time ever that one fan turned to another and muttered, darkly: Sure, I get it. All the fancy stuff is important to how the team plays. But can we not just pick a proper goalkeeper and start from there?

IMAGINED COMMUNITIES
IMAGINE COMMUNITIES

If a miracle is a story then the power is in the telling, and the retelling, and the retellings of the retellings. "I had never heard a soccer game announced on the radio before," says the narrator of *The Sunday I Became World Champion*, an autobiographical novella by Friedrich Christian Delius published in 1994. A pastor's son, he is listening to Zimmerman's commentary in his father's study and is taken aback: "Words kept coming up that had nothing to do with soccer ... miracle! ... thank God! ... This is what we all hoped and prayed for!" And then, most thrillingly of all "Turek, you're a devil of a fellow, you're a Soccer God!"

Previously a "timid" soccer enthusiast, our hero finds himself caught by this "blasphemous, scandalous ritual": he turns the volume down so nobody catches him, but at the same time he is unable to tear himself away. "From minute to minute I liked it better and better, having a secret god, a Soccer God alongside the Lord God." He looks up a picture of Moses but Moses is looking away, unconcerned; he waits for the crucifixes to fall from the walls and they do not. He sits in the seat where his father writes his sermons, and as Germany take the lead he realises that "This blasphemy was looking better all the time. [...] A Soccer God and an Underdog God." And the first commandment washes away in the rain.

The euphoria of the occasion allows our hero to forget his bodily ailments: stuttering, psoriasis, nosebleeds. (Maybe Lazarus forgot that he was dead, just for a little while.) The young child's body is freed from its cares; the young nation's body politic likewise. The old ways have been defied and the sacred places defiled, yet the walls have not come tumbling down. Instead lightness, freedom; liberation from the past and permission to enter the future.

Five years later, in his episodic and multivocal novel *My Century*, Günter Grass gave the 1954 chapter to an investment banker and financial adviser. He remembers listening to the game, huddled round the radio with a group of students, and he remembers his attempts after the game to persuade Walter and Puskás to collaborate on a range of wines and sausages: "a Fritz Walter vintage as a natural complement to Major Puskás's salami [...] thus reconciling the provincial hero and the citizen of the world and turning a profit into the bargain." Here the sporting miracle is tied explicitly to the postwar economic miracle, and what emerges from the victory isn't just a country, but a country of opportunity. Though neither Puskás, living it large in Madrid, nor Walter, retreated to his vineyard, can be persuaded to get involved.

Two decades earlier, the eponymous heroine of Rainer Werner Fassbinder's *The Marriage of Maria Braun* declared herself, with a broad smile, "the Mata Hari of the economic miracle." But come the film's denouement, Maria's success has rendered her charmless and brittle. The money has sharpened her edges and shortened her words. Her rich lover has died and left her everything; her exiled husband has returned; and West Germany are beating Hungary on the radio. She should be happy. And yet she cannot rest, so she flits from room to room, taking off her clothes and putting them back on again. She discovers that her lover and her husband had been in contact behind her back, that the former had arranged the latter's absence. Perhaps deliberately she leaves a gas hob open; perhaps forgetfully she lights a cigarette. The house goes up in flames as Zimmerman cries — a caustic, appalling juxtaposition — "It's all over! It's all over!"

The historian Joachim Fest once noted that West Germany's victory over Hungary "was in a certain way the birth of the federal republic," while '68 student radical turned MEP Daniel Cohn-Bendit has claimed that after 1945, "the German identity was broken and there were two things that rebuilt it. One was economic growth and the other was the 1954 football championship." And this rebuilding is the thread that runs through *The Miracle of Bern*, directed by Sönke Wortmann and released in 2003. As West Germany prepares for the World Cup, Richard Lubanski returns from 11 years in a Soviet POW camp to find his homeland and his family have both changed beyond recognition. His wife runs a bar, his eldest son is a guitarist with communist sympathies, his daughter wears colourful dresses and dances with soldiers, and his youngest son, born after he left for the war, is a Helmut Rahn fanboy who occasionally cries. "A German boy never cries," says Lubanski, shortly after striking his son in the face for some minor indiscretion. Meanwhile, West Germany manager Sepp Herberger is in Switzerland, praying for rain and struggling to keep Rahn and the press pack happy.

Peter Lohmeyer's convincingly hollowed-out Lubanski keeps the saccharine from reaching full Disney levels, but the ending goes the way the genre demands: triumph, reconciliation, forgiveness, lessons learned on all sides. See Lubanski, doing keepy-uppies with a knackered ball and learning to smile again. See Herberger, taking counsel from a wise old cleaning lady: "The ball is round," she says, "and the game lasts 90 minutes." See Lubanski, sobbing while his son consoles him. "I think German boys can cry now and then."

The tears were contagious. After attending the premiere, then-Chancellor Gerhard Schröder told the nation that the film had moved him to tears, and urged his fellow German men to join him. Millions watched it, although not everybody was buying the message. A columnist in *Die Zeit* wrote that "Wortmann's film is less about football than about this German feeling of having suffered rather than caused the Second World War. After a terrible defeat on the battlefield, at last they get their just rewards on the football field. The film tells the Germans they are right to feel this way."

Three years after Wortmann's film was released, Germany hosted the World Cup, the country's first major football tournament since reunification. A breezy attacking German side opened the tournament with a chaotic 4-2 win over Costa Rica, made it to the semi-finals, and took eventual victors Italy all the way to extra time in one of the great modern World Cup knockout games. They then defeated Portugal in the third-place playoff. No miracle this time, then, but another round of complicated conversations about positive patriotism and national pride, as German flags sprouted from windows and balconies. Ahead of the final, *The Guardian* quoted a 29-year-old engineer called Otto Hensch. "I never put up a flag before because it felt strange. Now I have had one in my window for three weeks. It is going to feel too empty if I take

it down, so I have decided I am going to keep it up for good."
(Once again, not everybody was buying it. Gary Younge wrote
that "The orgy of flag-waving patriotism spawned by Germany's
success is creepy [...] Brandishing your flag when your nation
is winning is opportunism; keeping it hoisted when they lose is
patriotism. Frankly, both 'isms suck.")

I must acknowledge that I am an outsider here, three times
over and more. Removed by time (I was born 29 years after this
game was played), removed again by geography (I'm writing this
from a shed in south London), removed once more by language
(I have no German, I have less Hungarian). And removed in a
more abstract way by the shifting meanings of all the component
parts of the equation. The idea of a nation has changed since
1954, when there was a whole other Germany. So has the idea
of a World Cup: in 1954 it was still a breezy, slightly shambolic
affair, with only hints of the modern, touring, corporate monolith
beloved of sportswashers everywhere.

And yet (here you may imagine me standing up, inside my
little shed, and perhaps trying to pace about, in this shed that's
one and a half steps long), and yet, for all that I and you and
everybody else knows that nations are made by geography and
economics and empires and material conditions; by lines on maps
and by lines in treaties; by expedience and opportunism; by
suits and uniforms; and by piles and piles of dead bodies, there
is something irresistible about the idea of a football match as a
national catalyst. (I sit down, triumphant, and hammer at my
keyboard.) No, a football *team* as national catalyst. For what is
a team but the soldering of the individual into the collective, the
gathering of the many into the one. Here is permission to come
together again, to work together. Here is the reassertion of the
possibility of comradeship, and here too the reassertion of its
centrality. Local heroes brought together into a national collective;
localities brought together into a nation. (Perhaps I punch the
air at this point.) As well as all that other stuff, a nation is a
story that everybody keeps telling one another. An imagined

community, as Benedict Anderson has it: museum, census, map ... and football team? When the broad mass of a nation gathers round a radio and hears their brave underdog boys snatch the prize from the greatest side in the world, why shouldn't that grip and twist the collective imagination in the same way as any story of any last stand, any doomed charge, any half-fact half-myth king. Countries don't just have borders. They have flavours.

(My back hurts.) Or maybe we should say: it is sometimes useful and sometimes consoling to pretend that this is what a nation is. To tell the story about the story, to regurgitate the national myth of a national myth. It is pleasing to imagine that the division between us and them is a thing made of heroism and togetherness rather than checkpoints and barbed wire and walls of brick and bureaucracy.

(My head hurts.) Or maybe we shouldn't? One of the most pernicious effects of misty-eyed nation-building is the way it forecloses on the possibility of imagining human communities apart from and beyond and above the nation. We can do better than borders, better than flags and anthems, and that means doing better than the stories that lock them in place and make them seem somehow natural, inevitable, correct. The one thing every nation is, above all else, is not any other nation.

And what did it mean to imagine a new German nation, a harmless German republic built from spirited sporting endeavour and plucky underdog stylings, so soon after the defeat of the Third Reich? The German national anthem, the *Deutschlandlied*, had been adopted in 1922 and was kept on in truncated form by the Nazis, who rather liked the first verse. That's the one that begins "Deutschland, Deutschland über alles". It shared anthem status with *Horst-Wessel-Lied* until the end of the war, at which point it was briefly banned. Then, with the founding of West Germany in 1949, an anthem-shaped vacuum opened up. But none of the proposed solutions managed to fill it: the West Germans tried carnival songs and folk songs, and a heavily religious alternative called *Hymne an Deutschland* totally failed to capture the public imagination. Eventually, in 1952, chancellor Konrad Adenauer succeeded in having the *Deutschlandlied* reinstated, albeit with a necessary compromise. Out went the impolitic, grossly nationalist first verse, and in came the third, which begins with the call of "Einigkeit und Recht und Freiheit". Unity, justice, freedom.

Do you know the third verse of your national anthem? After the 1954 final, the celebrating German supporters raised their voices to sing their anthem, and many and perhaps most sang the verboten first verse. (Grass's financier and his students do so without a moment's hesitation.) There was a scandal; some countries cut their coverage. You could call it an act of revanchist belligerence or an honest mistake; you could call it tactless. You probably wouldn't be completely wrong however you explained it, for there are lots of people in crowds and each carries with them their own imaginary nation. But it does rather illustrate the problem — not only a German problem, this — of trying to build that thing called patriotism, a nationalism that plays nicely with others, when the blood is barely dry on the tools available.

THE CHANGING OF BLOOD INTO FIRE

It wasn't just the wrong song that soured the aftermath. As Brian Glanville wrote in 2013, "That the West German World Cup winning team of 1954 beat Hungary in the final enhanced by drugs is something we have known for a long time. Indeed it was pretty plain soon after the final itself with tales — not least from an enraged Ferenc Puskás — of German players vomiting in their dressing room. When more than half that team succumbed to jaundice and were out for months it was plainer than ever that their remarkable second half rally against the Hungarians had a chemical basis. Just a few years ago, a dressing room worker revealed that he had found syringes below the floorboards."

Glanville was writing after the *Suddeutsche Zeitung* published leaked excerpts from an unpublished report that pointed to a widespread, state-sponsored doping programme dating back to at least the 1970s. The report also found evidence that some West German players had been using ephedrine at the 1966 World Cup, and going back further, that an unknown number of West Germany's 1954 finalists had been given Pervitin before the game.

The Wehrmacht called it "tank chocolate", the Luftwaffe called it "pilot's salt". The British wartime press called it "Germany's miracle pill", and chemists call it methamphetamine. If you put Pervitin into Google, you get a lot of headlines like "Inside the Drug Use That Fueled Nazi Germany", and a bit of clicking will take you to Norman Ohler's bestseller *Blitzed*, which avers that the whole of the Reich, from the frontlines to the home front and up through the echelons of power to Hitler himself, was high and bug-eyed for most of the war. And if you put Pervitin into your bloodstream then you will become more awake and more alert, you will feel neither fatigue nor fear, and you might even get better at football, at least for a few hours. Though you might not be great company afterwards.

What does this do to the miracle? It doesn't do anything in a legal, technical sense: you can't break rules that don't exist yet, and Fifa didn't bring in doping controls until the sixties. As far as I can tell there has never been any serious argument that West Germany's win should be struck from the record books and the medals removed to Hungary.

But does it ruin the feeling of it? It probably should, right? A miracle reduced to a conjuring trick; worse, a cheap conjuring trick, and poorly hidden. See the wires, see the mirror, see the trapdoor. And there is something desperately bleak about the use of Pervitin: like the anthem, an almost too on-the-nose reminder that new nations are mostly built from the left-over pieces of old nations.

So why doesn't it ruin it? In the course of writing this part I've been trying to whip myself up into some kind of outrage that might be commensurate with what was at stake. A doped World Cup final. A World Cup final, won by cheating. BY CHEATING! (Slaps self in face.) THE BRAVE AND BEAUTIFUL HUNGARIANS ROBBED OF DESERVED GLORY AND you know what, it's not really sticking. Presumably this is a consequence of time and distance. Everybody that played that day is dead, along with both the managers, the referee and both linesmen. And although this was the first televised final, the World Cup was yet to become a televisual event: that would only come in 1970, when Pelé gifted canary yellow to a chromatically starved Europe. All we have of this game are partial highlights in the Pathé news style, jerky footage of men with Brylcreemed hair, heavy shirts and weathered faces. They all look like they're smoking even when they're not. This is the ancient football of a bygone age, and this is the ancient doping that goes with it. We don't know what football's high-level doping programmes look like at the moment, because hardly anybody gets tested and even fewer people get caught. (Or because they don't exist. Maybe they don't exist.) But our lack of knowledge suggests we've come a long way from dirty syringes filled with wartime speed.

A miracle is already cheating. It's baked into the very concept. Some power, some other force comes along and suddenly the ordinary rules don't apply any more. And the quality of miraculosity is a sticky one: it survives through all the other explanations, taken singly or all at once, and it survives this one too. The story's the thing. Once everybody's decided that something goes beyond the capacity of rational explanation, there's no rolling that back.

Did the players know they were doped, if doped they were? It seems not. In 2004, West Germany's doctor admitted administering injections but claimed they contained nothing particularly exciting. "I injected the players with vitamin C to improve their stamina. You can't measure the effect, but the players believed in it." And then they provided the world with a miracle, and everybody believed in that, too.

~~SIXTH GOAL~~

~~But cram those tors back into your mouth and hold your national narrative horses: Hungary have only gone and equalised! There is a West German defensive line. It is not a particularly straight one. And into the unwanted space gallops the Galloping Major. He's hit cleaner finishes. He can't have hit many that important. It's the 86ᵗʰ minute, and Hungary are level!~~

IF YOU WANT A COUNTRY, YOU NEED A FLAG

Maybe the Puskás Award should be given to whoever scores the season's best disallowed goal?

It is very, very difficult, from the footage available, to come to any solid conclusion about whether Puskás was offside. (He says not. He would say not.) But what we have doesn't feel very offside, if we are trying to guess. Offside as an energy, offside as a vibe. Offside as pornography: you know it when you see it. If he was then it was marginal, if it was marginal then it could have gone the other way, and if it goes the other way that sends us spiralling out into a whole world of exciting counter-possibilities that generally come to rest with a Hungary victory. Hard to see how West Germany could have coped with the gut punch of being robbed of the victory at the very, very, very last. Some accounts of the game have Walter, ever the melancholic, turning to Rahn and lamenting "So it was all for nothing," only for Rahn to snap back "He was offside."

And what would that have meant for the fledgling republic, born and then unborn, glimpsed and then gone? Follow the logic through, and it's a little giddying to think that VAR might have preemptively toppled the FGR. Gunter Gebauer, philosopher and sports sociologist, has written that the win in 1954 "reshaped those qualities ascribed by Germans to their national character and blackened by the Nazi era into the new virtues of the period of German reconstruction." What if it hadn't? What kind of nation might have emerged from an economic miracle alone? To live an ordinary life is to wonder, from time to time, what might have been if a miracle had occurred at some ordinary conjuncture. To live with a miracle is to invert that wondering, to be haunted at every turn by the ghosts of lost mundanities. Perhaps a similar, subtly different story might have been told about the brave team that came so close, only to be defeated by the immortal Hungarians. A different country might have emerged, catalysed not by a miracle but by something more protean. What that might look like, what that Germany might taste like, is left as an exercise for the reader.

See the Hungarians. Look at their faces. Shock doesn't cover it: the bottom of the world has fallen out. The arc of history is being shattered and remade around them, without them. Nothing makes sense. And there is a sound rising, great and terrible. It is a slither and a hiss, many times over, multiplied up into a drumming of thunder. It is all the snakes in Ireland rushing as one to devour them. This is a miracle. Of course it is a miracle. But it is not their miracle.

NORTH KOREA

1

ITALY

0

NORTH KOREA	ITALY
1. Li Chan-myung	1. Enrico Albertosi
5. Lim Zoong-sun	9. Francesco Janich
3. Shin Yung-kyoo	11. Spartaco Landini
14. Ha Jung-won	8. Aristide Guarneri
13. Oh Yoon-kyung	6. Giacinto Facchetti
8. Pak Seung-zin (c)	4. Giacomo Bulgarelli (c)
7. Pak Doo-ik ⊗ (42')	7. Romano Fogli
6. Im Shung-hwi	17. Marino Perani
11. Han Bong-zin	14. Sandro Mazzola
17. Kim Bong-hwan	3. Paolo Barison
15. Yang Song-guk	19. Gianni Rivera

Manager: Myung Rye-hyun

Manager: Edmondo Fabbri

Ayresome Park

Middlesbrough,
England

ATTENDANCE
17,829

REFEREE
Pierre Schwinte (France)

TOBIAS JONES

The 1966 World Cup was far removed from the slick, glitzy tournament it has since become. Images of a youthful Queen Elizabeth opening the games make it look more like a school sports day, with hand-made flags and children sitting on easy-access fields.

The stadia weren't closed ovals, keeping out the reality of the world, but rectangles whose often unjoined edges allowed spectators to see the terraced houses and industrial chimneys beyond. There was a visual, as well as emotive, connection between the suburbs and what were still, back then, called "grounds". Football hadn't yet become an exclusive fantasy.

National anthems were played only in the opening and final games of that tournament because the presence of the Democratic Peoples' Republic of Korea had created a diplomatic conundrum: little more than a decade after the Korean War (1950-53) — in which Britain, the United States and their allies had fought against the Communist north, supported by the Soviet Union and China — Britain still didn't, diplomatically, recognise the nascent country. To have had the country's anthem played in the tournament would have been an admission that such a position was no longer tenable. In the West, the DPRK would become called simply North Korea.

Unlike today's World Cup matches, in which players are so familiar with the opposition because they either play in the same club team or have already played against each other repeatedly throughout the season, in 1966 there was almost complete ignorance about the opposition. A few last-minute training sessions might have been scouted, but Italians knew next to nothing about the team they had been drawn against in Group 4. Ferruccio Valcareggi, the Italian assistant manager, dismissed the North Korean players as *ridolini*, "little gigglers". The average height of the North Korean team was only five foot five — even the goalkeeper was only five foot seven — and more than one observer at the time called them "a team of jockeys".

Going into the tournament, the Italians were confident. In the four friendlies prior to the World Cup, against Bulgaria, Argentina, Austria and Mexico, Italy had scored 15 goals and conceded only one. The Italian team had some of the post-war greats in their ranks: Sandro Mazzola — son of the captain of the "great Torino", Valentino Mazzola, who perished in the Superga air crash of 1949 — had scored 19 goals for Inter in their title-winning 1965-66 season. His team-mate at both Inter and Italy, the lanky defender Giacinto Facchetti, had netted 10 goals that season. Gianni Rivera, the twisty midfielder from Milan, was the metronome.

In the mid-1960s, Serie A was the most international league in the world. In that 1965-66 season, its managers hailed from Sweden, Uruguay, Argentina and Paraguay, as well as, obviously, from Italy itself; there were players from Denmark, Germany, Brazil and even England (the great journeyman, Gerry Hitchens). There was something assured and educated about Italian football: it was cosmopolitan but also cagey, exuberant but always tactical, somehow noble but never immune to the dark arts of defending.

The North Korean team, by contrast, was only at the World Cup because of the absurdity of the qualifying process. The tournament organisers had decreed that only one team from the whole of Africa, Asia and Oceania could qualify for the 16-team tournament. In protest, African teams and South Korea refused to take part in qualifiers, meaning that Australia and North Korea played a two-legged knock-out game in Cambodia to go to England. Even though North Korea won 9-2 on aggregate, at the start of the tournament they were still 1,000/1 outsiders.

＊

By the end of the Korean war, the major cities, towns and factories of the Democratic People's Republic of Korea had been levelled. Photographs from the mid- to late-1950s show destitute children sitting disconsolately on hillocks of rubble. Flattened forests look like spilt matchsticks. The country's leader, Kim Il-sung, pioneered a frenetic rebuilding programme that went under the name of Chollima (a mythological winged horse which was said to cover 4,000 kilometres a day). Chollima echoed the Soviet's Stakhanovite ethic in which high-speed, incessant hard work would exponentially increase industrial production. The term became woven into North Korean life: one of the metro lines in Pyongyang is called Chollima and the winged horse is used on coins and postage stamps. The key elements were speed and personal sacrifice to a great national cause, so the DPRK's football team was nicknamed in North Korea "the Chollima team", with a song to match.

When the 74-strong North Korean contingent arrived in Middlesbrough, something happened that was as unexpected as it was uplifting. If there had been Establishment disdain for the delegation from an unrecognised Communist country, the reception in Teesside was very different. Lodging at St George Airport Hotel in Middleton, the North Koreans were invited to a civic reception hosted by the Middlesbrough mayor, Jack Boothby, who told the delegation: "You wear the same colours as Middlesbrough; we will shout for you". Over the decades, there have been many theories as to quite why a northern English town bonded so thoroughly with the diminutive, unknown Koreans. It might have been because of a fraternity between underdogs: Middlesbrough had just been relegated to the third tier of English football and the town hadn't even been due to host any World Cup matches. It was only a dispute between St James' Park and Newcastle City Council that had persuaded the tournament organisers to switch venues. The bond might have been forged because the North Koreans were defeated 3-0 in their opening game against the ultimate 'baddies' of the era, the Soviet Union. But the affection for the team grew also from an admiration for the way they played the game: fast, incisive, attacking football exemplified by daring and agility.

There were only 13,792 spectators present in the old Ayresome Park on 15 July to watch the North Koreans' game against Chile. Chile scored an early penalty and as the game drew towards its conclusion, the number of near-misses by the Koreans seemed to suggest that they were bound to suffer their second defeat and elimination from the competition. But the crowd was noisily partisan, cheering every North Korean interception and shot. When Pak Seung-zin scored an 88th-minute equaliser the Middlesbrough crowd went berserk. A sailor ran onto the pitch and afterwards, Boothby asked to go into the North Koreans' changing room to congratulate his guests on their draw.

"The crowd ... was as much responsible for the goal as the jubilant little Korean forward", the city's *Evening Gazette* wrote the next day. "When the equaliser came, some electric strip lighting in the Press refreshment room up in the stand at Ayresome Park was brought down by the stamping of a crowd that has well and truly 'adopted' the Asians ... The Koreans, obviously heartened by the fact that they were cheered every time they were on the ball, attacked with tremendous enthusiasm ..."

There were now just four days before the North Koreans were due to play Italy. Although the Italians had beaten Chile 2-0 in their opening game, they had lost 1-0 to the USSR. North Korea would need a win to progress, the Italians only a draw.

* * *

Edmondo Fabbri, the Italian coach, was born in 1921 in Castel Bolognese, half-way between Bologna and Ravenna. The last of six children (his sister had died before he was born), Edmondo was soon nicknamed *Mundein* (Mondino) because of his short stature. His parents were from a humble background: his father was a chicken-and-egg salesman, carting his animals from one village market to the next, and his mother worked in a factory. Later, his father would open a bakery and Mondino was forced to get up at 3am to help bake and distribute the bread before going on to school.

In the interwar years, Bologna were one of the strongest teams in Italy, winning the Scudetto (the Serie A championship) four times. Mondino grew up supporting Bologna, his favourite player being the legendary striker Angelo Schiavio, who over his long career scored 249 goals for the team. Mondino was a keen cyclist too, but soon gave up his bike for the ball. Playing for Imolese in a friendly against Bologna, he was asked at half-time if he would like to change sides, so — aged only 17 — he pulled on the red-and-blue colours of a shirt that, he said, fell down to his knees and covered his hands.

He was a right-winger, fast and direct. He was soon nicknamed *topolino* (Mickey Mouse) for the way in which he would scurry up and down the wing avoiding the big boys. In 1939, he was signed by Forlì on a contract of 400 lire a month. A year later, he moved to Atalanta for a 100,000 lire fee, earning 1,500 lire a month. He scored on his debut in Serie A aged only 18. At the end of that season, the newly-promoted Atalanta finished sixth, with Mondino scoring five goals. He did even better the following year, scoring a hat-trick at the San Siro in a 3-1 drubbing of Milan, and being called up to the Italy U21s (scoring, again, on his debut — his only appearance in an Italian team).

In 1942, Fabbri was sold to Inter for 225,000 lire, but after one season, football in Italy was suspended because of the war, and he was sent to Dalmazia for military service. After the war, he moved between various clubs — Sampdoria, Atalanta again (scoring 19 goals), Brescia (in Serie B) and Parma (in Serie C) where he scored 36 goals in 93 appearances. Watching footage from those years, you can always spot Mondino Fabbri: a good head shorter than the other players, barrel-chested with a scowl that just occasionally turned into a tight smile.

If his career as a player had been distinguished, his journey as a coach was meteoric. He took over Mantova in Serie D in 1957, and within five years he had led the team to the promised land of Serie A. Scorning the predilection for *catenaccio* ("chained-up", defensive football) prevalent in the late fifties and especially the 1960s, Fabbri set up his teams differently, urging them to attack and overwhelm opponents. After Mantova had defeated Legnano 8-2 in November 1958, his team was nicknamed *piccolo Brasile*, "little Brazil".

Mantova's rise was helped by investment from a local oil firm, but it was Fabbri who turned a provincial, Serie D side into a national sensation. He was described by one Mantova newspaper as "something more than a trainer: he's a conscientious, serious, affectionate father and at the same time severe. He knows how to instil in his players a fraternal spirit ... " As much as a tactician, he was a brilliant man-manager, scouting and mentoring the Brazilian forward, Angelo Sormani, who would go on to score 29 goals for Mantova before being sold to Roma for a then record half a billion lire.

Fabbri won the *Seminatore d'oro* (the "sower of gold") managerial award in 1962 but, after falling out with his club chairman, was suddenly sacked. In a public letter, he admitted to having a "strong, impulsive and vivacious character". By then, he had become slightly tubby. He habitually wore tinted glasses. He was invited to work as a scout at Inter, and briefly had a role at Verona, but in October 1962 was asked to become the Italian national manager on a four-year contract worth a million lire a month. He was only 40 and had, at that point, coached just one season at the top level of Serie A.

Nevertheless, things couldn't have started better. Fabbri's Italy beat Turkey 6-0. Shortly afterwards, in May 1963, they beat Brazil 3-0 with Sormani (an Italian citizen despite being born in Brazil), a 20-year-old Sandro Mazzola and the team's midfield 'director' from Bologna, Giacomo Bulgarelli, all scoring. Fabbri was credited with having created, at the national football centre at Coverciano, a team spirit not seen since the glory days of the 1930s when the *Azzurri* had won two World Cups. He used to wake up his players by blaring out the *Colonel Bogey March* outside the bedrooms in order to create a barracks atmosphere. "Of course, some people describe me as a 'dictator'," Fabbri once said. "Maybe that's true, but sport isn't politics: those with great responsibility need to have everything in hand."

He was extremely popular with the press, public and players. "Maybe the fact that I'm short makes me likeable", he joked. He had an attractive wife, three young boys and was revolutionising the Italian team. Italy hadn't qualified for the Swedish World Cup in 1958 and had been knocked out at the group stages after the disgrace of the 'Battle of Santiago' in 1962 in which two Italian players were sent off. Fabbri's innovation was, in part, to curtail the practice of calling up South American players of distant Italian heritage (called *oriundi*). Sandro Mazzola admired the way in which his coach had altered the mindset: "before him", Mazzola said years later, "four or five *oriundi* were fielded per game. And certain players would call in sick to avoid being called up for the *Azzurri*. Fabbri created a national team composed of Italians bound to the *Azzurri* shirt."

***

At 7am on the morning of 19 July, 1966 — the day on which Italy were due to play North Korea in the penultimate game of Group 4 — there was a catastrophic landslide in Agrigento on the southern coast of Sicily. Incessant, and sometimes illegal, building in the town meant that the mountainside was bearing weights it could no longer support. In previous years, huge blocks of flats had been built on the steep slopes so that a place once famous for its ancient Greek temple now looked like Lego blocks balancing on a ping-pong ball. That morning, cracks had appeared in roads and walls and only the astuteness of a dustman, who realised what was inevitably about to happen and quickly raised the alarm, prevented any loss of life.

The country's breakneck building had already been the subject of a *j'accuse* film, Francesco Rosi's *Hands over the City* (1963). The opening sequence, shot from above, shows mile upon mile of identikit, bland blocks of flats which, in previous years, had sprung up on the hills surrounding Naples. These were the years of the 'Sack of Palermo', a construction boom in which corrupt city councillors gave out building permits to Mafia-linked construction firms in the Sicilian capital. In the space of just a few years, the city — once an architectural jewel of the Mediterranean — became blighted by mile upon mile of concrete blocks. Something similar was happening in many Italian cities where a feedback loop was created: it suited politicians to issue as many building permits as possible to maximise the kickbacks they received from construction companies which were, often, in the names of people who had nothing to do with the building trade. The nominal owners of the companies were often simply fronts for criminals who wanted to keep their names out of the company's records.

In many ways Italy was, in the mid-1960s, experiencing its own version of a post-war, Chollima rebuild. The country was rapidly changing. In June 1966, the *Index Librorum Prohibitorum* (the Catholic church's "List of Prohibited Books" which were considered heretical or immoral) was, after four centuries, abolished by Pope Paul VI. It was a sign, perhaps, of the church's waning ability to ring-fence the intellectual tastes of a nation and to outlaw literary works which were considered deleterious to Christian morals and faith. Italy certainly wasn't a secular society — its leading political party was called Democrazia Cristiana, crucifixes still hung in every schoolroom and divorce wouldn't be legal until 1970 — but there was now a lively debate about the influence of the Vatican on Italian political life.

That debate was charmingly dramatised in the *Don Camillo* stories by Giovannino Guareschi. A satirist who had grown up along the banks of the river Po, Guareschi wrote hundreds of short stories in which a Communist mayor was constantly at loggerheads with a Catholic priest. Although ideologically opposed to each other — the one talking to his crucifix and the other to his comrades — they often compromised for the good of their little village. The stories were made into globally-successful films which revealed the fissures and fault lines in Italian society.

It was an era in which Italian film-makers were, arguably, making the most innovative and successful movies of the decade. 1966 saw the release of Sergio Leone's *The Good, The Bad and The Ugly*, Michelangelo Antonioni's *Blow-Up* and Pier Paolo Pasolini's *Uccellacci e Uccellini*. There was a creative confidence to the country which was reflected in Fabbri's tactics. He rejected the 'park-the-bus' football then fashionable at Helenio Herrera's trophy-winning Inter. "I have always tried to build a proactive national team in the offensive phase with a 'fluent' game," Fabbri explained. It was the sort of front-foot football that not only excited — there was also a clarity to what Fabbri wanted. He was repeatedly asked why he rarely selected the Inter greats like Landini, Burgnich, Buarneri, Bedin, Corso, Picchi and Sarti. Fabbri patiently explained that they had bad habits: "When someone on the pitch automatically plays 'catenaccio' applied by his club team, what can I do about it? If a child lives 11 months with his grandmother and one month only with his mother, he will end up picking up his grandmother's habits, even if they are wrong." So Fabbri decided to leave out many of the established stars of the generation, controversially favouring players from Inter's rivals, Bologna, a choice that was seen, by Milanese journalists, as a sign both of tactical naivety and of provincial bias.

Gianni Brera, Italy's celebrated post-war football writer, was particularly scornful. He called the tidy technical players Fabbri chose "little Abbots", implying they were well-meaning waifs who couldn't rough it in the arena of international football. Prior to the North Korea game, Brera even sent to Fabbri his suggested formation. By then Fabbri, having seen his team under-perform against Chile and lose to the USSR, was severely under pressure: "you can tell that great Milanese journalist", Fabbri said to the messenger, "that with this piece of paper he can clean his arse." The chances of a North Korean victory were, according to book-makers, 500-1 and Brera wrote in pages of *Il Giorno* that if Italy lost he would never write about football again.

* * *

In 1966, a ticket to the North Stand of Ayresome Park cost one pound. Almost 18,000 people filled the ground for the game. There were around 3,000 Italians in the crowd, mostly expats now living in England, but the rest were solidly behind the North Korean underdogs in red. Italy dominated the opening exchanges, getting into the box repeatedly only for Marino Perani to see his first shot saved by goalkeeper Li Chan-myung and his second screw just wide. Shortly afterwards, one-on-one, Perani again failed to find the back of the net.

Italy's captain was Giacomo Bulgarelli. Fabbri had been gushing in his praise of the Bologna player: he was, said Fabbri years later, an "extraordinary midfielder-director. I always considered him one of the most complete post-war directors, someone that the national team couldn't overlook. He was the starting point around which to build a team … he was two-footed, even if his left foot wasn't exactly enchanting, and he had the temperament and technical ability to orchestrate the team's play, both defensively and offensively. He possessed power and aggression, he had personality that he was able to transmit to his teammates, just as a team-leader should do."

But coming into the North Korea game, there had been concerns about Bulgarelli's fitness. His knee was aching and it was only a last-minute assessment by the Italian doctor that persuaded Fabbri that his talisman should play. In the 35th minute, Bulgarelli made a rash challenge, diving in feet-first, and came off worse. He lay on the grass and didn't get up. He was forced to leave the field in a game in which substitutes weren't allowed. Italy had to play almost an hour of football not just one man down, but missing their combative, iconic captain.

In the 42nd minute, it happened. A messy clearance fell to Im Shung-hwi who headed it forwards into the inside-right channel. Pak Doo-ik swung his right foot hard, slamming the ball towards the far corner of the goal. Perhaps the Italian keeper, Enrico Albertosi, could have got down quicker: by the time his body hit the ground, the ball was in the back of the net and Pak Doo-ik had his hands raised in the air, almost incredulous at what he had achieved.

The Italians seemed shocked by the energy of the North Koreans. At one point, Han Bong-zin chased a ball down so fearlessly that he smacked into the corner flag and snapped the mast in two. Throughout the second half, Italy pushed forward. Paolo Barison, Gianni Rivera and, again, Marino Perani all went close. "Behind me, the goal was small", the Korean keeper said years later. "Behind our goal was our nation. I knew if I conceded a goal, the reputation of North Korea would fall, we would have failed in the task set us by the Great Leader."

As the second half wore on, the Italians began trying to find individual solutions. Patient build-up play was replaced by desperation-dribbles and overly-ambitious through-balls. The partiality of the Ayresome Park crowd, excitedly cheering on every North Korean tackle, save and interception, seemed to drain the energy from the Italian players who, deprived of Bulgarelli's driving runs, started to appear fragile and lacking in both ideas and in confidence. When the final whistle went, they bent over, hands on their knees, as if cowed by exhaustion and shame.

The North Koreans' victory was both shocking and exhilarating. A photograph from behind the goal, showing Albertosi diving to his right, with an air-borne ball already beyond him and the North Korean players in the background, momentarily static and astonished, became one of the iconic images of that year. It seemed not only to encapsulate a redemptive

David-and-Goliath sporting story, but also to provide a humanising antidote to geopolitical narratives. North Koreans were supposed to be Communist automatons, but their football had been joyous: they seemed touched by the unexpected adulation from locals and played their games with exuberance. Off the pitch, too, they appeared not dastardly villains but humble, courteous guests who repeatedly sang their "friendship song" to the Mayor and people of Middlesbrough. Rather than reinforcing animosity, the North Korean team appeared capable of dismantling it. Years later, the goal-scorer Pak Doo-ik said that "playing football can improve diplomatic relations and promote peace".

**

If what happened against Italy seemed almost incomprehensible, what came next — not just in the following match, but in the months and years that followed — showed how a 90-minute game of football can change peoples' lives forever.

North Korea were due to play their quarter-final against Eusebio's Portugal at Everton's Goodison Park on 23 July. Thousands of Teessiders made the trip to Liverpool to support the country that had, by now, become 'their' team. It was the most extraordinary game of that entire tournament: North Korea started out fast, precise and ruthless. Pak Seung-zin scored in the first minute and then, in a three-minute burst half-way through the first half, the team went 3-0 up. The partisan crowd started chanting "we want four". It seemed inconceivable that these diminutive, unknown outsiders who had put Italy to the sword were now humiliating one of the tournament favourites.

It didn't last. At three up, many more experienced teams might have throttled back and thought about keeping a clean sheet, but the North Koreans lacked the cynicism to halt their style. They continued to push on, leaving spaces in behind which Eusebio began to exploit. He pulled two back before the break (one a penalty) and then scored two more (one another penalty) in the first 15 minutes of the second half. The Portuguese eventually won 5-3 and the North Koreans' adventure was over. They were lauded and applauded, but went back to North Korea and were, until 2002, never seen again.

***

What happened to Fabbri and the Italians was the opposite: predictably they faced public threats and press accusations. In the post-match press-conference after the Korean defeat, Fabbri barely looked at anything other than his shoes. "I won't hide my state of profound pain, but I am here to take full responsibility for what has happened ... "

The team flew back to Genoa's Cristoforo Colombo airport in an attempt to avoid the hostile crowds of Milan or Rome, but even though the plane touched down at 3.30 am, a crowd was present to shout *"bidoni, bidoni"* — "rubbish, rubbish" — as they stepped from the plane. Players were pelted with tomatoes and eggs.

Throughout that summer, fan fury continued to be aimed at Fabbri: there were paintings of a hanged stick-man on city walls with "death to Fabbri" scrawled next to it in white paint. When he went to the seaside with his family, the coach had to have a police escort. "I feel like I've been treated like a criminal," he said.

One guesses that Mondino Fabbri suffered what, in today's terminology, would be called a breakdown or clinical depression. He drove his car into a ditch. He went, with his son, to stay in a hermitage, Camaldoli, in Tuscany. He couldn't stop thinking about what had happened in Middlesbrough and began having delusions that his training camp had been deliberately sabotaged by the injection of secret pharmaceuticals into the bloodstreams of his players. That summer, he started to contact some of his key players, phoning them out of the blue or surprising them outside their houses. He interviewed them and took notes and began compiling a dossier which alleged that pink phials had caused inexplicable depression and tiredness. It was the only way, perhaps, that he could explain to himself what had become of him and his players.

He took his allegations to the press and, inevitably, a scandal broke. Many Italians were content to believe that the drugging of players was the real reason for defeat by the North Koreans, and if they weren't, it was a good story to talk about, another hypothesis amidst the thousands of others to explain it. But none of it made much sense. The notion that medical staff would collude with Fabbri's rivals, or with officials who were irate at the exclusion of Inter players, to drug players prior to a key World Cup match seemed fanciful. The team's doctor sued Fabbri for libel and he was pilloried in the press for his eccentric explanation for his team's failure. He was sacked and banned from football for six months. He was only 45 and his career appeared, in some ways, already over. His reputation was shot.

A year later, Fabbri was asked to take over at Torino. There he patiently created a style of play that was both eye-catching and, often, winning. He recognised youthful talent, as he had with both Mantova and Italy, and gave a debut to the future Torino legend Paolo Pulici. As national manager, he had given a debut cap to the brilliant, unorthodox winger, Gigi Meroni, and now Fabbri became his manager at club level. When Meroni was killed by a car in October 1967, aged only 24, Fabbri's eloquence in a moment of grief showed a man of granite kindness. People could see how hurt Fabbri was and how much he had become a paternal figure to his players.

When, in 1968, Torino won the Coppa Italia under Fabbri, it was a demonstration that the much-scorned manager was, still, a great coach. Two years later, when finally asked to manage his beloved Bologna, he coached them, too, to Coppa Italia glory. There he once again recognised and developed young talent, like the 21 year-old Beppe Savoldi. Years later, Savoldi warmly remembered Fabbri: "He was an innovator," Savoldi said, "attentive to formations and tactics. In training, he made us try out movements with other teammates, none of which we had ever done before. He also had a good cultural background. Every now and then he would quote a philosopher or a poet. I saw in him a life-guide, because it didn't end with the quotation of an aphorism. With his behaviour, he would put it into practice."

Even when Fabbri's teams didn't win trophies, he usually laid the foundations for his successors. The personnel and tactics which he had nurtured as Italy manager meant that the team, so ridiculed for their elimination in the group stages in 1966, went on to win the European Championship in 1968 with his protégés, Giacinto Facchetti, Sandro Mazzola and Gigi Riva, playing starring roles. He returned to coach Torino in the mid-1970s and there, too, he built a team which (inherited by Gigi Radice) went on to win the Scudetto in 1976, just a year after he had left.

But the North Korea defeat was a profound wound that never fully healed. Opposition fans would inevitably chant "Korea, Korea" every time he took his place in the dug-out and once he was even beaten up once by a Roma fan outside a ground. Perhaps worn down by that scorn, he retired early, aged only 56, retreating back to the small town of Castel Bolognese to tend his vineyard. Mondino Fabbri died in July 1995. At his funeral, his son, Roberto, confessed to Arrigo Sacchi (the great Milan coach who was, in some senses, a student of Fabbri's more expansive football) that "even after so many years, my father never managed to get over the trauma of Korea".

The great sports journalist and Torino fan, Gian Paolo Ormezzano, wrote a moving tribute to Fabbri in the pages of *La Stampa*: "Mondino", he said, "was propelled by his successes with Mantova into an orbit that was perhaps too big for him. Then he failed with the national team. Thinking about that defeat, the most atrocious in history, we all felt more competent and more capable than him to lead the Azzurri. Since millions of Italians continually pretend to be the national manager, he provided a convenient touchstone for our arrogance. And yet, Mondino knew everything about football. And he possessed a jovial morality. In the end, he would deal with even the worst of his enemies with a joke in Romagnolo dialect, without malice. And everything would end there. It would have been nice if, after Korea, we had all been able to do the same with him ... "

***

Far less was known about what had happened to the North Korean team. There were rumours that the players had been put in a labour camp for the decadence of late-night drinking after their victory against Italy. The North Korean defector, Kang Chol-hwan, who was interned in the Yodok concentration camp from the age of nine, claimed in his book, *The Aquariums of Pyongyang*, to have met the scorer of the equaliser against Chile, Pak Seung-zin, in the camp. Pak had been held there, claimed Kang, for over 20 years. It was a story denied by the North Korean authorities.

In 1995, Middlesbrough moved from Ayresome Park to the Riverside Stadium and the old site was turned into a Wimpey housing estate. But a few years later, the South African-born sculptor, Neville Gabie, decided to pepper the estate with bronze memories from the former stadium in an imaginative attempt to commemorate another era: a pair of football boots outside a front door where the centre circle used to be, a bronze cast of a football by the penalty spot, a coloured metal "scarf" where the corner flag used to be. Perhaps most evocatively, he placed a bronze puddle of mud, with indentations of studs, on the exact spot from which Pak Doo-ik had shot his winning goal against Italy.

In the late 1990s, at the same time as Gabie was negotiating with home-owners to place memorials to the sporting past on their property, the film director, Daniel Gordon, had an idea: he wanted to track down the original North Korean team that had so memorably bonded with the people of Middlesbrough. Teaming up with Nicholas Bonner, co-founder of a tour company, Koryo

Tours, specialising in North Korea, Gordon gained the confidence of the North Korean authorities and produced one of the most unusual and moving football documentaries ever made.

The Game of Their Lives never ducks the issue of a country in thrall to a personality cult: it mentions how every North Korean has to wear a lapel badge of either Kim Il-sung ("the great leader") or of his son. It shows how choreographed displays in the "mass games" (rehearsed for millions of hours) reduce human beings to miniscule pixels in sophisticated stadium displays. But rather than ridicule a society so remote from our own, the documentary simply observes it: the players, by then in their sixties and seventies, wear brown military uniforms with medals and seemingly over-sized hats. They weep in front of the statue of the "great leader". But despite the ideological distance from our own world, the power of the documentary lies (like that famous match itself) in its ability to humanise the participants: although superficially they seem stiff and starchy, in thrall to a barmy cult we can't understand, those players actually emerge as thoroughly human: Pak Doo-ik is shown in his spartan flat, laughing about how he can always avoid a parking ticket because of his footballing fame. The team sing their Chollima song again, each staring into the distance as if overwhelmed by the realisation that many decades have passed and that, despite singing about speed, they're now slow and elderly.

In 2002, the team was invited back to Middlesbrough. They visited Gabie's bronze puddle where the famous shot had been taken and, after a celebration dinner at the Riverside Stadium, were introduced to the crowd before Middlesbrough's home match against Leeds United. In the match programme, the North Koreans wrote about how the "cheering voices of the citizens of Middlesbrough remain fresh still in our memory ... we can clearly remember the people of Middlesbrough who had warmly welcomed us, enthusiastically supported us during our game against Italy and even followed us up to Liverpool." That unexpected bond between Middlesbrough and North Korea was cemented by the council hoisting — not without controversy — the flag of the Democratic People's Republic of Korea on 19 July, 2003, to commemorate the notorious match. In 2010, the Middlesbrough Ladies football team even toured the country, playing two matches in Pyongyang.

In Italy, meanwhile, they have begun to talk about the curse of 'the north': in 1958, Italy failed to qualify for the World Cup because it was, unexpectedly, beaten by Northern Ireland 2-1 at Windsor Park. Then in March 2022, Italy lost a World Cup qualifier, at home, to North Macedonia, meaning that they will be absent for the 2022 World Cup. It's as if that distant, fateful game against North Korea still reverberates, painfully, through the national, sporting psyche.

WEST GERMANY 1974

22 JUNE
GROUP STAGE

E.GERMANY
1

W.GERMANY
0

E. Germany	W. Germany
1. Jürgen Croy	1. Sepp Maier
2. Lothar Korbjuweit	2. Berti Vogts
3. Bernd Bransch (c)	3. Paul Breitner
4. Konrad Weise	4. Hans-Georg Schwarzenbeck OFF
12. Siegmar Wätzlich	*6. Horst-Dieter Höttges ON (68')*
18. Gerd Kische	5. Franz Beckenbauer (c)
10. Hans-Jürgen Kreische	8. Bernhard Cullmann
13. Reinhard Lauck	12. Wolfgang Overath OFF
14. Jürgen Sparwasser ⊗ (77')	*10. Günther Netzer ON (69')*
16. Harald Irmscher OFF	15. Heinz Flohe
17. Erich Hamann ON (68')	9. Jürgen Grabowski
20. Martin Hoffmann	13. Gerd Müller
	14. Uli Hoeness
Manager: Georg Buschner	Manager: Helmut Schön

Volksparkstadion

Hamburg, West Germany

ATTENDANCE
60,350

REFEREE
Ramón Barreto (Uruguay)

ADAM BUSHBY

> Truth be told, I was toying with starting
> this chapter with a date. Then I changed
> my mind. So I'd like to begin with a name
> instead. Jürgen Sparwasser. In fact,
> scrap that too. More of him later. I'm going
> to start with a country, Germany. Sorry,
> make that two countries, both called Germany.

The genesis of this unlikely story can be traced back to when Europe's borders were in a state of flux, redrawn following discussions between Churchill, Roosevelt and Stalin at Yalta. In the aftermath of the Second World War, Germany was carved up by the allied powers as a continent prepared for peace. "I don't think I'm wrong about Stalin," Churchill had said on his return to London, but he would confide his regret at trusting the Soviet leader to his private secretary John Colville just five days later. With tensions between the former allies simmering over the next few years, the German Democratic Republic (*Deutsche Demokratische Republik* or DDR) — East Germany — and the Federal Republic of Germany (FRG) — West Germany — came into being in 1949. One country cleaved in two. And, as a consequence, two national teams on very different paths.

In 1954, there was, unbelievably, a World Cup win for Germany. Well, the Western bit at least. Writer Friedrich Christian Delius described "a guilt-ridden, inhibited nation [that] was suddenly reborn". It was left to the one nicknamed *Der Kaiser* to exclaim: "Suddenly, Germany was somebody again." More of him later too.

It was a team of somebodies that would be undone at Wembley 12 years later in no small part by football's most famous linesman.

Four years after that, more than 100,000 would cram into the Aztec Stadium to witness the 'Game of the century' or '*Jahrhundertspiel*', with a truly remarkable five goals scored in extra time and West Germany on the wrong end of a seven-goal thriller against the Italians. Runners-up and semi-finalists in the two World Cup tournaments preceding their first on home soil. And when a Günter Netzer-inspired West Germany dismantled England in the Euro '72 quarter-finals, *L'Equipe* would gush about "dream football from the year 2000".

So that's more or less where we are in the summer of 1974. West Germany playing football from the future, Netzer looking like the messiah and occasionally acting like a naughty boy, Beckenbauer at his peak, Gerd Müller doing Gerd Müller things, and a supporting cast that were, more or less, at least the equal of any other national team in the world. But what of the other Germany?

***

Every good story needs a villain. Ours was born into poverty in a tenement in the working-class Berlin district of Wedding, son of a cartwright and a mother who died when he was young. Both were, crucially, ardent communists. This was pre-World War II Germany, back when it was but one country.

A murderer at age 24, for which many years later in a reunified country he would serve porridge, Erich Mielke was a man who survived and then thrived in the shadows. He survived Stalin's Great Purge, rising through the ranks while a fugitive in the Soviet Union, then as an operative of the *Servicio de Investigación Militar* during the Spanish Civil War. His Second World War ended with multiple Soviet military honours and a world view shaped and cemented through the lens of socialism. He then thrived in a new Germany.

From 1957 until the Berlin Wall fell in 1989, Mielke oversaw a vast, surreptitious operation as head of the Socialist Unity Party of Germany (*Sozialistische Einheitspartei Deutschlands*, or SED)'s

Ministry for State Security, better known as the Stasi. The Stasi was the DDR's largest employer by some margin. Quite how many is a secret that left this earthly plane in 2000 when Mielke was plonked six feet into the ground, but some historians posit that as many as half a million *inoffizieller mitarbeiters* (IMs, or unofficial informers) aided and abetted over 100,000 full-time officers and non-commissioned personnel. In a country of around 17 million people as of the 1970 census, roughly one in 170 was employed in an official capacity by the secret service.

Using figures cited by John O. Koehler in his book *The Untold Story of the East German Secret Police,* Stasi ranks swollen with IMs means that roughly every 66th inhabitant of the DDR was a cog in this unrelenting espionage and counter-espionage machine. "When one adds in the estimated numbers of part-time snoops," Koehler writes "the result is nothing short of monstrous: one informer per 6.5 citizens." As a comparator, the Gestapo had one officer for every 2,000 people. Mielke made it his life's mission to turn society itself into a prison, keeping the DDR's population at large incarcerated. He was very good at it.

The Stasi's tentacles reached into every nook of every community, Straße, household and football club. Some historians have said that, typically, one-third of a DDR-Oberliga squad's players worked in an IM capacity, more common in sides playing in European competition and, thus, travelling to the West. In 1974, this would be Dynamo Dresden, 1. FC Magdeburg, 1. FC Lokomotive Leipzig and Carl Zeiss Jena. Away days across Europe dangled the carrot of defection in front of young men who had dreams of playing for Juventus or Real Madrid, an unthinkable scenario for the DDR authorities. Erich Hamann, who would be so instrumental in the clash of the two Germanys, had been an IM of the secret police for five years prior to the tournament. Likewise, DDR manager Georg Buschner, operating under the imaginative codename 'Georg' between 1966 and 1971.

And then there was the psychological warfare waged on an entire nation. The practice was known as *Zersetzung*, general translation 'decomposition', under the auspices of which individual lives were disrupted, dismantled or smashed to bits. *Zersetzung* amounted to an assault on the mind: homes were bugged, people were followed, tires were let down again and again, houses were broken into where alarm clocks would be fiddled with, socks put in different drawers. Mielke oversaw the whole thing from his personal fiefdom; the bleak, sprawling complex of clad concrete buildings at Haus 1 on 103 Ruschestraße off Frankfurter Allee.

Konrad Jarausch, a historian at the University of North Carolina at Chapel Hill, has spoken eloquently of the subtle onslaught. "They beat people up less often, sure, but they psychologically trampled people," he says. "Which is worse depends on what you prefer." A gallows humour pervaded. An old DDR joke goes as follows: "Why do the Stasi work together in groups of three?" Answer: "You need one who can read, one who can write, and one to keep an eye on the two intellectuals."

Mielke's lasting legacy as far as the domestic league is concerned is as cynical and joyless as the man himself. A draw in Berlin being enough to win the DDR-Oberliga title in May 1978, celebrations were well under way in the dressing room of Dynamo Dresden. Then, Mielke's shadow darkened the door. He entered, ostensibly to congratulate them, gold medal around his neck like a dickhead, then soured the party completely by telling them to enjoy the glory while it lasted, as Berliner FC Dynamo would be champions next season.

True to his word and because he could, BFC Dynamo won the league the next season, and the next. And the next. And so on. They would win it 10 seasons on the bounce, amid allegations of crooked refs receiving brown envelopes and players throwing games. Then again, likely threatened with the sack or else a very public, state-led campaign of grinding your name into the dirt (or, if your Stasi file read that you weren't the breaking type, the same fate for a loved one), really, what would you do?

***

Going into the 1974 World Cup, German club football was undergoing something of a renaissance on both sides of the divide. Bayern Munich had dismantled Atletico Madrid 4-0 to lift the European Cup while less plausibly, 1. FC Magdeburg had beaten the mighty AC Milan 2-0 in the Cup Winners' Cup final. The average age of the 1. FC Magdeburg players was 23 and most remarkably, all of them hailed from within a catchment area of just $11,500km^2$; only Celtic, when lifting the European Cup in 1967, could boast that they had won a European trophy with a group from a smaller area.

In the middle of the 73-74 season, before the two Germanys put their stamp all over the European club tournaments, came the draw for the World Cup. What cruel mistress other than fate would draw two very divided sides of the same country against each other at the greatest footballing show on earth? She took the form of an 11-year-old choirboy on the night of 5 January, 1974. The baby-faced Detlef Lange plunged his hand into the glass bowl containing the four Eastern European nations and handed a capsule to Fifa's general secretary Helmut Käser. It was Group One. West Germany's group.

Chile were already there. Their inclusion had not been without incident. The 1973 play-off for a place in the finals should have seen the South Americans meet the Soviet Union. The Soviets objected to the choice of venue given the Estadio Nacional de Chile in Santiago had been used during Augusto Pinochet's recent *coup d'état* as a torture and execution site. It would be unconscionable to play in a stadium "splashed with the blood of the Chilean patriots," the Soviets would write to Fifa. The choice of venue remained, the Soviets stayed at home and were duly disqualified.

But back to Frankfurt am Main. Käser split the capsule, shifted slightly and handed the piece of paper to the outgoing Fifa president, Englishman Sir Stanley Rous. And just like that, it was so. Germany v Germany. East v West. Socialism v capitalism. Cue an uneasy silence shattered by the wild applause of the Colombian delegate, which was then amplified by the other suits in the room. Now what?

* * *

A fog of disbelief descended. In his capacity as Director of the German Gymanstics and Sport Association (DFV), Manfred Ewald was the top sports official in the DDR. And in this capacity, he was not a man joining in the clapping once news of the *bruderduell* reached his office, not that Ewald et al would look on the game as a duel of brothers. Ewald demanded that general secretary of the DFV, Günter Schneider, provide assurances that the DDR would beat the FGR — which he couldn't of course. When the financial penalties of withdrawing from the tournament were explained to him, Ewald furiously barrelled out of the room. One can imagine that it wasn't exactly a picnic in Miekle's office either.

"In East Germany, there was initially no reporting at all of the draw," German commentator Ralf Bosse told me. "It took a while before the DDR government knew how to deal with it."

Behind the scenes, a short, dour man was overseeing a dreary plan to ensure that the trip across the forbidden divide was a saturnine success; a success from *his* perspective, of course. *Aktion Leder* was the Stasi's response (literally 'Action Leather'). Mielke set the state's huge, clanking machine in motion.

Clandestine, of course, and forensic as ever, the operation laid out the intricacies of precisely what 'success' constituted. Declassified Stasi documents show that the East German 'fans' allowed to travel to the West were 1,500 carefully selected Communist Party loyalists from across the DDR who must "actively support the football team of the DDR politically and morally in the competition". Instructions for selection were strict: they could have no Western contacts, must be party members and must be married — the train of thought being that they wouldn't abscond if they had a spouse waiting for them back in the DDR. Crucially, "attempts by the enemy to poach participants" must be resisted. Everyone making the journey must return.

Success on the pitch was reaching the final eight. Not that anyone expected this achievement to include victory over the class enemy. "The officials were hoping it wouldn't be a disgrace," former Dynamo Dresden and East Germany striker Hans-Jürgen Kreische explained in a BBC interview. You see, the East German authorities had always resisted overtures from the West for a game. Until it became inevitable, as it had in the summer of 1974.

Ensuring that all representatives behaved in an exemplary manner was central to an efficacious *Aktion Leder*. The players were no different in this regard. The Stasi tried to recruit right-back Gerd Kische to snoop on his teammates pre-tournament, but he proved unmoving and then unamenable. However, Mielke's boys managed to 'reverse' a total of five players from the East German squad, in-keeping with the Stasi's plan to employ at least one active IM for every 10 tourists.

Arriving at Hamburg airport in their matching light grey jackets, green shirt and yellow ties, the DDR squad and management team were all smiles. The departure to their camp in Quickborn was delayed when a replacement bus needed to be found as the one emblazoned with the DDR name and flag went 'missing'. Given the FGR didn't even recognise the DDR as a proper country — *Bild* even referred to the East in inverted commas — this was hardly a surprise. No doubt the slight was documented in minute detail by one of tourists.

At their base for the first group stage, the Stasi agents among the entourage relaxed their surveillance a touch, presumably overawed by the chance to sample some of the pleasures of the West. With this new-found freedom, a trip to the Reeperbahn was organised by the owners of the Sporthotel in Quickborn. A night on the tiles beckoned. The West German hosts even offered everyone from the East German delegation a free TV. The officials declined — fraternisation with the West was a strict no-no, more so the receiving of illicit Western goods — but some of the players noticed that all the televisions were gone by the time they left.

A 2-0 win over Australia in the DDR's first ever game at a World Cup finals was followed four days later by a 1-1 draw with the Chileans in their second. A somewhat unexpected scoreless draw between their first two opponents had meant that the pressure was off by their third game, mere hours before kick-off. Both Germanys had already qualified for the knockouts. Just the thorny issue of the most politically charged football match of all time to traverse then.

Coaches of the DDR-Oberliga teams were invited to attend the German v German clash, but Hans Meyer, coach of Carl-Zeiss Jena, was notable by his absence. "On the day, I had stomach pains and had to stay home," Meyer later recalled. Meyer is well-known in Germany for his sarcasm and irony — he certainly wasn't ill on the day of the game. He had turned down the offer on the grounds that he had to catch a train from Gera at 4am, then "travel with the fans to Hamburg, wave my hammer and sickle flag, get stared at by the other fans like some exotic creature, get straight back on the train after the game, and then get back home in the middle of the night". He saw straight through the absurdity of the situation and presumably watched the game at home, *ohne* flag.

* * *

It wasn't a harmonious build-up to the finals for the World Cup favourites by any means. West German authorities wanted to avoid a repeat of the shocking violence of the Munich Olympics two years earlier when the Palestinian militant group Black September murdered five Israeli athletes and six coaches. The Chilean consulate in Berlin was fire-bombed shortly before the finals began so the South Americans trained on a pitch surrounded by barbed wire, while the Scots had concerns over the IRA and there were very real fears that the Baader-Meinhof Gang were planning something big after a threatening letter announced that the Volksparkstadion would be blown up. Security at the finals was beefed up in response. The West German base camp in Malente, to the north of Hamburg, resembled a "fortress", according to left-back Paul Breitner.

Looking beyond the barbed wire, the guard dogs and the armed guards, it's no exaggeration to say that on the day of the game itself, the FGR expected two points to be served with the largest piece of cake this side of Hamburg. "*Warum wir heute gewinnen,*" screamed the headline of the tabloid *Bild*'s front page. "Why we will win today".

The optimism in the FGR had not been backed up by performances on the pitch, however. They had stuttered to a 1-0 win over Chile that was greeted by catcalls from those in West Berlin's Olympiastadion. A 3-0 victory over Australia in the second match again failed to thrill the watching public. The composure associated with Beckenbauer deserted him when he gave away possession and was booed by the German crowd. *Der Kaiser* spat in disgust in the direction of the hisses.

Nor was all well behind the scenes in Malente. A few days before the tournament, a dispute over player bonuses had seen manager Helmut Schön pack his bags and threaten to leave the camp altogether. So too had Breitner, who was convinced to stay by Günter Netzer, Gerd Müller, Wolfgang Overath and Uli Hoeneß. Meanwhile, Beckenbauer was negotiating over the phone with DFB vice-president Herman Neuberger to raise the World Cup-winning bonus from DM30,000 per man to DM100,000. They would eventually settle on DM70,000 but not before Schön had berated his players. "All I ever hear from you is money, money, money!" It was a mess.

Not that it should come as a surprise that Schön was a little highly-strung in the build-up. The FGR manager was born in what would become the DDR and had managed in Soviet-occupied East Germany until overwhelming political interference made his position untenable and he fled to the West. As Uli Hesse explains in the brilliant *Tor!*, the West Germans "knew their Dresden-born coach wanted — no, needed — to win this match at all costs". All eyes turned to Hamburg.

***

Chants of "Deutschland, Deutschland" rang around the stadium before kick-off, though the choir didn't include the 1,500 DDR apparatchiks; they seemed content with waving their little flags — black, red and gold ones embossed with hammers and compasses. Müller rolled the ball to Overath and a game for the history books got under way.

In just the third minute, a neat one-two between Bertie Vogts and Jürgen Grabowski set an FGR break in motion. The little full-back found the feet of Müller, who flicked to Overath and a neat backheel saw Heinz Flohe speed into the box and smash narrowly wide, before pointing towards the corner flag in hope more than expectation. Croy's full-length dive had been more for the cameramen, sat in a row behind the keeper's goal, than for any perceptible threat.

A few minutes later, Beckenbauer set Müller scampering down the left, who rolled his marker and squared across the six-yard box for the onrushing Jürgen Grabowski. The cross evaded the outstretched Croy, but was fractionally behind the Eintracht Frankfurt winger who ended up on his backside as the ball bobbled inches wide.

The floodgates might have creaked a bit, but it wasn't all one-way traffic. A better first touch by Gerd Kische after being set free by Kreische may well have seen the DDR get their noses in front. It was Kreische's turn to get a face full of egg when Reinhard Lauck cut back far too easily past Beckenbauer for the DDR number 10. Bernhard Cullmann stood stock still, unaware that the forward had stolen in behind him. Kreische had enough time to put his foot on the ball, climb into the crowd, grab one of the little flags being waved by his countrymen, get back on the pitch, give it a wave himself, then get down on all fours and nod the ball over the line. Instead, he did none of those things, belting the ball high, high over the bar. The West replied, Müller hitting the post. It was scruffy as only Müller did scruffy. Goalless into the break ...

It was still goalless in the 78th minute. But the eagle-eyed among you will have noticed I promised you more on Jürgen Sparwasser. Enter our hero.

* * *

After catching a tame header by Cullman, Croy launches an attack with a quick overarm throw to substitute Hamann on the right. Striding forward with the freedom of Hamburg, Hamann keeps going with a neat run from Lauck creating space in front of him. Hamann angles a long diagonal into the path of Sparwasser.

Using the element of surprise, Sparwasser opts to control the pass with his face, a move of deceptive finesse actually because, let's face it, footballers don't usually use their faces at all. He races diagonally from left to right, past both the flat-footed Horst-Dieter Höttges and Vogts. He arrows towards Sepp Maier's goal ... he can't ... can he?

"Sparwasser."

Another touch away from Höttges and Vogts ...

"Sparwasser!"

He has to shoot.

"Und ..."

Shoot man, shoot!!

"Tor!!!"

He has you know!!!!

Sparwasser arrows the ball past Maier into the roof of the net and with it secures one of the great World Cup upsets. It is when watching the goal in slow motion from behind Maier's goal that the deftness of Sparwasser's shape to shoot can be appreciated. Imperceptible at first, he cocks his right leg back

but holds off connecting for a split-second, long enough to sit
Höttges on his arse and daring Maier to commit to a dive, which
he does. Bang!!!!!

Sparwasser does a tipple tail then wheels away like a puppy
chasing a roll of toilet paper. "Never before in my life have I done
a somersault," he would later say. He ends face down on the turf
on the touchline, surrounded by his ecstatic team-mates, overcome
with the emotion of it all. Now it is cries of "Heja, heja DDR!"
that ring crisply through the still night air.

"Following the final whistle all the players swapped shirts,
although we didn't do it on the pitch because officially it was
forbidden," Kreische remembers. "But we got on very well. We spoke
the same language after all. It was a hard but fair battle."
'Spoke the same language'. Let that hang in the air for a few
seconds. German was the first language of both Germanys. This
game pitted Germany against Germany. One saw the other as
an aberration, while one saw the other as the enemy. And that's
really quite astonishing when you think about it.

* * *

Fritz Walter, the hero of the miracle in Bern, pulled no punches when
assessing how the West had lost the clash of the Germanys. In his
book, *Fußball-Weltmeisterschaft 1974*, he wrote: "The DDR
victory was a tactical one, and Buschner's team carried out his
plan so successfully and effectively that the West German eleven
fell prey to a state of confusion after an hour, and staggered to
the end of this tortuous and depressing 90 minutes in a state of
complete disintegration."

If Schön was receiving a mauling in the press the next day —
"Not like that, Mr. Schön!" *Bild* blazed on the front cover — his
East German counterpart was revelling in the upset. "We've won
the group and that's an outcome far beyond our dreams." Finding
it hard to keep a grin from spreading across his face, Buschner
invited the international press to watch his team train the next

day. "We welcome everyone, cosmopolitan as we are."

Buschner also noted how sportsmanlike both teams had been: "The most important thing about the game for me was the amicable and sporting spirit the game was played in, and that everything people had tried to impose on it from outside had no effect on the teams — on the field and afterwards there was absolutely no animosity." It seems the DDR players had taken the brief to be the personification of socialist values to heart. Whenever Konrad Weise brought down Gerd Müller, he would extend a hand and enquire: "I hope you're not hurt?"

The DDR, buoyed by their monumental success in Hamburg, travelled to Hanover for the second round where a functional, but increasingly agricultural Brazil beat them thanks to a touch of class from Rivelino's free-kick. The beautiful Dutch side outclassed them 2-0 in the pouring rain in Gelsenkirchen four days later, suffocating them with their press, and a creditable 1-1 draw against Argentina saw the side return home, beaten but unbowed. No matter. *Aktion Leder* had been an overwhelming success. The class enemy beaten and no man left behind.

Meanwhile, defeat to the DDR had "sent Helmut [Schön] into such a hot funk that someone had to cut his dinner into tiny pieces and spoon-feed him like a child" in the words of *The Guardian*'s Scott Murray. The story goes that Beckenbauer took a central role in reforming the side. Rainer Bonhof and Bernd Holzenbein came in and the Germans improved markedly, defeating Sweden, Yugoslavia and Poland (just) to set up a final with everyone's favourite team, the Dutch.

When Johan Neeskens casually makes it 1-0 to the Netherlands, the first German to touch the ball is Sepp Maier, the goalkeeper, after 80 seconds. Then the Dutch forget to score a second and the rest is history. FGR captain Beckenbauer would later state that the loss to the DDR was pivotal for his team: "The Sparwasser goal woke us up. Otherwise we never would've become world champions." Both Germanys had won in the end.

**

Miekle, Ewald and co were satisfied. Progression to the next round? Check. Everyone accounted for? Check. ITV's Keith Macklin declared: "If there has been any political gain at all from this game of football, it's certainly gone East." The opportunity to immediately exploit the victory over the old class enemy was one missed by the SED though, with Mielke's scrupulous plan seemingly missing one vital ingredient — what to do if they actually won. It would be left to the Olympics to project East Germany's sporting soft power. As it was, the people celebrated the win in Hamburg in the comfort of their own living rooms. They would be left with re-runs of *that* Sparwasser goal for 14 years until Unification Day on 3 October, 1990.

Meanwhile, there were noises off in the West. A conspiracy theory that excuses an embarrassing defeat is just oh so convenient and the story went that the FGR threw the game against the East to avoid the irresistible *Oranje* in the second round. "The funny thing is that this conspiracy theory is now widely accepted," says Hesse. "Everybody seems to have forgotten that the final games in groups 3 and 4 were played on the day after the West met the East, meaning nobody knew where the Poles would end up. Or the Dutch, for that matter." Philosophically, he adds: "I suppose if you're a footballer who seriously contemplates taking it easy to gain an advantage, you have to take into consideration that others might do the same."

**

There is a danger that within a system so completely melded to the collective that individual stories are lost. The SED put deference to the state at the centre of its political project, but for some, force of personality had too much propulsion to be cowed. Football was no different in this regard and so we turn to some examples where these positions intersect, those liminal spaces between state and society, we and I.

"It should have been clear to everyone that the DDR had great players, such as Jürgen Sparwasser, Joachim Streich, Dixie Dörner [the elegant sweeper, idolised by Mattias Sammer, missed the '74 World Cup due to a bout of jaundice] and Jürgen Croy, a first-class goalkeeper. The DDR had great quality," Bosse explained. Croy, a man whose imposing presence between the sticks was a fixture for the DDR between 1967 and 1981, won 86 caps for his country in that time, starting with a clean sheet (Sweden 1-0) and ending with one (Cuba 5-0).

He was by far and away the greatest goalkeeper the DDR ever produced and, despite Dino Zoff and Sepp Maier receiving far more plaudits internationally, he remained peerless. To the chagrin of the party bosses, Croy later explained in an interview with German football magazine *11 Freunde* that there were routinely two or three large clubs in the West fishing around for his transfer. But he knew the consequences to his loved ones would be dire so he never gave the idea anything other than a passing thought.

As a one-club man at the unfashionable Zwickau, Croy also faced pressure at home, with one of the Dynamos Berlin or Dresden, Lokomotive Leipzig or 1. FC Magdeburg touted as desired destinations. The seventies was a time when players were simply delegated to preferred clubs and Croy was one of the top prizes in the DDR. Remarkably, he stood up to the vice president of the football association, Franz Rydz, at a face-to-face meeting in Berlin when the issue of moving on was raised. It was relayed in no uncertain terms that he could be drafted to the army and end his career in the footballing no-man's land of Thuringia.

But the goalkeeper had something the Stasi hadn't bargained for. Not only had he the public backing of manager Buschner at national level, but he could call on the support of the mayor of Zwickau, numerous local officials and, above all, the workers at the VEB Sachsenring automotive factory, who had vowed to go on strike in a bid to keep their prize asset in the city. The Stasi relented and Croy stayed put.

He would end his career with just two FDGB-Pokal wins, in 1967 and 1975, as well as a Cup Winners' Cup run in the 75-76 season that saw Zwickau beat Panathinaikos, Fiorentina (Croy would score the winning penalty) and Celtic, before losing to eventual winners Anderlecht in the semi-final. Never one to put personal gain ahead of the collective, Croy was just happy that his friends were able to rub shoulders with the greats. "In the national team, I was able to regularly cross swords with world stars. But for my team-mates, meetings with Giancarlo Antognoni, Kenny Dalglish, Rob Rensenbrink and Arie Haan were something very special."

Even in retirement, Croy would never leave the hometown that meant so much to him. "I have never regretted the decision to play for Zwickau," he told *11Freunde*. "I had lots of fun with the team, had great team-mates and a very professional environment. My family liked living in Zwickau. It was never vital to earn 400 marks more playing in Dresden or Leipzig. At the time, I felt it was more important to be close to the fans. I simply saw a connection that I had with these fans, who gave me so much." Never one to blow his own trumpet or else kick up a fuss, Croy always knew that quiet resistance can carry just as much noise.

***

For most fans, who they support is unequivocal and so their enemies are written in stone and remain a constant, in a football sense anyway. For some, it's not so simple. And when a country gets ripped in two, it's not simple *in the slightest*. State as system and symbol goes *pretty* far, but it still only goes *so* far. Fealty to the flag will always be limited by the fact that it does not concern itself with subjective experience and lifting back the curtain (both iron and personal) was integral to what I wanted to achieve with this story. For what is football less the feelings it stirs and the memories it conjures?

Published in 1999, *My Century* by Nobel Prize for Literature winner Günter Grass charts 100 years in the form of a year per chapter. Using his supreme artistic license, Grass explores the poignant, existential experience of German chancellor Willy Brandt-aide-cum-Stasi agent Günter Guillaume when Germany faced Germany in 1974. "Which side was one for?" asks the prisoner Guillaume from his cell. "Which side was I or I for? Whom was I to cheer on? What conflict broke out in me, what forces pulled at me when Sparwasser shot his goal?"

Not everyone was conflicted though. Alexander Osang, the pre-eminent, multiple Egon Erwin Kisch Prize-winning journalist was born in East Berlin and spent his formative years growing up in a now-defunct country. He told me that he didn't know how East German he was until the '74 World Cup.

Osang was born in 1962, a year after the wall was built. On the evening of 22 June, 1974, he was 12 years old and watching the *Sport Aktuell* programme with his father. He would recall how deeply personal it all felt and that as an East German, he had always felt like an "outcast". It was a description that peppered our conversation. That is until Sparwasser changed everything. "I jumped around the flat and screamed," he remembers. "We beat them. I felt *I'd* beaten them."

It may have pitched siblings against each other and been billed as such in the intervening years, but it also saw generations baffled by each other's allegiances. For Osang's father, "the concept of 'East Germany' was very artificial. Very temporary". For the son, however, it was everything. The older man was German and the younger East German. One country for one, two entirely detached entities for the other.

The night East overcame West informed more than just Osang's formative years. It was *his* victory won by *his* people. He would write in his chapter on Germany for '*The Thinking Fan's Guide to the World Cup*': "With reunification there came an opportunity for change — but I couldn't let go of the past. I watched the 1990 World Cup semi-final, between Germany and England, on a big screen in the Berlin Lustgarten, with thousands of people. England's Paul Gascoigne cried, and I cried too when Germany won. I stood among rejoicing German fans, very alone. I couldn't watch the final against Argentina."

It wouldn't be until the 2002 World Cup in Japan and South Korea, travelling around the former for a few days with Beckenbauer in his role at *Der Spiegel*, that Osang could finally throw his personal albatross into the sea. "It was as if an iron ring exploded around my heart," he explained to me. "It was the first time I could embrace them, that I could support them." Germany would reach another final that year. It was ever thus.

Although historian Ilko-Sascha Kowalczuk sits on the other side of the political divide to Osang, he too was born in East Berlin and remembers similar feelings of joy when Sparwasser's shot beat Maier and hit the back of the net, telling me: "I was seven years old. We watched the game together with the extended family at an uncle's house. When Sparwasser scored, even those who were usually always against the DDR, always against the regime, cheered. In many sports competitions between the DDR and the Federal Republic, most people were in favour of the West, but not so much in this game."

When asked about Osang's description of feeling like an "outcast" and whether or not this was still a powerful emotion into the 2000s, Kowalczuk had a different perspective. "Osang, as an adapted SED supporter, may have felt that way — but not me. In 1992, in London, where I lived for some time, I experienced how the European Championship went and Germany lost in the final: that was my defeat. Likewise, 'I' became world champion in 1990. I think absolutely most people felt that way."

"In respect of 1974, one aspect is quite important," according to Kowalczuk. "In the Federal German media, there was an argument about how the DDR v Federal Republic match would be commented on, because in the Federal Republic, the only thing that was ever used to describe them was 'Germany'. Now, one could actually say, badly: 'Germany against DDR'. This was a perennial issue and had occupied many critical East Germans because many said: 'We are Germans too, why do you exclude us from your concept of Germany?'"

Two East Germans, two ideas of East Germany.

***

There was also a chance encounter on a Lufthansa flight between Hamburg and Düsseldorf a few days after the match that would have lasting repercussions for a member of the triumphant DDR team fraternising with the class enemy. Hans Apel, FGR Minister for Finance, took his seat next to a younger gentleman. Apel was a suave man, a confident man. It wasn't long before he introduced himself and they got to talking. The younger man laughed incredulously when he found out who he was sat next to. So too the older man. "You're one of the players?" Kreische nodded.

Their paths had crossed as Apel was on his way to the West German capital Bonn, via Dusseldorf, while Kreische, along with his team-mates was en route to Hanover, with Brazil waiting for them at the other end. Apel had something he wanted to get off his chest before the two went their separate ways. "One thing is absolutely clear," he stated. "West Germany will never win the World Cup." Kreische disagreed. "Excuse me but you're just talking nonsense," Apel insisted. "Perhaps you're too polite to tell me how bad this team is. Let's make a bet. Five bottles of whisky."

Kreische would sheepishly explain that he did not have the means to make good on the bet should he lose but Apel reassured him. "Who cares? I have enough whisky. I don't need it. But you'll get yours if you win."

And so it was that a few days after West Germany got their hands on the World Cup trophy, Kreische would get his on five bottles of Scotch. "It was absolutely forbidden to have any contact with anyone in West Germany," admitted Kreische. "But I was allowed to keep the bottles. I shared them with my friends. It was good whisky. Black and White."

It was just another day ending in 'y' for Apel, who forgot all about the wager until a letter arrived to his office. "I got a typed letter, a peculiar letter," Apel said. "Kreische later told me it was written by the secret service, and he had to sign it."

Kreische had thought that his place in the national team and his status at Dynamo Dresden would surely preclude him from any serious consequences, save for perhaps a telling off. How wrong he was. For one sentence in particular had alerted the Stasi in Apel's letter accompanying the Black and White: "I hope that we will meet again soon."

Kriesche wouldn't be at the Montreal Olympics in 1976 when the DDR won football gold, despite scoring 24 times as his club won the league title and the cup. He retired two years later, aged 30. When he gained access to his Stasi file in 2014, he was unsurprised but vindicated. "Sportsman Kreische is not acceptable to represent East Germany at the Olympic Games," it read. Such a simple and random human interaction and such an obscenely overblown reaction to it. Welcome to life in the DDR, where all were prisoners in an invisible exercise yard.

Kreische came to have a pragmatic view of the wager, however. "Why should I mourn or regret something that happened so long ago?" he asked, perplexed. "Since then, I met Apel and we became really good friends. He regretted that the whole thing had harmed me a lot."

***

The dread of a visit by a Stasi agent to the door of a footballer was always a low, muffled drumbeat. It was ominous then when such an official made contact with Uwe Rösler when still a teenager, making his way at Lokomotive Leipzig in the late eighties. "I was approached by the Stasi like many, many other players," he told me. "I was a young player, just coming into the first team at 18 years old. Obviously, for them it looked to them like I was an easy victim."

Rösler was understandably afraid but had faith in his coach, Hans-Ulrich Thomale, telling him everything that had taken place in the confidence of the manager's office. "He spoke to the right people to leave me in peace and I was very lucky. I didn't suffer any punishment for speaking to a third person about the approach and I am very thankful to the coach that he helped me."

It was still happening in 1987 just the way it had in the seventies; *Aktion Leder*, Croy, Hamann, Kreische and who knows how many others whose names are lost to history. "There was psychological pressure because they made it clear that when you don't work with them, you work against them. And when you work against them, they finish you career."

Did he see it as normal, given that his was the experience of most players? "No, nobody spoke about being approached because you weren't supposed to speak to anyone when you were approached." It was a conspiracy of silence. Everything about it extreme, familiar only in hindsight, when stories could be compared and patterns found.

Rösler would follow in Sparwasser's footsteps, leading the line at 1. FC Magdeburg and scoring 19 times in 50 games. He was too young to remember the most famous goal in East German history but he would appear in the second most famous game — a 2–0 victory against Belgium in 1990; the final time there would be an eleven put out by the DDR, coming just a couple of weeks before reunification.

The importance of being representatives of the state by proxy never dulled in that time. "When we played against other countries, especially those from the West, it was a political event; which system is the better one," Rösler explained. His role, like that of Sparwasser before him, was clearly defined and only partly on the pitch. "We were diplomats in tracksuits." As the Bard would tell us: "there's the rub."

**

There is a popular German book by Elke Wittich called *Wo waren Sie, als das Sparwasser-Tor fiel?* — 'Where Were You When Sparwasser scored?' Peter Ducke, or 'Black Peter' because of his dark hair, knows exactly where he was. He watched Sparwasser score his defining goal from the East German bench. It is not a happy memory.

In Black Peter's counterfactual, the book is entitled *Wo waren Sie, als das Ducke-Tor fiel?* and it is he who has scored the winning goal. Ducke's World Cup ended before it began, however. In a game for Carl Zeiss against BFC Dynamo in February, Ducke would come off worst in a challenge with the keeper. A torn meniscus meant that the DDR footballer of the year in 1971 would endure a race against time to be fit for the '74 finals.

It was a race he made but Ducke wouldn't start any of East Germany's six matches in 1974, meaning 1974 would never be *his* World Cup. In his prime, Ducke was a wanted man, not that he was any the wiser. Only when he accessed his Stasi file did the extent become apparent. "I had inquiries from Barcelona, Marseille, even from South America and England. My eyes fell out! I knew nothing about it. These offers have always been kept from me."

In a candid interview with *Bild* to mark the 40th anniversary of East v West, Ducke couldn't hide the disappointment that he feels to this day. "[Watching] was hard," he says. "If I had been fit, I would have played. Then Jürgen would probably never have scored that goal. After that I had a lot of trouble dealing with it. Everyone just talked about Jürgen. I was the one who determined our games. But I just sat on the bench, watching others become heroes."

"I often wondered what would have happened if I had played," Ducke ponders. "It still haunts me to this day. This win was probably my biggest defeat."

* * *

Speaking of which, whatever happened to Herr Sparwasser? Taking part in a veterans' tournament in Saarbrücken, West Germany, he would quietly, purposefully slip away from the camp, as he had evaded his marker on that famous night in Hamburg. Just a year before the wall fell, the 40-year-old Sparwasser walked into a police station and sought asylum. Former ski-jumper and 1976 Olympics gold medallist Hans-Georg Aschenbach was another high-profile sportsman to defect to the West in 1988. "We were warriors deployed on the political front, fighting for the nonsense of socialism," he concedes in his autobiography, before adding: "My skis were the weapons."

Meanwhile, Croy, ever the diplomat, stayed. "Of course it was glorified by the politicians, but that happens everywhere," he said. "All countries try to take political advantage of sports success."

Sparwasser would perennially joke that if his tombstone read only "Hamburg, 1974", everyone would know who was buried beneath. His comments though were laced with just a hint of bitterness. After all, this was a man who had three Oberliga title-winning medals, four FDGB-Pokals, one Cup Winners' Cup, an Olympic bronze medal from Munich, 133 goals in 298 games for 1. FC Magdeburg and was one game shy of reaching half a century of caps for his country, scoring 14 times. Still, one goal would come to define him.

How Peter Ducke would love to have swapped places with him. A three-time East German champion and cup winner with 153 goals for FC Carl Zeiss Jena and one more for the national team than Sparwasser; still it was that night in Hamburg and watching Sparwasser, arms aloft before the ball has even hit the net, that continues to haunt him. Little did he know that the goal haunted the scorer too.

Free of the antennae of the Stasi, in an interview to mark his 70th birthday, Sparwasser would elaborate. "That goal was the beginning of the end; my end in the DDR," he would say with some sadness. "Because many were against the regime, the hatred grew even greater after the goal and erupted on me. Whenever I went to Dresden, Leipzig or Jena with Magdeburg, I was booed from then on."

It's clear that Sparwasser was just another hostage to fortune, a pawn in a rigged game. "It's well known that a lot of East Germans back home stood for and sang the West German national anthem," he remarked to another interviewer: "No wonder they were pissed off at my goal. In terms of my standing in East Germany, my goal ultimately did me more harm than good."

Poor Sparwasser even had to scotch rumours that he'd been given special privileges as reward for his winner. "Rumour had it I was richly rewarded for the goal, with a car, a house and a cash premium. But that is not true." Jealousy stalked him everywhere. He'd become a scapegoat when he should have been a hero.

On retirement, he wished to remain in his role as football instructor at the Erich Weinert Academy, where he was happy. The Stasi wanted him to coach 1. FC Magdeburg. He refused and so was blocked from promotion at the Academy. "If they hadn't forbidden me to do that, I would have stayed in the East," Sparwasser confided. It is precisely because of this claustrophobic atmosphere of casual, calculated cruelty that this underdog story, that Sparwasser's story, that all of these stories, enter into the realm of the remarkable. It's a football story, it's a spy story, but fundamentally, it's a human story.

***

By 1989, open acts of defiance against the regime built by Erichs Honecker (leader of the SED) and Mielke spread like wildfire. Chants of "We want to leave" were suddenly replaced with "Down with the Stasi" and then climactically "We are the people." A protest march of 70,000 in Leipzig in October became 120,000 the week after and 300,000 the week after that. Time nor tide waited for Honecker and he was booted out of office by his own party members.

As the border guards stationed on the Berlin Wall began to open checkpoints on the evening of 9 November, tens of thousands of *Ossis* swarmed through gaps in the concrete to be met by jubilant *Wessis*. The beginning of the end had come to one of the most shameful symbols of the Cold War.

Berlin was sliced down the middle by a wall of brick and wire for 10,316 days. Astronaut Andre Kuipers took a photo of the German capital from the International Space Station more than 30 years after the wall fell. Seen from high above on a clear night, Berlin's east glows amber, lit mainly by older sodium-vapour lamps, while the west's environmentally conscious policies, spearheaded in the seventies, are reflected rather aptly in greener tones. The demarcation snakes along the lines of the wall; the humble light bulb illuminating a city and a country's complex and troubled past all the way from space. History moves on but familiar ghosts remain.

In the 41 years that there were two Germanys, East would play West competitively only once. Fate briefly had designs on a rematch, moving the pieces once more by drawing Germany and Germany together for the 1992 European Championships qualifiers; but reunification put paid to that.

They would never play each other again at full international level after 22 June, 1974. DDR one, FGR nil. Crystallised, for the ages. For all the FRG's World Cup and Euro triumphs, for all its Beckenbauers, Müllers, Matthäuses and Klinsmanns, the DDR would forever have Jürgen Sparwasser and one unforgettable night in Hamburg.

ARGENTINA 1978

SCOTLAND
3

NETHERLANDS
2

SCOTLAND	NETHERLANDS
1. Alan Rough	8. Jan Jongbloed
3. Willie Donachie	2. Jan Poortvliet
4. Martin Buchan	5. Ruud Krol (c)
13. Stuart Kennedy	17. Wim Rijsbergen
14. Tom Forsyth	20. Wim Suurbier OFF
6. Bruce Rioch (c)	7. Piet Wildschut ON (44')
8. Kenny Dalglish ⊕ (45')	6. Wim Jansen
10. Asa Hartford	10. René van de Kerkhof
15. Archie Gemmill ⊕ ⊕ (46'p, 68')	11. Willy van de Kerkhof
18. Graeme Souness	**12. Rob Rensenbrink ⊕ (35'p)**
9. Joe Jordan	13. Johan Neeskens OFF
	14. Johan Boskamp ON (10')
Manager: Ally MacLeod	**16. Johnny Rep ⊕ (72')**
	Manager: Ernst Happel

Estadio Ciudad de Mendoza

Mendoza, Argentina

ATTENDANCE
35,130

REFEREE
Erich Linemayr (Austria)

DAVID WINNER

> You probably recall the most celebrated
> moment of the match. It might not be
> the country's best-ever World Cup goal,
> but it is the best loved.

Our dark-shirted hero has already scored once for a 2-1 lead. Now he picks up the ball just outside the corner of the penalty area and begins his famous slalom past a bunch of illustrious defenders. The solo climaxes with a clever finish against a goalkeeper who played in the last World Cup final. For a small country perennially in the shadow of its larger neighbour, this great third goal in a bittersweet 3-2 victory has become something of a symbol of national identity. The commentary makes it even nicer. Sadly, after the disastrous earlier group matches, the goal isn't quite enough to take the scorer's team to the next round, but at least the players can now fly home with pride.

In popular culture, the moment has left its original context (the stadium in Argentina where Scotland famously failed against Peru and Iran) and entered the realms of myth, legend and YouTube clips. But film director Danny Boyle never considered using the footage for the sex scene in *Trainspotting*. Neither Scotland's midfielder Archie Gemmill nor TV commentator Archie Macpherson have ever been asked about it. And no-one in Holland mentions it either. This is because everyone has their own nostalgias and blindspots concerning the 1978 World Cup, and in the dark circumstances of that time and place, this is but a trivial example.

As you will have spotted, the goal I just described is not Archie Gemmill's against Holland in Mendoza in the first round, but Hans Krankl's winner for Austria against West Germany in Córdoba in the second. Gemmill did, too, collect the ball just outside the corner of the penalty area, cut inside, slalom past famous defenders and beat a World Cup Final goalkeeper (in his case, Holland's Jan Jongbloed rather than Germany's Sepp Maier). The main difference between the two goals is that Gemmill, in blue, beat three defenders while Krankl, in red, only managed two. Scots have paid homage to Gemmill's "wonder goal" in literature, on film, in ballet, and with a permanent exhibit at the Scottish Football Museum at Hampden Park. Austrians celebrate Krankl's solo as the key moment of *das Wunder von Córdoba*, their most memorable football victory over their neighbours. Both goals became part of national folklore in part because of their famous soundtracks. For Krankl, Austrian radio commentator Edi Finger screamed *"Tor!"* six times in a voice cracking with pure joy. For Gemmill's masterpiece, Archie Macpherson ... well, we'll come to that.

The way we remember the tournament is reminiscent of the film *Rashomon*. Akira Kurosawa set his masterpiece in feudal Japan, but the location and even the story are less important than philosophical questions of truth, memory and reality. *Rashomon* doesn't exactly tell the story of a murder and a rape. It gives us four incompatible, contradictory versions of the crimes. We first hear from the rapist who may also have been the murderer; then from the raped woman who may have killed her husband; then from the dead man himself, who speaks from beyond the grave through a medium. Finally, we hear from a supposedly neutral observer who saw the whole thing. He seems a decent enough chap but is behaving rather oddly and has, we eventually learn, reason to feel ashamed. The piece is not so much a whodunnit as a what-happened. Who did what? Who did nothing? Was there a betrayal? Whose point of view is the most important or valid? Are we, as mere observers, in a position to pass moral judgment?

Setting the Austrians aside, there were three nations implicated in the Scotland-Holland match in Mendoza on 11 June, 1978: the participants and the host. Each had their own narratives and realities. Each would develop their own stories and understanding of what occurred. One nation won but lost. Another lost but won. And the third won the most and lost the most. Along the way, there was quite a lot of rape and murder.

***

For Scotland, the main themes of the game would be hubris and possible redemption. Two weeks earlier, the team had left Prestwick Airport amid scenes of patriotic delirium. Scotland had one of their most talented squads ever and had qualified for the World Cup for the second time in a row. Having beaten European champions Czechoslovakia en route, they were legitimately among the tournament dark horses. England, for the second time in a row, had not qualified. This delicious reversal of normal fortunes helped inspire a flowering of Scottish pride and optimism. Support for the Scottish National Party had been growing, and the public took the national team to their hearts. Goalkeeper Alan Rough remembers crazy scenes on the way to the airport for the flight to Argentina: "I lived in Ayrshire on the road to Glasgow and part of the road is called the Fenwick Moors. It's in the middle of nowhere, but it was lined with supporters all the way to Prestwick. It was incredible." Everywhere he looked he saw kilts and tammies and football strips. Children sported T-shirts bearing the words: 'We're going to win the World Cup'. People sang patriotic songs, including Andy Cameron's novelty hit *Ally's Tartan Army,* celebrating manager Ally MacLeod, which includes the lines: "We had to get a man who could make all Scotland proud/He's our Muhammad Ali; he's Alistair MacLeod." A day earlier, 30,000 fans had paid to cheer and wave flags at the team as it paraded in Hampden Park and rode an open-top bus. At the airport, there were so many fans that Rough didn't get a chance to say goodbye to his wife and son.

The send-off was the culmination of what author Graham McColl called a "six months'-long festival of Scotch kitsch". MacLeod had promoted a carpet company by sitting on a rug, wearing a poncho and a sombrero, and holding a pistol. The players had posed behind a Chrysler Avenger car promising "Style, toughness. And a championship performance."

For months, MacLeod had toured Scotland whipping up support for his side and talking up its chances. At one point, he'd predicted: "You can mark down 25 June, 1978 as the day Scottish football conquers the world." On other occasions, he would more modestly say only that Scotland would come back with a medal. The commentator Archie Macpherson often accompanied him. He remembers: "We would get to a hotel where I would be the MC and people would be standing on the tables cheering him on like he was an evangelist. I thought: "Ally, if you fall you're gonna make Icarus seem like a swallow."

Macleod's confidence was rooted in events of the previous summer. After beating England at Wembley (happy Scottish fans had torn up the Wembley pitch), they flew to South America to play three games. The most controversial was in Chile, at the national stadium in Santiago which had been used as a concentration camp after Pinochet's coup four years before. 30,000 people signed a petition urging the Scottish Football Association to call off the match, and Labour politician Ian Mikardo urged the team not to play "on a blood-soaked pitch". But the Scottish Football Association (SFA) refused to budge. In the stadium dressing room, Alan Rough saw bullet holes on the wall where prisoners had been executed. "We were warned not to go by a lot of people who knew what was going on there, but being a sportsman, when you were asked to go and play football you went and played football. When we got there there was a curfew at 10pm for everybody." Had they had known how bad things were, most of the players would not have gone.

In Holland, before the World Cup, the *cabaretier* Freek de Jonge led a campaign for the national team to boycott the competition because of Argentina's dismal human rights record. But there was nothing comparable in Scotland. "I don't remember anyone saying anything like that at all," says Rough. "There was a lot about

Chile the year before, but nothing about Argentina." Scotland had won 4-2 in Santiago and were relieved to fly on to Buenos Aires for their next match. Apart from a false bomb alert at the Boca Juniors stadium before the match, the city seemed calm and nice. The players had no way of knowing they were close to mass murder in progress. The years 1976 and 1977 were the bloodiest of Argentina's 'National Reorganisation Process' and the stadium was about a mile from the Club Atlético clandestine detention centre where, in batches over a period of 18 months, nearly 2,000 people were tortured and raped, then taken away to be murdered.

Scottish attention focused on the pitch, where MacLeod's team played brilliantly, survived cynical fouling and bad refereeing, and had the best of a 1-1 draw. Archie Macpherson considered it "the most brutal game I had witnessed" and Scottish journalists walked out of the post-match press conference in protest when Argentina coach Cesar Luis Menotti refused to answer their questions about his team's violence. But Ally MacLeod was elated. If Scotland could outplay Argentina in the Bombonera, he reasoned, there was no limit to what they might achieve. A few days later, in Rio, he surprised journalists by suggesting the match against Brazil at the Maracana might be a preview of the World Cup Final. Scotland lost 0-2 but MacLeod remained bullish. "Scotland were robbed, really robbed in Buenos Aires," says Macpherson. "They'd played extremely well. That was the genesis of Ally's expectation that Scotland would win the World Cup. His blethering started after that game."

Fast forward a year, and things started to go wrong as soon as Scotland landed in Argentina. When they reached their base, the Sierras Hotel in Alta Gracia outside Cordoba, crowds of locals and a pipe band turned out to greet them, but the team bus broke down. The beds at the hotel were hard and short, the bedrooms had no windows, there was no water in the swimming pool, and the training pitch next door was rutted and unplayable. The players were also in a simmering dispute with the SFA about bonuses, and the press began to print false stories about the players drinking heavily. On the plus side, some of the TVs worked, even if the programmes were in Spanish.

Their first game in the tournament was against Peru, a team MacLeod was not worried about. Three months earlier, he was too busy with his commercial activities to accept Macpherson's offer to accompany him, all expenses paid by the BBC, to watch Peru and Argentina play each other in a friendly. McLeod considered Peru's best player, Teófilo Cubillas, "the Peruvian Pele", old and unthreatening. It was quite the misjudgement. In the match, Scotland took an early lead and missed a penalty, but in the second half they were run ragged by their skilful opponents' quick, short-passing game. Cubillas scored two brilliant long-range goals as Peru won 3-1. The press and the Tartan Army were horrified.

Before the match, Macpherson had been disturbed by a scene he'd witnessed outside the stadium. "I went to see Scotland training. We followed the team bus in a taxi, and as we got out of the taxi, there were 20 men standing with their faces to the wall with their arms up above them, like hostages, and two guys at either end of the line holding guns. I found out that they were workers on the stadium, and they were still there when we came out. They must have been there like that for an hour. That gave me a little chill up the spine."

He and other journalists did make references to human rights abuses. Dutch magazine *Vrij Nederland* sent two reporters: one to cover the football, the other, Frits Barend, to report on the political situation. Indeed, Amnesty International had urged journalists to go to Argentina and to keep their eyes open. John Simpson, in his 1985 book *The Disappeared*, co-written with Jana Bennett, reflected that the campaign encouraged sports reporters "to look beyond the confines of the football field a little, and the result was that a great many of the background articles written in the Western European press about the World Cup betrayed some awareness somewhere of the overall political atmosphere in which the finals were being played. But for those who had read and heard stories about the savage guerrilla warfare in Argentina's towns and cities, and had been nervously expecting to see some evidence of it, there was a surprising air of peace and acquiescence everywhere they went ... In part, the surprise arose from the natural slowness of foreigners to keep up with the changing situation in Argentina."

Few realised — or could have realised — the scale of the horror. At the match against Peru, for example, unnoticed by Scottish players, officials or journalists, a particularly sinister figure wearing a white suit sat in the VIP box, alongside the presidents of Argentina, Peru and Fifa. His name was General Luciano Benjamín Menéndez and he'd been busy with 'anti-subversive' activities in Córdoba for years. Under the previous regime, he had organised death squads and Nazi-style book burnings. Now, as head of the Third Army Corps, he controlled implementation of the 'Process' over a huge swathe of the country, including Córdoba and Mendoza. Menéndez personally supervised torture sessions and mass executions and had set up the secret La Perla concentration camp outside the city. He also had a number of World Cup-specific initiatives. For example, in the unlikely event that Montoneros guerrillas sabotaged the tournament, he had arranged for 50 selected hostages to be murdered.

In the crowd, a related drama unfolded. Few inmates survived La Perla, but Héctor Kunzmann was one. Years later, he recalled his experience of being taken from there to the Scotland-Peru game by his captors. The match "was a torture all in itself", he said. "They took you to the games so you could point out people, acquaintances. And if you didn't point them out, they paid attention in case someone got close and said hello. If that happened, they took the poor guy to La Perla. You wanted to be invisible so no one could see you. That was the terrifying thing: the fear that some friend, some friend from the neighbourhood or from militancy would end up in a concentration camp just for saying hello. Luckily, it didn't happen."

Losing to Peru was bad enough for the Scots, but after the match things got worse. Winger Willie Johnston failed a random drug test and was sent home. The squad now found itself under siege from hostile tabloid reporters. At a press conference, MacLeod joked that his only friend was a dog the squad had adopted as a mascot. As he patted it, it bit him.

Fortunately, the next game was against Iran, so Scotland were virtually guaranteed to pick up two points. Team captain Bruce Rioch had injured his ankle in training, so he watched the game on television. "What's the worst horror movie you've ever seen?", he asked himself 40 years later. "Scotland versus Iran". Again, Scotland scored first. Again, they were pegged back, and feebly slumped to a 1-1 draw. On the touchline, in what became one of the defining images of the tournament in Britain, the TV cameras spotted Ally MacLeod holding his head in despair.

Now the Tartan Army turned properly mutinous, surrounding the team bus and hurling abuse at him and his players. The poet and novelist William McIlvanney had joined the thousands of Scotland fans who spent vast amounts of money they could ill afford to get to Argentina. After the failures against Iran and Peru, he wrote, the pain of their alienation from the team became "extreme". Even if Scotland were somehow to qualify, "the feeling will remain that a betrayal has taken place". The fans blamed the man they now called Ally McClown. Someone shouted at MacLeod: "You promised everything, you gave us nothing."

* * *

Holland, losing finalists at the last World Cup, were having no fun either. Their best player, Johan Cruyff, had refused to travel to Argentina (he didn't want to abandon his family and feared four weeks away might jeopardise his marriage). And their second-best player, Wim van Hanegem of Feyenoord, had pulled out of the squad at the last minute, at the airport. Playing "total football" without Cruyff would be impossible, but that was the least of their troubles. Instead of cheering crowds to wave them on their way, the squad were hustled through Schiphol Airport to avoid a crowd of demonstrators urging them to boycott the tournament. The journey to the southern hemisphere took the best part of two days, and when they reached their base, some of the players began to envy the missing stars.

As Iwan van Duren and Marcel Rözer recorded in their book *Football in a Dirty War*, the Potrerillos Hotel was in a beautiful spot about an hour and half's drive from Mendoza. It was also cold, isolated and lacked basic facilities. The beds were hard and short, there was no water in the swimming pool, the phone lines were down, and the TVs didn't work. The squad was riled by false press stories about players chasing chambermaids. Heartthrob Johnny Rep, the only member of the squad with an all-female fan club, said the stories couldn't be true because the chambermaids were old. The story may have stemmed from the Dutch habit of wandering around naked. The hotel was surrounded by mountains, a lake, and three cordons of soldiers who slept in ditches and warmed themselves beside open fires. Some players were woken each morning by donkeys knocking on their windows and braying.

The biggest problem was isolation. Arie Haan, who didn't play in the Scotland game, explains: "We Dutch players love life, we like to have contact with people, to be friendly, to walk in the city, not to be in a prison in a hotel. It's not our way to prepare for a game. In Mendoza, we were in the mountains, 1,500 metres high and we always made a joke. For an old German — I don't say the name, you can imagine — who went to Argentina after the war, it was a good place to hide." Some players wanted to go home. René van de Kerkhof, injured in the first match, became so homesick he started packing his suitcase, burst into tears during a press interview and had to be heavily sedated.

Meanwhile, the training pitch at the hotel was bald in patches and the players kept having to climb down a hill to retrieve balls. The team's gruff, chain-smoking Austrian coach Ernst

Happel spent most of his time playing cards, barely talking to anyone. On one occasion, captain Ruud Krol approached him, hoping to discuss a new problem. Without looking up from his cards, Happel waved him away with a curt "nein". Like MacLeod, Happel considered the Peruvians too old to be dangerous and regarded Iran as nobodies. Luckily for him, Holland played Iran first and beat them 3-0 without difficulty. Forewarned by the Scots' experience, the Dutch knew what to expect from Cubillas and co, and played out a 0-0 draw. Happel had tinkered with the formation, but found no satisfactory solution. His attempt to use Rob Rensenbrink in Cruyff's role foundered on the obstacle of Rensenbrink not being Cruyff. The Dutch were also dismayed by the state of the Mendoza pitch: the thick long grass played havoc with their passing game. Back home, the public was unimpressed. Despite the presence of Rep, Rensenbrink, Krol, Neeskens and others from 1974, the Netherlands were a shadow of the Total Football team of that joyous tournament. They didn't even have their fans with them.

Everything would now turn on Scotland v Holland. Assuming Peru beat Iran (which they did), Scotland had to win by at least three goals. Any other result would send the Dutch through. Back in Britain, the words of two TV commentators would frame the memories of the game. David Coleman covered the game for BBC Network, meaning everywhere except Scotland, which heard Archie Macpherson.

The brand new stadium in the San Martín park was built especially for the World Cup. The military regime had bulldozed a community to make way for this prestige edifice, which stands near a university and a hospital. In 1978, it was about a mile and a half from "D2", the province's largest and busiest clandestine detention centre, situated in the Police Palace on Belgrano Avenue.

This is relevant because shortly before kick-off, there was a peculiar moment in Coleman's commentary. The players were on the field and Holland had won the toss, but kick off was delayed because a marching band dressed all in white was slow to leave. Coleman, therefore, filled in. First, he reminded his audience of Scotland's "marvellous record" since 1974: played 28, won 17, drawn seven, lost four. Still waiting, he moved on to local colour. "Looking at it from a distance, this looks one of the best pitches we've seen at these World Cup matches. Incidentally, the stadium, set right at the foot of the Andes, with Chile just across the border ... [*keep going, David*] ... Mendoza the great, er, wine area of Argentina ... The stadium itself, all the, er, entrances are overhead entrances, and the stadium itself is set in a natural bowl ..." At this point, the camera cuts to the VIP section of the crowd and we see a man with a long, pinched face, black brilliantined hair and thick moustache. He looks bored and a little uncomfortable. He is the tournament's key figure: General Jorge Rafael Videla, president of Argentina. Videla is on screen for a full six seconds, but Coleman doesn't refer to this or say anything about him. After a long-seeming silence: "It really is a beautiful setting."

In 1979, a US defence intelligence agency report described Videla as "a genuinely nice" and "very polite" religious man with "a spontaneous smile and handshake" who was "inclined to be timid". In the same vein, the Dutch ambassador Dorone van den Brandeler reported to his government that he personally knew general Videla to be charming and deeply religious. Photographs of him in the late seventies in the Getty Archive show him variously playing golf, wearing impressive military uniforms and looking dignified on state visits to Spain and Japan. There's even a picture of him, taken for *Paris Match* magazine in January 1979, showing the president enjoying breakfast on the lawn of his Buenos Aires mansion with his wife Alicia. The couple wear pale blue while the house and servant who brings them coffee are dressed in white: the colours of the Argentinian flag. In soft focus in the foreground we see pink roses, an artful reminder of the Casa Rosada, the presidential palace.

By 1979, the genuinely nice, polite, patriotic, religious president with the cute garden had presided over a system that led to tens of thousands of rapes, murders, disappearances and other crimes during a reign of terror that still traumatises his country. Sitting just out of shot to Videla's right in the Mendoza stadium was another general, Albano Harguindeguy, the interior minister known as 'The Butcher' or *El Genocidio* — the genocide man — the main ideologue of state terror.

Videla was the leading figure in the military coup that seized power in Argentina in March 1976. The takeover was widely welcomed at first. Having lived through two years of anarchy under previous president Isabel Perón, most Argentines believed things would get better. A rising tide of kidnappings, bombings and assassinations from the revolutionary left had spawned vicious counter-terror from the right. Burned, bullet-riddled bodies turned up on the streets of the capital almost daily. There were 1,500 political murders in 1975, but things were about to get worse. Argentina had plenty of experience of military dictatorships — in the past, 'subversives' were locked up. The new regime had a different plan: physical annihilation of everyone they disliked.

The D2 in Mendoza was part of this secret 'National Reorganisation Process'. Outside of the capital, it and La Perla were among the busiest of the junta's hundreds of clandestine killing centres. Dragged from their homes, workplaces or streets, victims, most of them in their twenties, were usually brought there in unmarked Ford Falcon cars. Routinely, they would be tortured and subjected to sexual violence and would reveal names of friends who would, in turn, be kidnapped and tortured. Across the country, by the end of 1977, almost all members of the two main leftist guerilla groups, the Montoneros and the Marxist ERP, were dead. Yet the terror rolled on, devouring an ever-lengthening list of targets: trade unionists, students, lawyers, artists, writers, priests, Jews, psychoanalysts, schoolchildren. Sometimes, entire families were butchered. When relatives tried to obtain information about missing loved ones, the authorities denied all knowledge. The missing became known as *desaparecidos*: neither alive nor dead, said Videla, but "disappeared". We'll never know for sure how many victims there were. The usual given figure is 30,000.

And how did the World Cup fit into this? Argentina had been awarded the tournament in 1972. After initial doubts over the cost of hosting it, in 1976, the junta decided it could use the event to project a benign image of the country and themselves to the world. As the Argentine journalist Ezequiel Fernández Moores put it, "the 1978 World Cup was the most obvious political manipulation suffered by sport since the Olympic Games of 1936 in Nazi Germany." Simply put, the men who organised mass murder also organised the football, and they manipulated the tournament as best they could to get the result they wanted — Argentina crowned as world champions. National euphoria following this triumph may have extended the life of the dictatorship by several years.

Much has been written about the tainting of the tournament, though few dirty tricks have been conclusively proved and probably never will be. Referees in various matches gave surprising decisions in Argentina's favour, one post-match drug test revealed an Argentine player to be pregnant, and so on. Peru are widely thought to have been bought or pressurised into throwing their final game so Argentina could reach the final (Argentina, needing to win by four goals, won 6-0). There have been studies, too, of the reaction of the public in Argentina. How much did they know? Could they have behaved differently? The attitude of audiences in the outside world might also be worth investigating.

One relatively unexplored aspect is the way football rites were woven into the fabric of repression. Mario Villani, a physicist, was held in five camps in and around Buenos Aires: Club Atlético, el Banco, el Olimpo, Pozo de Quilmes and ESMA. It seems he survived because he was able to repair his torturers' stolen radios and TV sets (military perpetrators usually looted and trashed the homes of the people they abducted). In the camps, "transfer" meant death. Villani, who died in 2021, considered himself already dead while in captivity, but somehow was never "transferred". He happened to be in El Banco during the World

Cup and speaks to us now from beyond the grave, as it were, through the medium of an interview he gave in the mid 1990s to Marguerite Feitlowitz for her book *A Lexicon of Terror*:

"The guys running the camp decided that as this was an historic event for Argentina they would arrange for everyone to 'enjoy' it. In quotes. Or maybe not in quotes. See? The limits become blurred. Back and forth between the double message. They didn't have the means to put together an auditorium or viewing room. So they brought in a TV (stolen, of course, and repaired by me) and put it up on a high platform at the end of a long corridor … They opened our cells, let us raise our *tabiques* [blindfolds] to our foreheads and sit in the doorway on the floor. Still shackled, still cuffed, we watched the game. And [cheered] the goals. The whole thing was very mixed-up. It's not that they said: 'Now, you're required to cheer the goals'. But these were people who if they hadn't been *desaparecidos* would have been home, or at the stadium, watching and cheering. Some — whether they knew it or not — had already been programmed to die, were in fact scheduled for the next transfer. So, the whole thing took on a different meaning, to be there, perhaps on a death list, cheering the goals. It was extremely cruel because the sensation you have is that the outside world has disappeared. That you've left the world. And so these signals from the world are very … I don't even know how to put it."

It's distressing to think that the football co-existed with such horror, but it did. And when we think of the tournament, the two things inevitably flow together: football and repression belonged in different worlds, yet cohabited. We can't be sure, but it seems prisoners didn't get to see matches not involving Argentina. What, one wonders, would they have made of *Escocia-Holanda?* It helped determine which team Argentina faced in the final. And it was a remarkable match.

For Scotland, MacLeod finally did what journalists had been urging: he dropped the ineffective Don Masson and put Liverpool's Graeme Souness into midfield for his first cap. The effect was immediate: Scotland dominated the Dutch from the start. Tom Forsyth and Kenny Dalglish both had the ball in the net for disallowed goals, and Bruce Rioch hit the bar with a header. For Holland, Johan Neeskens, who wasn't really fit, went off injured after 10 minutes. Against the run of play, Holland took the lead with a penalty, but Scotland equalised a few minutes later, Dalglish volleying in from Joe Jordan's knockdown. After the break Scotland continued to dominate and Archie Gemmill scored a penalty. Something was stirring, and the Argentinian crowd was cheering for the Scots.

In the 68th minute, the most momentous 240 seconds in modern Scottish football began. On the right, three Dutch defenders stopped Dalglish and the ball broke loose. Archie Gemmill got to it just before Wim Jansen. The marvellously sonorous Coleman became excited: "*Good play by Gemmill!* ... [He's moved inside and turned to beat the wildly lunging Ruud Krol] ... *And again!* ... [Gemmill has somehow evaded the last defender, Jan Poortvliet, by nutmegging him and Dalglish with the same touch and is now alone in the penalty area with only the goalkeeper to beat] ... *THREE — ONE!!* ... [Gemmill took a touch, opened his body and curled the ball past Jongbloed's shoulder] ... *A brilliant individual goal by this hard little professional has put Scotland in dreamland! The miracle is beginning to happen! They need one more to qualify!*"

On the Dutch bench, coach Ernst Happel turned to his assistant Jan Zwartkruis and said grimly: "We can pack our bags now, Jan". But Dreamland was a vaporous, delusional realm. Before Gemmill's goal, Scotland were focused, vigorous, irresistible. In the afterglow, they floated. Two minutes later, full-back Tom Forsyth, under no pressure, almost headed an own goal, missing by inches. Coleman yelped in panic. And two minutes after that, Johnny Rep, alarmed by the turn of events and determined to do something about it, ran all the way back to his own half to pick up possession. Scottish players mostly stood and watched as he played a languorous one-two with Krol and began to surge towards goal. Still no Scotsman reacted. At the last, Gemmill woke to the danger and charged across to stop him. Too late. Rep hammered a shot and Gemmill's attempted block only made things worse: in touching the ball he made it spin so it dipped and plunged into the top left corner of Alan Rough's goal. Recently, I asked Rep if he meant it. "OF COURSE! You have to have a little luck to score a goal like that, but it's a FABULOUS goal!" Rough still can't believe he didn't save it. "I got a good hand on it. Four fingers! I was sure I'd pushed it over the bar. Then I turned round ... I'm still not sure how it went in". Anyway, the Scottish momentum had been broken. The mood in the stadium abruptly deflated. There would be no Miracle in Mendoza after all.

So near yet so far. Typically Scottish. A glorious failure. A heroic failure. The nation that always snatches defeat from the jaws of victory just did it again ... clichés aplenty would roll around that moment, and eventually they would crystallise around the words of the other Archie.

Macpherson's commentary on Gemmill's goal was also excellent: "Good play by Gemmill ... *great* play by Gemmill!! Can he do it? He's done it! Oh, a *great* goal! Oh *superb*!!", and one day about 18 years later, in Paris, where he was working for Eurosport (on occasion with Johnny Rep), he received a call from Danny Boyle, a filmmaker. Boyle was shooting a movie version of a novel by Irvine Welsh called *Trainspotting*. Would Archie be willing to come to London to re-voice his commentary on Gemmill's goal? He recalls: "I didn't argue with him too much because he told me what they were going to pay me, so I just accepted. So I went into this dungeon-like editing room. You know, typical thing in Soho. And I did it several times and he wanted me to push it, *push it*! Which I did. I was taking the money and running. He also sent me, in fairness, the script, which I didn't read. I might have flipped over the first two pages, and that was that."

Some time later, Archie got a call from a newspaper. Did he know his voice was the soundtrack to a sex scene in a new film? He did not. "'Well you'd better go and see it'. So I thought, 'yeah,

I'd better see it'. I went to one of these marvellous cinemas in the Champs-Élysées, with French friends. And after they had watched it ... I *rose* in their estimation! I mean, I was giving a background to a sex scene that John Williams' music couldn't have bettered!"

In the movie, it's actually three interconnected sex scenes after the scene in the nightclub. Renton has just met Diane and they're having a wild time on her bed. Meanwhile, Lizzy and Tommy are about to have sex when Lizzy says she wants to watch the sex tape they've made of themselves. A third friend, Spud, is so drunk he's passed out. Boyle cuts wittily between the three locations as Blondie's *Atomic* chugs away on the soundtrack. Tragically, earlier in the film, Renton switched the Tommy/Lizzy video for a '100 Great Goals' compilation, so in their moment of passion, the couple find themselves watching Gemmill's goal and hearing Macpherson's innuendo-laden, brand-new commentary: "Scotland charging forward again, and there's the captain, Archie Gemmill, picking it up from the outside. Oh, I think he wants to go himself. How *far* is he gonna go? *He's going all the way!* And he *SCOOOOOORES!!* Oh, what a magnificent goal! Gemmill at *his very best*! What a *PENETRATING* goal that was!!" As the ball hits the back of the net, Renton has his orgasm, augmented by footage from a different match entirely in which a stadium full of Argentines wave blue and white flags. Renton falls back happily exhausted and delivers the punchline: "I haven't felt that good since Archie Gemmill scored against Holland in 1978!".

Trainspotting was a hit and helped to turn the memory of Mendoza into something jokey, artistic, almost cosy. An attitude of wry nostalgia partially sanitised the whole affair. The impression conveyed was that Scots had come to terms with Argentina and were essentially cheerful about it. This was later enshrined as a kind of official memory. In the late nineties, Gemmill himself appeared in a comedy re-enactment of the goal on David Baddiel and Frank Skinner's *Fantasy Football* show, gamely mugging along with jokes about baldness, with Ally MacLeod depicted as a proboscis monkey. The goal was later turned into a mini-ballet and incorporated into a travelling show, featuring an audio piece mixing crowd noise with the original Coleman and Macpherson commentaries. Rewriting history, the goal *itself* was now "The Miracle of Mendoza". The Scottish Football Museum created a popular interactive permanent exhibit of the goal in which visitors could retrace Gemmill's steps, marked by footprints on the floor, and photograph themselves evading life-size models of Dutch defenders.

But there was a darkness to that *Trainspotting* scene, as well as humour. Renton's betrayal — the switching of the tapes — triggers Tommy's descent because Lizzy leaves him. Having been the only healthy member of the group of friends, he rapidly slides into heroin addiction and death. An earlier scene between Renton and Tommy conveys a particularly bitter view of the nation. Tommy takes his mates to enjoy fresh air in the great outdoors and asks if it makes them feel proud to be Scottish. It does not. "It's shite being Scottish!" says Renton. "We're the lowest of the low, the scum of the fucking earth, the most wretched, miserable, servile pathetic trash that was ever shat into civilization. Some people hate the English. I don't. They're just wankers. We, on the other hand, are colonised by wankers. We can't even find a decent culture to be colonised by. We're ruled by effete arseholes. It's a shite state of affairs to be in, Tommy, and all the fresh air in the world won't make any fucking difference."

Back in 1978, the aftermath of the Holland match had been bitter too. On TV, Coleman suggested the victory over Holland restored pride after the humiliations against Peru and Iran. Rough reckons defeat by Holland would have been seen as "a national disaster" but the victory turned the tournament into "a massive disappointment". But veteran sports columnist Hugh MacDonald remembers feeling the opposite: "Beating the Dutch was looked upon as a final fucking insult because it showed precisely what we could have done. People thought Peru would just lie down for us. Then we entered into this kind of gnashing-of-teeth self-flagellation after the draw with Iran, saying 'we're no fucking good anyway', and 'we just have to accept we're just fucking shite.' And then you go and beat Holland!? And beat them in spectacular style! It's not just the Gemmill goal. They *demolished* them! Dalglish was Dalglish. Souness was Souness. You know this team could have…" [his voice trails away at the thought of how far Scotland could have gone, which was far]. "I can remember being in the pub with the Holland game and a lot of people being really angry. 'I mean, fuck me, we do it when it doesn't matter … '" Very few people now mention beating the Netherlands. Everybody still talks about Peru and Cubillas, and Iran. The Dutch game comes a very poor third and will only maybe be mentioned because of Archie's goal. There's still a real kind of national self-loathing about the whole thing.

"In the microcosm of that game, you've got the whole Scottish character and Scottish politics and history. You could write a bloody good book on that game, taking in Scottish culture, Scottish political aspirations, the 'Scottish cringe' as we call it. For all our obvious belligerence, we shrink before others. It's self-doubt. We criticise things about ourselves instead of taking them forward. Some historians would say it goes back to Flodden and Culloden. We celebrate our defeats much more than we look at successes. 'Argentina '78' became a shorthand for Scottish failure, for Scottish coming up short. When the deck was laid and we had our cards, we just came up short."

Return was not at all like departure. Alan Rough remembers looking out of the window as the plane began its descent to Prestwick and wondering what the huge dark shape beside the runway might be. As they got lower, he realised: "It was a kind of unwelcoming committee for us". Were they carrying pitchforks? "Not quite that bad but they were quite vocal. Unfortunately, most of [the abuse] was directed at Ally. He got the brunt." He'd gone from being the most popular person in Scotland to the most unpopular? "Correct. But I never heard him saying we were going to win the World Cup. He might have said it at a press conference, in front of the media. But he never said it to us in any team talks at all. But that's what he was like. He would just build everything up. It was incredible he got the whole nation involved in football. And we were on a good run before we got to Argentina. We were a very good side with a good track record."

Archie Macpherson reflects: "Ally was a victim of hubris, and we all must leave it there. He did not deserve the hatred that was poured out against him by so many people. I did feel sorry for him, particularly when journalists who had praised him to the highest savaged him brutally. That I couldn't take." And the fans? "Absolutely." MacLeod, an essentially sweet and good-hearted man by all accounts, was broken by the experience, though he recovered a little in public affection before he died of Alzheimer's in 2004. The SFA, whose amateurish approach had caused many of the team's problems, appeared to try to pin the blame on Willie Johnston, claiming that Fifa had docked two points for his drugs transgression, so beating Peru would have made no difference. Fifa had done no such thing.

The political consequences are too complex to calculate. Some historians argue that Scotland's failure in Argentina led to a low turnout in the devolution referendum of March 1979. (The proposal got a majority of votes but failed to pass the turnout threshold). If that vote had gone the other way, how would Margaret Thatcher, who came to power two months later, have dealt with a strong Scottish independence movement? Would English nationalism have emerged sooner in reaction? And if Holland and Scotland had both played to their potential in the first round, Peru would not have topped the group or even reached the second round. The most notorious game in World Cup history would never have taken place because it's hard to imagine the Scots or Dutch rolling over, as Peru did, to let Argentina win 6-0 and reach the final. Argentina's junta would not have enjoyed the political bounce they got from winning the World Cup. And would it even have occurred to them to try to rekindle patriotic fervour by invading the Falklands/Malvinas in 1982? That would have affected British politics. Without the Falklands War,

Margaret Thatcher, desperately unpopular at the beginning of 1982, may have lost the 1983 election. As it was, she won by a landslide. The consequences still reverberate.

The Dutch didn't exactly plunge into mourning after their defeat. Three days later, in Córdoba, having brought youngsters Ernie Brandts and Jan Poortvliet into the team and switched to an old, familiar 4-3-3, they hammered Austria 5-1. It was almost Total Football reborn. Next came a replay of the 1974 final — a 2-2 draw with West Germany, effectively knocking the Germans out. In the quasi-semi-final, Holland beat Italy 2-1, Haan scoring one of the great long-range goals of history. "We were very happy we lost against Scotland," he reflects, "because in Córdoba we had a much better hotel, and a much better situation." But didn't you stay at the Sierras Hotel in Alta Gracia? "I don't remember the name." The Scots *hated* it there. "Well, let's say it like this: we went from very bad to only bad." A big improvement? "Could be! Anyway, the big change happened because we moved hotel. We were much freer there." They also changed things on the bench. Ernst Happel was demoted somewhat and his assistant Jan Zwartkruis, who'd led the team through qualification, was given more power. The exact nature of the new arrangement is hard to pinpoint. In his autobiography, Zwartkruis claimed he essentially took over with Happel staying on as figurehead. Others dispute this, pointing out that Happel was ruling on tactics and picking the team.

The Dutch very rarely think about the Scotland game because they have their own 'what if' moment that year. At 1-1 in the final against Argentina, in injury time, Rensenbrink hit the post. Johnny Rep, reflecting the atmosphere of fear and intimidation the Dutch experienced that day, still insists they would never have been allowed to win the game and might even have been killed if they had. But that was surely impossible. The whole world was watching on TV, and whatever the generals wanted there was no way to manipulate events so crudely. Ezequiel Fernández Moores has suggested a Holland win might even have had the opposite effect and endangered the regime.

But none of that happened. Argentina scored twice in extra time (the third goal involving a double handball) and Videla presented the trophy to captain Daniel Passarella. Videla later invited his team to one of his palaces to thank them and give them silver cigar cases. Meanwhile, the country celebrated fervently, and the generals reaped the political reward. Videla was replaced in 1981 but the junta remained in power until 1983 when, after their disastrous Falklands gambit, they fell. Democracy returned and the long battle for justice began. Under the first post-dictatorship president, Raúl Alfonsín, prosecutions of the regime's murderers started, but faltered under pressure from the military. The next president, Carlos Menem, tried to put the past to bed by issuing blanket pardons. Under the Kirchners, the search for justice resumed. The pardons were annulled and a belated attempt to grapple with the horrific legacy of the so-called 'dirty war' began. Hundreds of trials followed and former death camps, such as La Perla near Córdoba, the D2 in Mendoza, and "Argentina's Auschwitz", the ESMA former naval mechanics' school in Buenos Aires, became museums and memorial centres. In 2010, Videla and Menéndez were pictured together again, this time in a courtroom where both were convicted of crimes against humanity. Videla died in jail three years later, Menéndez five years later, while serving 14 life sentences.

Meanwhile, Argentinian football struggled with the legacy of 1978. For decades, there was a reluctance to admit anything had been amiss. Over the last 15 years or so, a much more nuanced, ambivalent feeling has developed. Some old Argentina players have spoken of their shame at realising how they were used by the regime. "We can only ask for forgiveness," said goalkeeper Ubaldo Fillol. There have been ceremonies and events and expressions of solidarity with families of the regime's victims, including the Mothers of the Plaza de Mayo (and now Grandmothers) who bravely campaigned for their 'disappeared' children during the dictatorship.

In 2018, Arie Haan and Ernie Brandts returned to the country with a Dutch TV crew, and met their opponents from the final. They also met the Mothers, who told them their presence in 1978 had helped focus world attention on their plight. (One of the Dutch players, Wim Rijsbergen, injured against Scotland, had secretly visited the Mothers at the time). Haan and Brandts also visited the ESMA, barely a kilometre from La Monumental, where Holland had played Italy and Argentina. "It was very emotional," Haan says. "You think 'we were playing not far from here'. They told us how the [prisoners] could hear the stadium and they showed us where they were held. It was unreal. It was true but you couldn't understand it. They showed us everything. The torturers had nicknames so afterwards nobody could identify them. The people being tortured had sacks over the head so they couldn't see. All this stuff was told to us and then you feel it even more. In your mind, you go back to '78 and think, 'my God, what was happening here?'"

Did you see the old Argentina players as enemies? "No, no, no. The players had nothing to do with it. It was outside their control. Menotti was in Buenos Aires and there were a lot of players from this time. Fillol was there, and Passarella. Normally, he doesn't give interviews but one evening we were with him. He organised everything and it was very nice. We talked about the final and about the referee and everything. You know, after it is finished, we are normal people. We can talk with each other, and we like it. We like each other in principle. There is a lot of respect among the players.

"In Holland, we still think the referee was bad. But when you look at the game again, I didn't see so much that was going wrong. The big thing was how Argentina got to the final. It's much more what happened in that game. But in principle, you have a referee, and you have the other team, and we all do our best. We play football, we win, lose or draw and after the game, especially when it was years ago, you can talk easily about it. Maybe I'm a little bit different. I know some other players who still have some hate, but I never had this. We have the same shit over Holland-Germany. But the game is over for me."

As part of the trip, he and Brandts travelled to Mendoza, and, at the stadium of the long grass and of Archie Gemmill's goal, the two Dutchmen met Leopoldo Luque, one of Argentina's strikers in '78. The old foes posed for pictures together, smiling and holding replicas of the World Cup trophy and the shirts they wore during the tournament. Luque, who died of Covid in 2021, had become an outspoken member of the movement to address the horrors of the dictatorship and he often worked with the D2 Memorial Centre.

It used to be customary to end match reports with a list of the players on each side, but there's another 11 whose names deserve to be known. At the main entrance to the Mendoza stadium, not far from the spot where Videla sat, a wall plaque commemorates victims of a unit called Special Group 78 (GE78 in Spanish). As part of local preparations for the World Cup, the unit had been created in December in 1977 to hunt down potential opponents of the regime who had survived earlier round-ups. A former Montonero called Juan-José Galamba had managed to escape the first wave in Mendoza and was still in hiding. GE78 operatives located and kidnapped him and all the friends and acquaintances who had sheltered or had contact with him in the previous two years. In late May, days before the tournament started, they were 'disappeared' permanently, probably tortured before being murdered. I think of the 11 as the ghostly third team in the stadium on the day Scotland and Holland met. These are their names: Margarita Dolz, Raúl Gómez, Aldo Patroni, Gustavo Camín, Mario Camín, Daniel Romero, Juan Carlos Romero; Isabel Membrive, Víctor Hugo Herrera, Juan-José Galamba, Ramón Sosa.

SPAIN 1982

16 JUNE
GROUP STAGE

ALGERIA
2

W.GERMANY
1

1. Mehdi Cerbah	1. Harald Schumacher
2. Mahmoud Ghendouz	15. Uli Stielike
5. Chaâbane Merzekane	20. Manfred Kaltz
4. Noureddine Kourichi	4. Karlheinz Förster
16. Faouzi Mansouri	2. Hans-Peter Briegel
8. Ali Fergani (c)	6. Wolfgang Dremmler
15. Mustapha Dahleb	3. Paul Breitner
10. Lakhdar Belloumi ⊗ (68')	14. Felix Magath OFF
14. Djamel Zidane OFF	*8. Klaus Fischer ON (83')*
9. Tedj Bensaoula ON (63')	**11. Karl-Heinz Rummenigge (c) ⊗ (67')**
7. Salah Assad	9. Horst Hrubesch
11. Rabah Madjer ⊗ (54') OFF	7. Pierre Littbarski
12. Salah Larbès ON (88')	
	Manager: Jupp Derwall
Manager: Rachid Mekhloufi	

Estadio El Molinón

Gijón, Spain

ATTENDANCE
42,000

REFEREE
Enrique Labo Revoredo (Peru)

RAPHAEL HONIGSTEIN & PAUL DOYLE

As he kicked a ball around the streets of Marseille, a nine-year-old Zinédine Zidane used to tell his chums that he was a cousin of Djamel Zidane. It was a forgivable fib.

Djamel Zidane hails from Algeria's Kabylie region, as does Zinédine's father, and he played with a two-footed elegance not a million miles from the style that a grown-up Zizou would later elevate to a new level of mastery. In 1982, it was only natural for an excited kid to talk up his supposed links to a member of the team that played its way on to the lips of every football fan in the world.

Coincidental namesakes aside, the ties between the Algerian national team and the people it represents are exceptionally strong. The two are bound by a history that few, if any, other countries can match and that, if opponents cared to look, would forewarn against underestimating Algeria.

West Germany did not care to look before their opening game in Gijón. And why would they? Goalkeeper Harald 'Toni' Schumacher told everybody that the reigning European champions would score "four to eight goals" against these unknown minnows on their way to lifting the World Cup. Jupp Derwall, the West Germany coach, hadn't even tried to brief his team about the opposition's strengths. "My players would only die of laughing if I showed them a film about the Algerians," he said. When a Brazilian journalist wondered whether he would take a draw in the opening match, Derwall repeatedly refused to answer, dismissing the enquiry as a "childish question" and said he'd take the "first train back" if his side were to lose the game. After the game, the utterly dejected 55-year-old told reporters he would have bet his life on West Germany winning.

This kind of arrogance was typical of a side that severely overestimated their powers. Derwall, a genial man who liked to sing German folk songs after a few drinks, believed that star players like Paul Breitner, Karl-Heinz Rummenigge (both Bayern Munich), Horst Hrubesch and Felix Magath (both Hamburger SV) needed only to be given maximum freedom to perform. The team took full advantage. During their Black Forest training camp at Schluchsee, soon dubbed "Schlucksee" (from *schlucken*, to gulp), players spent their evenings drinking, playing poker and entertaining female tourists staying in the same hotel; the German FA had forgotten to block-book the entire establishment. "Some were fucking the whole night and then crawled to training next day like a wet dish rag," Schumacher wrote in his autobiography, years later.

Football's governing body had also neglected to adjust the calendar in the run-up to tournament. While most European leagues had finished in April or mid-May at the very latest, the Bundesliga's last match day was on 29 May, a mere two-and-a-half weeks before West Germany's first game in Spain. German FA president Hermann Neuberger revealed that Derwall had initially asked the league to play on until 5 June. He evidently hadn't thought a pre-tournament camp all that necessary.

Having arrived in Spain, the national team manager had his unruly team train "like an amateur side," a reporter from *Der Spiegel* wrote in astonishment, "a few corners, a few shots on goal, a few two-against-fives". Players also spent hours sunbathing on the beach next to their Príncipe de Asturias team hotel. This overly relaxed attitude was strangely enough seen as the height of professionalism at the time: Breitner, who had returned to the national team after a seven-year absence, was convinced that top players didn't need to prepare properly nor restrain themselves off the pitch in order to perform. He led by example in that respect and his team-mates duly followed.

Hamburger SV right-back Manfred Kaltz happily confessed that he had "little idea" about the Algerian players he was about to face.

The one piece of intel everyone in the German camp did seem to remember was that it was Ramadan — and that the Algerians' fasting would surely see them suffer physically on the pitch. But once again, the *Nationalmannschaft* simply hadn't done their homework. "Ramadan only starts [six days later] on 22 June," forward Lakhdar Belloumi said after hearing of his opponents' misplaced assumptions. "In any case, we will only celebrate once our work is here done. And that might take a while."

The German players may have been blissfully ignorant, but France's Michel Platini had enough of an inkling about Algeria's potential that when asked just before the World Cup draw whether he fancied France being pitted against them, he replied: "I'd be happy to face anyone except Algeria."

Back then, Platini played for Saint-Étienne so he was no doubt familiar with the story of Rachid Mekhloufi, who, along with Mahiedine Khalef, co-managed Algeria at the World Cup. Mekhloufi had been a rising star at Saint-Étienne before sensationally fleeing France, along with a slew of other top players, in order to join Algeria's struggle for independence. Theirs is a story that conferred a special symbolic power on the national team and gave deeper significance to Algeria's appearance at their first World Cup — on the 20th anniversary of an independence so proudly and traumatically achieved.

Algeria's war for independence from France began in 1954. The colonial regime omitted no atrocity as it sought to suppress the rebellion. In an attempt to rally international support, and with media anticipation of the 1958 World Cup building, Algeria's *Front National de Libération* (FLN) hatched the idea of forming a national football team to demonstrate Algerian talent and unity, a showcase of what the country could achieve if allowed to harness its own resources. Algeria could call on many fine players, the best of whom played for French clubs and, in some cases, for the national team. The FLN's plan was to persuade those players not only to sacrifice the fortunes they could earn in Europe, but also to risk imprisonment or worse, by sneaking off to Algeria to play for the football wing of the liberation movement or, as the colonial authorities saw it, for the propaganda arm of an organisation waging war with France. In the first wave of defections, 10 professional players answered the call, slipping away from their clubs as part of a caper that no thriller movie has ever surpassed.

The commanding Monaco centre-back, Moustapha Zitouni, turned his back on a potential transfer to Real Madrid in order to spirit himself out of France and lead the FLN's team. He was accompanied by three other Monaco players, including the midfielder Abdelaziz Ben Tifour, who had played for France at the 1954 World Cup. The Toulouse forward Saïd Brahimi was another to have been capped by *Les Bleus*, scoring for them against Iceland in the qualifiers for the 1958 World Cup before he, too, took stealthy flight to join the FLN. Another Monaco player, Hassen Chabri, attempted to follow suit but was caught at the France-Italy border and sent to jail for nearly a year, accused of trying to smuggle arms.

Mekhloufi took perhaps the biggest risk of all. The 22-year-old was not only a striker for Saint-Étienne but also on the books of the French army, whom he had helped to win the World Military Games in 1957. If he had been caught defecting, he would have been court-martialled. Yet in April 1958, he plotted to make his get-away to Algeria immediately after playing a league game for his club against Béziers. Mekhloufi did his utmost not to arouse suspicion before the game and, as if to show it was business as usual, he opened the scoring in the match. But then came an unforeseen snag: Mekhloufi suffered a head injury in an aerial duel and had to be taken to hospital. Improvising nimbly, two FLN agents disguised themselves as nurses and sprung him from the hospital. They helped him to sneak across Europe and over to Tunis, home of the provisional Algerian government.

Amid rabid French protests, Fifa refused to recognise the FLN team, but over the next four years it travelled far and wide to play exhibition matches, from the Middle East to Vietnam, Hungary and Yugoslavia, their playing style as adventurous and uplifting as the anti-imperialism message they were promoting. "When people, even in France, saw me and other professionals they knew well playing for that team, they understood the people fighting for independence were not just some bandits, it was a noble cause," explained Mekhloufi years later. Ferhat Abbas, the first president of the Provisional Government of the Algerian Republic, later said the FLN team's contribution to the independence struggle was so big that it spared the country about a decade of further bloodshed.

On the 20th anniversary of their independence, with Mekhloufi in their dugout and a backroom staff that included several other ex-FLN players, such as the coach Abdelhamid Zouba, Algeria's players were not going to take things lightly. "Because of this history, the bond between the Algerian national team and our people is uniquely strong and we took the comments by the Germans before the game as a slur on our population," Belloumi explained in an interview with one of these authors in 2010.

"We had our parents at home, but we players also considered that we had our parents with us at pitch-side," added Belloumi. "Those guys from the FLN were like our second fathers — in their day they abandoned fame and fortune to fight for their country and we were carrying on that fight. We were already a tight-knit group, but we were given extra motivation by the Germans, especially as we were very conscious that 1982 was the 20th anniversary of our independence. We were determined to uphold the dignity of our people." Defender Nordine Kourichi, too, stresses the importance of recent history to the team. "The Algerian Revolution started in 1954 against France and was one of history's greatest struggles for liberation," he says. "Each member of the national squad, technical staff and the organisers vividly remembered the final years of occupation and the jubilant days of independence in July 1962. We were all triggered by a sense of urgency to perform and rise to the occasion".

Of course, it was not just patriotic pride that fuelled Algeria. The team that reached the World Cup were also exceptionally gifted, the most skilful generation the country had produced. Belloumi, a sharp and zippy striker, was a prime example. There was also his fellow forward Rabah Madjer, the energetic and suave midfielder Salah Assad, the rampaging full-back Chaâbane Merzekane and the dinky and dangerous midfielder Moustapha Dahleb. Dahleb was so irresistible that the Algerian government were moved to alter state policy so that he could play.

In the 1970s, as the recently liberated country pursued a bespoke socialist model of development, the Algerian government sought to foster the domestic league and discouraged calling up foreign-based players for the national team. And home-based players found it difficult to move abroad, as Ali Bencheikh realised when the country's president, Houari Boumédiène, personally intervened to block his mooted transfer from MC Alger to Real Madrid. State policy seemed fine when Algeria triumphed in the 1975 Mediterranean Games, which were staged in Algiers and culminated in a glorious victory in the final over France's Olympic team (the logo for that tournament, a Fennec, or desert fox, gave Algeria the nickname that they still use today). Officially, the domestic league was entirely amateur but that was mostly a sham; top players were paid salaries, but for jobs that they seldom did as pseudo-employees of big state companies. After the swelling of national pride at the Mediterranean Games, Algeria craved an even greater international exploit. Reaching the 1978 World Cup became a cherished, realistic target.

To attain it, the national federation was given permission to call up players based abroad: Dahleb, then illuminating Paris Saint-Germain (PSG)'s midfield, was the first to be summoned. To no avail, initially, as Algeria were knocked out of the World Cup running by Tunisia, who went on to take Africa's only spot at the 1978 edition.

Tunisia would represent the continent with honour, radiating enterprise and technical poise as they became the first African country to win at the World Cup thanks to a swish 3-1 victory over Mexico. They then lost 1-0 to Poland before missing out on progress to the next round despite a valiant 0-0 draw with West Germany, a match flush with pointers for what would transpire four years later. Some of those pointers were apparently ignored. But one lesson that could not be denied was that Africa deserved more places at the World Cup.

Even before that, the new Fifa president João Havelange had promised, when running for election, to allow an extra African team into the 1982 tournament. Though he was castigated for that commitment in the wake of Zaire's sorry display in 1974, Tunisia's performances in Argentina had shown that one more place was the least Africa merited. Algeria and Cameroon would ram that truth home in Spain.

First Algeria had to get there, which would take some doing. But the golden generation was beginning to bloom and the manager, Evgeni Rogov, a Soviet presumed to be in line with government's socialist principles, was given permission to augment his squad with a few more players from foreign clubs. That allowed Djamel Zidane to be recalled after a six-year absence brought about by his move from MC Alger to Kortrijk in Belgium. Algeria made smooth progress through the first qualifiers, but that earned them a two-legged playoff showdown with the opponent they dreaded most: Nigeria, who had walloped them 3-0 in the 1980 Africa Cup of Nations final in Lagos and reached the playoff by ending Tunisia's hopes of making it to two World Cup in a row.

In October 1981, Algeria returned to Lagos for the first leg of the tie. This time, in front of 80,000 aghast locals, they made light work of the Super Eagles, an explosive shot by Belloumi and a neat flick by Zidane giving them a 2-0 win. Then came the home leg, on a brand-new grass pitch laid over its limestone predecessor to favour a swift passing game. A friendly match arranged to inaugurate the pitch went badly — Algeria lost 3-0 to PSG — but the hosts thrived when it mattered most: Belloumi struck early, rifling in off the post from the edge of the box. Felix 'One-Blow' Owolabi pulled one back for the visitors with a close-range header before Madjer ruthlessly punished a mistake at the other end to crown a 4-1 aggregate win. Algeria were World Cup-bound. "The win over Nigeria was a sweet revenge for 1980 and told us we could do something. We were a team growing in power," recalled Belloumi.

Rogov was soon replaced as manager, Mekloufi stepping up from the number two role with Khalef to support him. It was the very opposite of a trend that would emerge in later years, whereby African countries shed local coaches immediately after qualifying for major tournaments to bring in European technicians reputed to be more savvy.

Three months before the World Cup, Algeria registered another rousing win over Nigeria, beating them at the Africa Cup of Nations in Libya before falling in the semi-final to Ghana. They probably would have prevailed over Ghana if captain Ali Fergani had not lashed out and incurred a stupid red card when Algeria were leading 2-1. It later transpired Fergani had been playing despite an injury, and straight after the game he travelled to France for an operation to ensure he was in peak condition for the World Cup. That was Algeria's date with destiny.

Europeans may have looked down on African football, but Algeria arrived at the World Cup with no complexes. Most of their players made their living with Algerian clubs, but experience told them they were not inferior to European players. "In those days there were no visa issues so as teens many of us had travelled and played against Europeans — we knew they weren't better than us," Merzekane later explained. Before departing for Spain, they drew further confidence from warm-up wins over the Republic of Ireland and an array of European clubs, including Lyon and Benfica. "The warm-up matches were a remarkable revelation of our talent and abilities to the team, as well as the Algerian people," defender Noureddine Kourichi said. "During the five-month period leading to May 1982, we played over a dozen warm-up matches against respectable teams, ranging from

Brazil's Atlético Mineiro to Real Madrid, Republic of Ireland and Peru, all of which we beat. Mineiro had a few players from that golden Brazilian national squad of 1982, while Real Madrid had the likes of Santillana, Juanito and Camacho, who were in the European Cup final one year earlier, not to mention Ireland's players who starred in the English League."

Kourichi recalls putting a photo of the German squad next to his bed as an added source of motivation. "But Mustapha Dahleb, a key player of Paris Saint-Germain, was my roommate, and he reminded me to approach the Germany match like any other. It was important to reach that optimal balance between strict preparation for the match and trusting in our way of playing. We were also emboldened after seeing various photos of members of the German squad strolling around the pool with their wives, while we were fired up during our warm-up matches".

Still, a few jitters would have been pardonable as Algeria lined up to face West Germany, the reigning European champions, in their first match at their country's first World Cup. Yet Algeria were anything but nervous. They tore into West Germany like men on a mission they knew they could accomplish. "We went out to attack them, to play with our style: Algerian vivacity," said Merzekane, who personified this style more than anyone, constantly forcing Breitner backwards with powerful surges from deep. "We knew he liked to attack, that he was the best in the world at it, so we set out to exploit that — that was part of our tactical triumph," continued Merzekane. "But we also dominated them technically and physically." Dominated is a stretch, but certainly Algeria were the better team in the first half, with West Germany and Breitner in particular looking sluggish as the sins of Schluchsee came back to haunt them.

"Algerian football is known for skill and trickery, but we knew that would not be enough against [West] Germany when they came at you like a bulldozer if you blinked," Kourichi says. "Our plan was to combine rapid passing with nimble dribbling and ball-control. Our readiness to attack from the first minute was exemplified by Merzekane, our right wing-back, who was always attacking. So, we basically faced the European Champions with three defenders, Mansouri, Guendouz and me. Mansouri, the left wing-back, reminded me to tell Merzekane to keep coming back after his many deep runs."

West Germany, who had so often relied on superior fitness and will-power in the past, were severely lacking in ideas. "In midfield, nothing at all happened," *Kicker* magazine wrote in their match report. Up front, it wasn't much better. Rummenigge, the two-time Ballon D'or winner (1980 and 1981), could hardly run because of a muscle injury, while Hrubesch was expertly marked out of the match by Kourichi. "I tried to give him as little room as possible on the ground or in the air, until he slammed the floor in frustration," the former Bordeaux player says. He had faced the tall centre-forward before, eight months earlier in the second round of the UEFA Cup, but with less success, as Hrubesch scored twice in the second leg to win the tie 3-2 on aggregate for his Hamburger SV side. This time, Kourichi had the upper hand.

"They wanted to tire us, they felt we would fold physically," Dahleb said. "But we were just waiting for them, ready to pounce on the break." At the break, Khalef told the team they should go for it even more in the opposition half. "With a bit more pace and energy up front," he said, "you can beat them".

His players took note. Madjer gave them the lead in the 54th minute, poking a rebound into the net at the end of a sweeping break after Schumacher could only parry a shot by Belloumi. On Algerian TV, a commentator named Mohamed Sellah was so enraptured that all he could shout was "Belloumi, Madjer! Belloumi, Madjer! Belloumi, Madjer!", an ecstatic synopsis that immediately entered Algerian folklore.

After the goal, Algeria kept coming, the crowd oléing as slicksters in green-and-white buzzed and cut through their illustrious opponents. "The crowd were a definite boost for us," Kourichi remembers. "The familiar chants of the Algerian fans never stopped, but the roars from the Spanish crowd grew louder with every run we made. Added to passing ability of our midfielders Dahleb and Fergani and the sharp runs of the wingers Madjer and Assad, we became hard to stop."

Merzekane and Assad, in particular, were uncontainable, inspiring whoops of glee from fans as they deepened West Germany's torment with every burst and pass. But West Germany did not wilt, at least not immediately. Rummenigge, for once, stole a march on defenders to stab in a low Magath cross for the equaliser in the 67th minute. But anyone who thought that heralded an inevitable return to the natural order was about to be proven wrong again.

One minute later, Algeria ripped through West Germany with a wonderful nine-pass move, Assad flying down the left on the overlap before receiving the ball and fizzing it across the face of goal. Belloumi slammed it home. "Belloumi does it! Belloumi does it!" chanted Sellah as if entering a euphoric trance.

"It was the perfect goal, one of the best moves of the whole tournament," recalled Merzekane. "And after that we didn't hang on, we continued to attack and we could have won by three or four." Merzekane almost scored the third goal himself, charging forward from his own box before being thwarted at the other end by Schumacher. In Britain, the wowed ITV commentator, Hugh Johns, proclaimed Merzekane "one of the discoveries of the World Cup". Algeria didn't increase their lead, as it happened. "They tried to fight back, but our goalkeeper Mehdi Cerbah, one of the shortest men on the pitch, played his part, frustrating successive attempts from Littbarski, Hrubesch and Rummenigge," Kourichi says. He could see that the Germans were getting increasingly desperate. "Schumacher was shouting at Kaltz, and I later heard Schumacher being angry in the changing room as well." In the end, 2-1 was enough to secure a famous win. In Algeria, and in Algerian communities in cities across the world, people poured into the streets to jubilate.

"The Germans didn't show us any respect, we were angry about that," Khalef said. "For that reason alone, this victory feels good. Even European champions shouldn't look down on Africa as if there's no football being played there."

Twelve-year-old Ashraf Laidi visited Algeria's base camp after the game with his father, a diplomat who knew the Algerian ambassador in Spain. The team were staying in Ceseda, 30 minutes outside Gijón, in villa that belonged to a local ophthalmologist who used it as a holiday home and for family get-togethers. Celebrations were controlled — "they're only drinking cola," a visiting reporter from *Kicker* magazine noted — but Laidi remembers a great sense of pride and achievement. "Algeria's first game in the World Cup, and we beat Germany. Everyone realised that they had pulled off a feat, something that would go down in the nation's history." The Algerians were very humble in their moment of triumph. Laidi recalls his father asking Dahleb for a photo and addressing the player as *la vedette*, the star. "You are the star," Dahleb replied, pointing at the boy.

Following the win, 40,000 Algerians flooded into Spain. The players could not avoid being a little affected by the euphoria. Five days later, they seemed drained, even a touch complacent, against Austria. They lost 2-0. "That's where we showed our inexperience," Belloumi explained. "We should have kept a cool head before that game and probably changed a couple of players but, in fairness to the Austrians, they had studied our style and knew we could be vulnerable on the counterattack." In contrast to the Germans' snootiness, Austria's manager, Georg Schmidt, had been monitoring the Algerians since the Africa Cup of Nations in Libya and knew their strengths. "Our loss to Austria was a partly a result of lack of concentration and few tactical changes in the second half, which cost us the game. We remained dominant throughout the game, but it was not enough," Kourichi recalls. Germany, meanwhile, bounced back with a 4-1 win over Chile, Rummenigge scoring a hat-trick.

Algeria were back to their swashbuckling best for the group dénouement. They raced into a 3-0 lead against Chile, Assad netting twice while Tedj Bensaoula, who started in place of the injured Belloumi and teed up the opening goal with a sublime pull-back, drilled in their third from 20 yards. A rash foul by Mahmoud Guendouz gave Chile a route back in the second half, and when Juan Carlos Letelier dribbled his way through the defence to make it 3-2, the seemingly rampant Algeria found themselves hanging on.

They got the win, but the two goals they let in proved costly, as Algeria were denied a place in the next round because of goal difference. Algerians still debate to this day whether their team was partly culpable for that. Even the players cannot agree. "We showed our inexperience, we should have seen that match out and preserved our three-goal lead," Belloumi said, while Merzekane took the opposing view: "Some say we should have stopped attacking, but we had come to the World Cup to show the Algerian style and we weren't about to start playing defensively." Kourichi says the team were essentially left to their own devices. "None of the coaching staff pressed us to score more goals or said anything about the importance of goal difference. I personally was urging my team-mates to go for more goals and I even made a few runs into the Chilean box."

Of course, goal difference only mattered because the next day, with the benefit of knowing the exact score that would suit both teams, West Germany and Austria contrived for the last group game to end with a 1-0 win for the Germans. That result looked conveniently likely from the moment Horst Hrubesch opened the scoring in the 10th minute. Fans in Gijón howled at the blatant lack of effort from both sides as time ticked towards the score that would send the two European teams into the next round and Algeria out of the tournament. Algerian fans in the crowd burned peseta notes to show they interpreted what had happened as corruption, and the Spanish paper *El Commercio* famously ran the match report in their crime section. "A disgrace," German TV commentator Eberhard Stanjek called the game. He remained silent in protest through most of the second half. Derwall's side improved over the course of the competition to make it to the final, lost 3-1 to Italy, but their reputation was forever tarnished by a hat-trick of transgressions: the naked arrogance of the Algeria defeat, the collusion with Austria, and Schumacher's brutal foul on Patrick Battiston in the semi-final against France.

Several German players have since apologised publicly for the cynicism they showed in the Austria stitch-up, but at the time none offered any remorse. "I can't worry about the crowd's reaction," midfielder Wolfgang Dremmler said after the final whistle, "people fly down here to see the game at their own risk." The head of the Austrian delegation, Hans Tschak, added insult to misery when he made this barely believable declaration: "Naturally, today's game was played tactically. But if 10,000 'sons of the desert' here in the stadium want to trigger a scandal because of this it just goes to show that they have too few schools. Some sheikh comes out of an oasis, is allowed to get a sniff of World Cup air after 300 years and thinks he's entitled to open his gob."

Merzekane said in 2010 that such a deranged comment, on top of a shameful performance, gave Algeria a measure of satisfaction. "We weren't angry, we were cool," he said. "To see two big powers debasing themselves, in order to eliminate us, was a tribute to Algeria. They progressed with dishonour, we went out with our heads held high."

From all over the world came calls for Fifa to sanction the Europeans or even order a replay but in the end, all the world's governing body did was rule that henceforth, the last pair of games in every group must be played simultaneously. That had been the norm at the previous tournament and did not necessarily guarantee there would be no cynicism — West Germany had demonstrated that in 1978 by toning down their efforts in the closing minutes of the match against Tunisia so that Poland, who were leading at the same time against Mexico, would top their group and thus meet Brazil and Argentina while the Germans got a notionally easier route — but it at least made anti-competitive arrangements more difficult and risky. "Our performances forced Fifa to make that change, and that was even better than a victory," Belloumi said. "It meant that Algeria left an indelible mark on football history."

Algeria yearned for more tangible recompense for a thrilling generation. There were frustrating third-place finishes at the 1984 and 1988 Africa Cup of Nations, either side of another, less glorious appearance at the World Cup, as their 1986 odyssey yielded a draw with Northern Ireland and defeats by Brazil and Spain. In truth, the '86 team did not play with the same vim and flair as the '82 side, and there was discord in the camp as some home-based players fell out with some Europe-based ones, who now made up half of the squad as the government, partly in gratitude for the performance in Spain, allowed stars to move abroad.

Madjer proved that Algerian players could still upset the elite — Germans again, as it happened — by backheeling in a magnificent winner for Porto against Bayern Munich in the 1987 European Cup final. And then, in 1990, Algeria at least got the consecration they craved, beating their old rivals Nigeria in front of over 105,000 fans to be crowned African champions on home soil.

Sadly, football joy did not now reflect political reality. In 1992, Algeria sunk into a horrifying civil war pitting the government against various Islamist rebel groups. A glittering end to a golden football era for the country could not prevent a plunge into over a decade of violence that ruined millions of lives and dreams.

It would take until 2014 before Algeria would make positive impact at a World Cup again. Kourichi was the assistant coach when Les Fennecs came very close to dumping the eventual tournament winners out in the last 16 in Porto Alegre. But revenge for the disgrace of Gijón narrowly eluded Vahid Halilhodžić's team — a much more likeable German side squeezed through in extra-time.

"I have had several achievements in international football of which I'm highly proud, such as being a member of the first Algerian national team qualifying for the World Cup, making history in 1982 and being assistant manager in 2014, when we made it to the second round of the World Cup at last," Kourichi says, looking back with fond memories. "But 1982 tops it all. My father was an immigrant, he had arrived at Ostricourt, in the north of France, from Msirda, a village in Western Algeria, in 1949. He worked six days a week, 14 hours a day in the coal mines. To see his tears of joy and pride after our historic victory over [West] Germany in Spain was my ultimate moment of deep honour and accomplishment."

Kourichi also made history in another way. France-born, he was the first binational football player to make the Algerian national team. "I'm proud to have been the first in that list," he says. Two more generations have followed in Kourichi's footsteps. Who knows what Algeria might have achieved on the world stage if a certain nine-year-old kid from Marseille had turned out for them too.

SPAIN 1982

25 JUNE
FIRST GROUP STAGE

N.IRELAND
1

SPAIN
0

N.IRELAND	SPAIN
1. Pat Jennings	1. Luis Arconada (c)
2. Jimmy Nicholl	6. José Ramón Alexanko
5. Chris Nicholl	2. José Antonio Camacho
12. John McClelland	5. Miguel Tendillo
3. Mal Donaghy ▉ (61')	3. Rafael Gordillo
8. Martin O'Neill (c)	4. Periko Alonso
10. Sammy McIlroy OFF	16. Tente Sánchez
14. Tommy Cassidy ON (50')	15. Enrique Saura
4. David McCreery	7. Juanito
9. Gerry Armstrong ⊗ (47')	9. Jesús María Satrústegui OFF
16. Norman Whiteside OFF	*20. Quini ON (46')*
13. Sammy Nelson ON (70')	11. Roberto López Ufarte OFF
11. Billy Hamilton	*17. Ricardo Gallego ON (77')*
Manager: Billy Bingham	Manager: José Emilio Santamaría

Estadio Luis Casanova

Valencia, Spain

ATTENDANCE
49,562

REFEREE
Héctor Ortiz (Paraguay)

ROB BAGCHI

> It was 40°C in Zaragoza and the midsummer Andalusian dust chafed the throat. But it was still not hot enough to stop Billy Bingham striking a match and holding it so close to his face it would have singed a virgin smoker's nostril hairs.

The pipe lent the Northern Ireland manager an avuncular air but it was not a gimmick. You could often smell him before you saw him emerging through a pungent, indigo fog of, perhaps, a woodwork teacher's Three Nuns, a postmaster's Gold Leaf, an angler's St Bruno, a GP's Condor or whatever other lethal brand was at hand. It was not an altogether unpleasant aroma, but it clung to his clothes and tinctured the hair. A pipe is a smart prop, masking its true purpose — to deliver nicotine to the addict as quickly and efficiently as possible, mainlining it if you will — and camouflaging any abrasiveness of character by imbuing him with a kindliness and gravitas inspired by our enduring affection for JB Priestley, Bing Crosby and Eric Morecambe; the Brotherhood of the Briar. It's an example of virtue by association; charm shrouds the grit.

You have to be patient to be a pipesmoker. All that ritualistic tapping, poking, shredding, rubbing, prodding, tamping, toasting and, at last, inhaling, gives one time to think. Time to ruminate. Time, like Harold Wilson toying with Robin Day, to come up with an answer.

Northern Ireland had embarked on the 1982 World Cup, their first finals appearance for 24 years, with a straightforward strategy to qualify for the second phase from Group E: hold Yugoslavia to a draw, beat Honduras and, if they really had to, scrape something from their final match against the hosts, Spain.

Part one had gone to plan. Their diligence and discipline had stymied a prodigiously talented Yugoslavia, but a rancid blend of profligacy and heat exhaustion had eroded their early lead over Honduras in an absolute dog of a game. The two points they had bargained for from the Concacaf champions had been halved by Antonio Laing's equaliser and given the Spain game a significance they had intended to negate. In four days, a team that had seldom ventured beyond binary scorelines for years, and almost never positively, would have to defeat a team striving to become the fourth home winner in five World Cups. Or, even more improbably, manage a high-scoring draw. For Ballymacarrett 'Bing' at the final whistle in La Romareda, this was at least a three-pipe problem.

Northern Ireland had held off Sweden and Portugal to make their second World Cup, finishing behind Scotland in the qualifying group after Gerry Armstrong's goal earned them a 1-0 victory over Israel in their last match at Windsor Park. Five of the qualifiers had taken place in 1981, the 13th year of the Troubles and spring and summer of the hunger strikes. Between beating Portugal 1-0 in Belfast at the end of April and losing in Stockholm by the same margin at the beginning of June, four Republican prisoners had starved themselves to death. Six more would die before Scotland's visit in October in a wild year of more than 80 confirmed sectarian murders by paramilitary organisations. The sense of escalation, of parts of the six counties, its borderlands and city streets being turned into charnel houses was distressingly palpable on a personal if not collective level. Mass unemployment was ransacking British society, but in Northern Ireland, factory closures had become a contagion. On the eve of the World Cup, unemployment among adult males in Belfast stood at 19.8%, in Cookstown 36.7% and in Strabane a barely conceivable 46.3%. Assailed by harrowing sectarian strife and the poverty and loss of purpose unemployment wreaks, despair was natural but not all-pervasive. Hope, defiance and determination to weather everything for love of place and people sustained the communities.

Northern Ireland, winners of the annual Home Championship in 1980, were dreadful in the 1982 tournament. They were not as complicit as England and Scotland in wishing the competition away, but Bingham, forgivably, used the opportunity of matches against their three oldest rivals to assess how some of his fringe picks — Glentoran's Jim Cleary, Coleraine's Felix Healy and Bobby Campbell of Fourth Division Bradford City — might cope if, by some grotesque misfortune, he had to call on them in Spain.

Bingham was not strong-armed into giving Irish League players international opportunities. He did not have to be. As a former Glens player and Linfield manager, he had his own loyalties and knew his duty. England trounced them at Wembley in February. Sammy McIlroy scored to earn a 1-1 draw with Scotland two months later in Belfast, but in their last match before facing Yugoslavia, they went down 3-0 to Wales at the Racecourse Ground, watched by a desultory crowd of 2,315. In four matches since beating Israel, including a 4-0 rout by France in Paris, they had shipped 12 goals and scored only one. Malcolm Brodie, who would flip and flop from castigation to exaltation and back again so pricelessly over the next six weeks, wrote in the *Belfast Telegraph*: "Never has any side embarked on the World Cup finals adventure so demoralised as Northern Ireland after this utter humiliation by Wales. Indeed, they could be a positive embarrassment in Spain next month unless there is a dramatic improvement in the mediocrity which has characterised performances since qualification." Small wonder their World Cup odds drifted out from 100-1 to 150-1.

Their enjoyment of the Home Championship, usually such a valued challenge for the players, was blighted by a dispute over the bonus sheet for Spain. The Irish FA proposed a sliding scale of £600 each per match for the starting XI, £400 for the five substitutes regardless of whether they came on and £200 for the six left out of the matchday squad. The negotiations meandered on for months, neither side wanting to appear unreasonable in public though the usual argument was briefed to the press by the association: the shirt should mean more than mere money. It is always presented as an incontrovertible proposition and one with which supporters and patriots readily sympathise, pride convincing them to commit to a notional sacrifice rather than an actual one. For the players, of whom only a handful were well-off even by the standards of the day, it was as much about principle as cash. Their efforts in qualification had wet the IFA's beak in the Fifa pond. A considerable take from the tournament was coming the association's way no matter what. It was just a question of equitable distribution. In the end the players smoothed the rancour among themselves, agreeing to pool everything and split it 22 ways.

That problem was resolved in Brighton, where Bingham set up camp at the Metropole Hotel and University of Sussex's sports ground at the beginning of June. The month before, the captain of England, Kevin Keegan, his team-mate Trevor Brooking and Scotland's Graeme Souness had all said that they were prepared to forego the World Cup if the government issued a formal instruction to the FA, SFA and IFA to boycott it over the participation of Argentina following the invasion of the Falkland Islands. For 30 years after the war, it was generally accepted that, like the 1980 Moscow Olympics, the government was happy for the usual gobshite backbench MPs to advocate a withdrawal but would not make the mistake of establishing a precedent by officially interfering. Yet when the papers were unsealed in 2014, we discovered that the prospect of pulling the three teams out had been on the cabinet agenda and that the Secretary of State for Environment, Michael Heseltine, the sports minister's boss, had told his colleagues: "We should be ready to adopt that course at short notice if the situation worsens and in the light of public opinion." From the sinking of HMS Sheffield on 4 May until the ceasefire and surrender of the Argentinian forces on 14 June, the day after César Luis Menotti's defending champions had kicked off the opening match of the tournament, a government embargo on the three teams' participation was always on the cabinet table. Only victory removed all lingering threat.

Northern Ireland's greatest player was a less apocalyptic spectre for Bingham but a looming presence all the same. George Best had inherited Bingham's green number 7 shirt, his debut coming the game after Billy's last cap. The manager had selected him 15 times during the 20 games of his first spell in charge of the national team from 1967–71, the golden age of Best. Had he been fit and available, he would doubtless have played all 20. There was no animosity between the two. Best would turn 36 the month before the 1982 finals began, but that did not prevent the boosters among his many friends in the media pressing his case, essentially on grounds of entitlement rather than plausibility. Bingham's entire managerial career had been based on athletic endeavour, positional discipline and counter-attacking. It was opportunistic, not free-wheeling nor, God forbid, sentimental. Nonetheless, Bingham travelled to Easter Road in October 1981 to watch Best play for his club, San Jose Earthquakes, in a friendly against his previous side, Hibernian. Best reckoned Bingham judged him on the company he kept on and off the field. He was still a capable midfielder if a crambazzled shadow of the indomitable sprite that won the hearts of millions. But San Jose — and Hibs for that matter — were rubbish, and by May 1982 he had played no proper football, if you could call it that, since the end of the 1981 NASL season, the previous August. Periods of hope and recovery that winter would end in depressive binges and, although he felt Best could provide valuable impact from the bench during the final 15 minutes of a game, Bingham knew the high summer temperatures in Spain would only underscore the damage the drink had done to him. Besides, how would he be able to resist the clamour for a romantic gesture if he took Best and named him among his five substitutes, and not antagonise his own supporters and the wider world? Worse still, if he were among the six who did not even get stripped for the match, how would he ever move off the subject before or after? There were no upsides to the gamble because Best's mental and physical shape were not up to playing at a World Cup nine years on from his last First Division outings. The hair was still inky, the skin bronzed and the smile as bashfully charming as ever, but for all his love of the game, breezy confidence in his own unique talent and seriousness of purpose on the occasions he was focused, Best was finished. Despite the urgings of journalists, TV personalities, Pat Jennings and Sammy McIlroy, Bingham left him out of the 40-man preliminary squad. Being the ringmaster at a circus is one thing; being the daft bugger who merrily sticks his head in the lion's mouth is quite another.

If the finest discovery of Bob Bishop's exemplary 30 years as Manchester United's Ulster scout was too careworn for Spain, his latest find was considered too much of a fledgling. Norman Whiteside had celebrated his 17th birthday on 7 May, 13 days after he had made his first-team debut as a £16-a-week substitute against Brighton at the Goldstone Ground. On his first start in the final match of the season, he scored at Old Trafford and the Stretford End opened its heart to him. 'The Boy Wonder' had played only 105 minutes of first-team football but one look at him instantly brought to mind a line of William McIlvanney's from his novel *Docherty*: "He's no' a boay. That's three men dressed up as a boay."

The Shankill Skinhead was a raw-boned forward of uncommon strength, skill and will, with an immaculate first touch and spatial awareness. His left-foot shot reminded older Manchester United fans of Jack Rowley, who belted the ball so hard it could rip the nine-inch stays holding the nets to the turf out of the ground. And while Whiteside was as good in the air as one would expect of a lad built like that, it was his vision and unflappability that made every club in England covet him from the age of 11. When Tottenham's Paul Miller and Graham Roberts, as tough a top-flight centre-half pairing around that year, attempted to intimidate him with a threat to break his neck if he came near them, he laughed at them. Only a chronic knee problem, which led to the removal of a cartilage, had thwarted his progress — and would eventually end his career by the age of 26. Had he been able to remain as swift as the schoolboy sprint champion he once was, Whiteside would have been one of the greatest. Instead, with tibia grinding on to fibia for nine years, pain and swelling gradually eroding his mobility, he had to settle for merely world-class.

Whiteside's place among the 40 players originally put on standby made few waves. There was safety in numbers among the many 'unknowns' on the list. The joke was not that Bingham had called up a kid, but that he'd actually managed to trawl 40 possibles. Whiteside learnt of his call-up for the 22 in San Diego on his first post-season tour with Manchester United. Eric Harrison, his youth team manager, had worked alongside Bingham at Everton and had furnished his old friend with every mouthwatering detail of Whiteside's progress since recovering from his latest bout of knee surgery. Jim McGregor, United's physio, doubled up as Northern Ireland's trainer and was also in Bingham's ear. Both men let Whiteside know quite early that he was in the frame and when he received Bingham's invitation, he was unfazed. Mind you, nothing to do with football has ever fazed him. I have never met a player in 25 years of football writing more confident in his own ability and determination to succeed. "I grew up on the Shankill Road. I saw people get drills through their kneecaps," Gary Bailey says Whiteside told him when refusing to take part in a humiliating, first-team dressing room initiation rite. "Why would I be frightened of you?" Not that it was true, Whiteside cheerfully admits. But he was never above a mindfuck, even at 16.

The last time Whiteside had checked into the Metropole on Brighton's seafront was the night before his league debut. Now, fresh from California, he was back. The weather was glorious on the south coast that fortnight, hotter than the Algarve where Scotland prepared. Strenuous physical training had been the making of Bingham as a player. From the age of 15, he had worked with Buster McShane, a Belfast gym owner and bodybuilder who would go on to coach Mary Peters to pentathlon Olympic gold. Whiteside, whose knee and hip problems had left him, in his words, "running like a robot", had been due to take part in one-to-one sprint tuition with Peters that summer, but instead found himself in East Sussex undergoing the schedule originally devised by her mentor in the 1940s. Bingham, a Southport resident, ran his players on the dunes of the Lancashire seaside town when managing the local club and, later, Everton. But in Brighton, he engaged the university's best middle distance runner to act as a pacemaker and stuck predominantly to the track, building stamina with distance work and sharpness with the old favourites: a medley of 1x800m, 2x400m, 2x 200m, 2x100m and 4x60m. Whiteside says he had never been fitter nor would be again. The World's Strongest Man contestants were also staying at the Metropole. The Northern Ireland players were not inhibited by their fellow guest's muscles, only their chestnut hue. "I looked like the Milky Bar Kid next to them," Whiteside says.

There was a reason they didn't bronze. Bingham, ever the hustler, was a partner in a chemist's shop in Southport and used the opportunity to shift some of his stock. The players were grateful to be handed bottles of sunscreen and aftersun by their manager after training one evening, less so when he charged them £6.50 a pop. Poor Noel Brotherston was doubly kippered when Bingham asked him to try on a pair of sunglasses, which he reluctantly did, only to be polite. "That's a fiver, please Noel," Bingham said and duly collected. We cannot know for certain but it is highly unlikely any of the other 23 World Cup managers that summer would have been Del Boying Ambre Solaire and Foster Grants to a captive market. Long live Hooky Street.

Their camaraderie, already substantial, grew over the 10 days. There was a blend of religions and backgrounds. The only preponderance was the number of affectionately denominated 'Big' men over 'Wee' ones. 'Big Pat' Jennings, 'Big John' McLelland 'Big John' O'Neill, 'Big Chris' Nicholl, 'Big Billy' Hamilton, 'Big Norman' Whiteside, 'Big Jim' Platt, 'Big George' Dunlop and 'Big Felix' Healy outnumbered David 'Wee Dee' McCreery nine to one. Jennings, Mal Donaghy, the captain Martin O'Neill and Gerry Armstrong were all Catholics, but from diverse environments. Armstrong and Donaghy grew up in the snug, nationalist communities of West Belfast, O'Neill, their brightest mind, in Kilrea, no more than a village to the north of Belfast and east of Derry, and Jennings in Newry. The goalkeeper had a bass voice so sonorous whales could hear it at the bottom of Carlingford Lough and a delivery as ponderous as *Derry Girls*' Uncle Colm. But to Whiteside, from the Shankill stronghold in West Belfast, and McIlroy, McCreery, Hamilton and McLelland from the loyalist heartland in the east of the capital, the veteran goalkeeper, their one true star even if he had missed the last six months of Arsenal's season with injury, was a father figure, no matter his church.

There was no boozing after training. With all the salt tablets and 10 pints of water Bingham insisted they took on board, there was little room. But most congregated in the Metropole foyer, despite wives and children being put up at adjacent hotels, ordering pot after pot of tea, nattering away and buttressing their bond. Both that and the training forged confidence. "Physically we were more than ready," says Whiteside. "But it also gave us a bedrock of belief in each other which built every day as we witnessed our team-mates getting stronger, growing closer. We were like one big, tight family."

They arrived in Valencia on the day the Argentinian garrison at Port Stanley surrendered, and trained at Levante's ground to a strict timetable. In the morning, they took the bus across town to Estadio Ciudad de Valencia for a gentle session of jogging, shape and set-piece work. Back at the hotel they did ancient but effective PE jerks in the ground before lunch, took a siesta, woke to a light tea before going back to the stadium for a full-on, intensive session at 9pm, the kick-off time for their three group matches. Bingham said he knew Whiteside would start the moment he saw him play on the fields of Falmer. One moment in particular stood out. "I beat Big Pat in a training match in Brighton with a curling shot that was similar to the one I scored in the 1985 FA Cup final," Whiteside says. "I bent it round him and he couldn't get near it. As Billy told it at one of our reunion dinners, from that point on I was on the teamsheet."

It was a decision that inspired the famous headline in the *Belfast Telegraph* on the morning of the Yugoslavia game: 'Belfast boy beats Pele.' At the age of 17 years and 41 days, Norman Whiteside became the youngest player in World Cup finals history, a record he holds 40 years and nine editions on. His inclusion demanded a tactical tweak to 4-3-3, with Whiteside on the left, Armstrong on the right and Hamilton through the middle. It was not rigid. McCreery sat the deepest of the midfield three and O'Neill and McIlroy, attacking midfielders by nature, enjoyed the freedom to go forward, knowing that every one of the three front men could and would cover. Likewise, if Jimmy Nicholl bombed on, McCreery would shift to the right, O'Neill would fall back and Armstrong hold the line. In that heat, Bingham knew sprinting long distances necessitated taking a breather and other players pitching in for the one raiding upfield. Shuttling runs like modern full-backs, up and down the whitewash at full pelt, were impossible, so the players would whirl between positions to help out. When the opposition had the ball, the forwards and midfield would merge, not becoming 4-5-1 as one might expect but 4-6-0, challenging them to play through the congestion. When Northern Ireland won it back, the aim was to maximise the strength of Hamilton and Whiteside to hold the ball up and lay it off to harness the ability of Armstrong, O'Neill and McIlroy to make third man runs beyond. It was not designed to be pretty, only effective. The DeLorean was the most beautiful thing to come out of Northern Ireland in 1982, not the national side — but look how that ended.

Bingham was a practical man and counter-attacking is the practical football man's method. They all bought into it and ran themselves so relentlessly against Yugoslavia, Hamilton shed 12lbs. Packing midfield and handing the initiative to your opponent to attack also forced their playmakers to probe around the press, which slowed the tempo. With only two points for a win, draws were not yet devalued currency, which also bred caution. Bingham was happy with a point which matched the one Spain had taken off Honduras the night before.

That Honduras comfortably held Spain, who needed Roberto López Ufarte to dive and 'win' a penalty, which he scored himself to burgle a draw, should have alerted Bingham to the deficiencies in his scouting report on the Central Americans. Instead, they were persuaded that Spain had been rattled by first night nerves and Honduras, spurred on by the occasion, had been inspired by cup fever to play in a way they could never manage again. He must have thought he was right when Gerry Armstrong put Northern Ireland ahead in Zaragoza in their second group match after only nine minutes with a tap-in once both McIlroy's inswinging free-kick and Chris Nicholl's header from the rebound had thumped into the bar. They dominated the first half and both Hamilton and Armstrong should have extended the lead but after the break they played into Honduras's hands. When two counter-attacking sides meet, it's a test of nerve. Rather than inviting Honduras on to them, as Whiteside recalls, "we tried to steamroller them with hard running and crosses into the box, but they undid us with dainty footwork and short rhythmic passing, which made us chase shadows. We grew ever more frustrated and tired." Managers were more fatalistic back then about their influence on the play once matches had kicked off, half-time talks and substitutions apart. A more demonstrative manager than Bingham, and certainly a modern one, would have pointed both index fingers at his temples, football's universal mime demanding concentration. But it would have been pointless. Exhaustion plagued them. And the suffocating heat. Jennings' extraordinary hairdo, which had kept his ears covered for the last 12 years with a helmet of waves, like side-crimped Cornish pasty crusts, resembled Jheri curls.

By the time he was taken off after 65 minutes, five minutes on from Antonio Laing's header which had made it 1-1, Whiteside was dissolving. In the 1970s, Dave Thomas of QPR, Everton and England forsook shinpads and had his socks wrinkled around his ankles, exposing great swathes of naked shin that were fleshy bullseyes for full-backs' studs, his pace and wizardry notwithstanding. That night, Northern Ireland looked the same, sweat pouring down their legs like condensation on a window pane, socks slung low, protection discarded in vain hope of some comfort from a breeze that never came. Wilting under the heat and pressure, they scuffled hard for a draw which, given Spain's 2-1 victory over Yugoslavia 24 hours earlier, demolished Bingham's original computations. Fortified by a toot or two on his pipe, he told reporters: "It will take a lot of effort against Spain, but we are still in with a shout. We now have to face the fact that we must win our last game, against the host country on their own ground, and that's a difficult task. But when the will is there, and the desire is strong, everyone knows that we will really give it a go."

The squad made the last flight back to Valencia from Zaragoza with minutes to spare. McIlroy and Sammy Nelson, an unused substitute, had taken two hours to dribble out enough to satisfy the post-match drugs testers and finally dashed to the airport, utterly spent. Having written off Tuesday as a rest day, training geared up again on Wednesday and Thursday. They returned to their hotel from their 9pm session on the eve of their match against Spain to watch Yugoslavia beat Honduras with an 87th-minute penalty. The following afternoon, West Germany and Austria would stitch up a farcical 1-0 victory for the Germans which meant both would qualify for the second round at Algeria's expense. Until the Disgrace of Gijón, it was routine to have the third round of deciding group fixtures kicking off at different times and on different days, and Northern Ireland went to bed knowing that a win or a draw in which they scored a minimum of two goals would see them through. They were not daunted by Spain as a football team for the simple reason that they had seen them play. Other considerations weighed heavier on their thoughts that night.

The hosts were not the Spain of tiki-taka. La Furia Roja owed more to the brutality of the present and past Liga game than its future beauty. The back four — José Camacho, Miguel Tendillo, José Alexanco and Rafael Gordillo — were a formidable unit and the two centre-backs, along with midfielder Periko Alonso, Xabi's father, were masters of niggling provocation, what old players called "marking the inside of your shirt". Making a nuisance of themselves by holding on to an opponent's jersey or shorts, they also bumped players before the ball came to knock them off their stride, nipped their upper arms, raked down the shin to plant their two heel studs on to metatarsals or tackled from behind or the side, one leg braced like a harpoon to take ball or man before the full weight of the defender's body followed in for the demolition. So violent at times was their approach, encouraged by their Uruguayan manager Jose Santamaria, it flirted more with nihilism than workaday cynicism. It did not help that their two most creative players, Joaquín and Jesús María Zamora, the heartbeats of Sporting Gijón and Real Betís respectively, were struggling with injury, nor that Quini, their quick, resourceful Barcelona striker, who had been held hostage by bungling kidnappers for 25 days the previous year, could not displace Jesús Satrústegui in his manager's affections.

Disharmony was not confined to the team and its tactics. Underneath the elegance of Madrid's Gran Vía, the vibrancy of Las Ramblas and the gaudy gaiety of the Benidorm strip, Spain was riven by inflation at 14% (compared with the UK's 5.4), unemployment which had leapt from 11% in 1980 to almost 16% in 1982, and the intensification of ETA's Basque separatist campaign of terrorism targeting police and civil guards. Every team at the World Cup was accompanied everywhere by motorcycle outriders and police officers with assault weapons slung casually over one shoulder. Northern Ireland's players saw more guns in Valencia that year than they had encountered in a lifetime in Belfast. Moreover, just a year earlier, Spain had withstood the Tejerazo, an attempted coup by right-wing military officers. On 23

February, Lieutenant-Colonel Antonio Tejera, waving a pistol and wearing his three-cornered hat, led 150 Guardia Civil members into the Congress of Deputies and held the elected representatives hostage for 22 hours. Democracy was barely six years old in 1981 and, over a tense day and night, there was genuine unease about its survival. A co-ordinated putsch in Valencia, however, was the only supporting move and the following morning, after King Juan Carlos had appeared on TV at 1.15am to denounce the plotters, Tejera surrendered. The coup might have been a dud, but disquiet remained and both monarch and government saw the World Cup generally, and the red shirt principally, as a way to bind the country together in a show of patriotism, diluting the nationalism of some regions and the fascism of the past. Consequently, Spain's players were on £25,000 a man to win the group and £250,000 each to win the tournament. They were no longer footballers as such, but avatars of the new Spain.

That is what worried Bingham and his players. If victory was politically significant, how far would they be prepared to go? There were mutterings about 'Spanish practices' and 'Spanish customs' after López Ufarte was awarded the penalty that secured the draw with Honduras, grumblings which were multiplied when they were given another one for a foul that had blatantly occurred outside the box during their defeat of Yugoslavia. The pejorative terms were not properly applied. But they were too good not to misappropriate as a catch-all for Iberian corruption. One of the first British footballers to play in European competition once told this author that after playing an away leg against a Spanish side, they were royally entertained at the traditional post-match banquet. Afterwards, the president took them off to a nightclub that turned out to be a "knocking shop" and one or two of his team-mates "went upstairs to be entertained". He could never be sure whether it was genuine hospitality, insurance should the president need to call in a favour or simply to have something over them, to weigh on their minds, before the second leg. That wasn't what was happening during the World Cup but those old war stories about the Spanish game bred suspicion and conspiracies that infected Jimmy Hill's co-commentary.

Something more tangible was going on, though. O'Neill sounded the warning on their return from Zaragoza. "We don't fear the Spanish team one little bit but we are all afraid of the fans. They have a big influence on the referees here. I have travelled around the world playing and watching football, but never before have I seen a crowd put so much pressure on the man in the middle. They just control him."

Valencia had been a canny choice as the venue for Spain's three group games. They did not want to run the gauntlet of the Madrid public and their white handkerchiefs before they had found their feet and Seville, home of their diehard supporters, would have been a furnace in June. Valencia had the right mix of city and coast, exuberant fans who could match the passion of Seville, and it was the home of Manolo, the team's most famous supporter and his, depending on your taste, immortal/infernal drum, *El bombo de España*. It would take a special kind of referee not to be influenced by the occasion. Fifa appointed Paraguay's Héctor Ortiz for what turned out to be his one and only World Cup finals match.

Northern Ireland's own travelling support were bolstered for the final group game by scores more coming the long way via Liverpool, or by bus from Larne to Stranraer and down through Scotland, England, France and Spain. Among them was Whiteside's brother Ken, who rang in sick and was unfortunate to be spotted on TV by his boss who subsequently docked his wages. Others flooded in for the day from Fuengirola, Torremolinos and Marbella. They were outnumbered at least 10 to one yet still made themselves heard, singing *When Irish Eyes are Smiling* and the diddly-dee World Cup anthem *Yer Man*. While many of them were shaking off the rust from their limbs after their long journey south and slaking their thirsts in the late afternoon, most of the players were around the pool at the hotel. Bingham had outlawed sunbathing for all but an hour each day. It was usually a time for piss-taking and relaxation. Naturally, this time they were more preoccupied and spoke about the game. Everyone had his say and eventually it was O'Neill's turn. Armstrong remembered it word for word: "Look, it's as simple as this. We are not good enough to beat them two- or three-nil so forget about it. Look at the way they played the other night, like a team under a bit of pressure. What we've got to do is keep them under pressure for the first 25 minutes, not allow them too many chances, let the crowd turn against them when they aren't having any joy with us, and you know what we're like, we'll create three or four chances on the counter-attack and we'll stick one of them in. That's how we'll beat them." O'Neill doubled up as the squad's bookie. Considering how it all panned out, you would have to be pretty cavalier to lump on against him after that.

Bingham named the same XI for the third successive game and kept his team-talk simple, preaching patience and pride. He reminded them who they were playing for, the people of 'Our Wee Country' and their families. He spoke of hope and community, of peace, of everything their compatriots had endured for the past 13 years and what their presence there meant back home. He could have pointed out (but did not) that more video recorders were rented that week in Belfast than in the build-up to the wedding of the Prince and Princess of Wales. Before the peroration that left Whiteside with goosebumps in defiance of the heat, Bingham told his players to swamp midfield to force their opponents to hit the ball over the top, believe in the counter-attacking plan and, above all, maintain a high defensive line because the Spanish players would look to dive and the referee might not be able to brave the cacophony of 45,000 overwrought home fans.

Few pundits gave them a prayer. On the BBC, Lawrie McMenemy spoke for them all when he said: "Northern Ireland are such a tiny soccer nation they have won to get here really. Spain have done so badly and have had so much stick even from their own supporters that I think Ireland could just get the backlash tonight." Indeed, John Motson said their task was "monumental", but Jimmy Hill nipped down to the tunnel to grab a quick word with McIlroy after the warm-up, who told him they had banished all negative thoughts. "It's Northern Ireland," said McIlroy. "Anything can happen."

The BBC and ITV get behind every home nation at international tournaments. It makes political and commercial sense. Yet it is often forgotten that in 1982 most of the country did too, with the obvious exception of the Scots rooting for the English. Back in England, those of us who had been forced by 1974 and 1978 to have a broader sense of British identity than exists today, readily embraced Scotland in West Germany and Argentina. Naturally, we would have preferred England to be there but in their absence we transferred our allegiance to Willie Ormond's Scots, essentially Revie's Leeds in navy blue, and Ally MacLeod's magnificent spoofers. Even though England were present, millions tuned in to do the same for Northern Ireland now.

The noise was deafening from the start. Manolo, sustained by regular squirts from his wine skin, beat merry hell out of his drum. He was joined by 45,000 shrieking home fans and seemingly as many air-horns. Northern Ireland dropped back as instructed and Spain proceeded to create a number of chances: Alonso shot wide, Jennings raced out to dive at López Ufarte's feet, Satrústegui missed the target with two headers and Alexanko flashed another header over the bar. Watching the game again on a dodgy DVD, analogue pictures grainy and almost pixelated on a digital screen, I had forgotten all that. Forty years had washed the details away and all that remained was a vague impression of lawlessness and ultra-violence that had been veneered by the result.

There were not enough cameras to capture all the fouls. Tendillo and Alexanko clumped Hamilton and Whiteside in the calves and ankles when they had their backs to goal or kneed them in the buttocks or punched them in the small of the back. They went over the ball targeting the shins or the top of the foot when faced up. If they went up in an aerial challenge, Northern Ireland's players were clattered by braced forearms and elbows wielded like maces, or rabbit punched on the top of the head. Down by the left corner flag, O'Neill was felled by Alonso's hack across his ankles after a sliding tackle had wiped out McIlroy, who later had his achilles raked by Enrique Saura as he turned to lay it off. They dished plenty of it back too. "Me and Billy were big, brawny Belfast guys who knew precisely what their game was," said Whiteside. If they could leave a mark, they did, Hamilton particularly relishing getting his own back on Tendillo by catching him in the bollocks. Only McIlroy took retaliation too far, responding to Saura's assault by stamping on him with the referee barely two yards away. The card should have been red, but he escaped with a yellow. Saura got off scot free.

A minute before half-time, McCreery, who was everywhere that night in the performance of a lifetime, slalomed his way down the inside-left channel but before he could wrap his foot around the ball to centre it, Alexanko blindsided him, dipping his shoulder to pole-axe the wee man, smashing into his clavicle, snapping his head back and leaving him in a heap. Ortiz did not even have a word with Alexanko and simply awarded a corner. "They are pushing the referee as far as they can," said Motson. He was only partially right. There was no limit to how far they could push.

At half-time, Northern Ireland were bruised, but not bowed. They had barely created anything apart from Whiteside's 20-yard shot and his cross from the left byline through the six-yard box that eluded Hamilton. Bingham praised them, said the tactics were working and warned them not to give the referee the slightest pretext to punish them. Two minutes into the second half, Gordillo went on a run up the left, played a one-two with López Ufarte and ran into Jimmy Nicholl. The Spain left-back held him off, turned away and rolled a casual pass out to his winger. Armstrong had tracked him back and picked his moment perfectly to spring into a lunge and intercept with his right toe. He set off on a muscular charge, prodding the ball ahead, tacking infield then out, riding Sanchez's wild swipe at his heels. Whiteside kept pace with him but stayed on the left to keep Camacho out of Armstrong's way while Hamilton sprinted into the hole Gordillo had left on the Irish right. Armstrong spotted the run and flicked the ball to him. When Tendillo came over on the cover, Hamilton used his momentum and a stiff left arm to the solar plexus to hold him off and wriggle free to cross with his right. Whiteside was poised to make a back-post run but it did not have the height to reach him. It was more of a dink than anything.

It was at that point that Spain's goalkeeper, Luis Arconada, would ensure his name would be eternally linked with Armstrong's. There was no white shirt within eight yards of him and Alexanko could have hooked the cross away, but Arconada decided to go for it, misjudged the curl and found he could only reach it with the weakest part of the hand, the tips of his fingers. All he did was divert it straight to Armstrong who put his laces through it. Arconada had scrambled back to his feet but had not regained his balance and the shot went through the keeper's legs, bisecting Alexanko and Camacho behind him. "And Arconada … Armstrong!" said Motson, his voice pitching upwards with each of the last two syllables. There was a gasp from the crowd and then silence. Armstrong, spooked by the lack of positive reaction, thought it had been disallowed. For the first time all night, the players could hear themselves. It was only when Whiteside yelled "Gerry, Gerry, it's a goal" and jumped on his back that he allowed himself to believe.

If the game finished that way, both sides were through but with the crowd on their backs, Spain had to try to save face. Northern Ireland weathered an onslaught for the next 15 minutes. Jennings, Chris Nicholl and McLelland were outstanding and their team-mates did not rise to any of the provocation, the diving, fouls or gamesmanship. With a third of the game left, Donaghy shepherded a ball out for a throw-in by leaning into Camacho. Both stumbled into an advertising hoarding and when they stood up Donaghy pushed him in the chest. Although his team-mates would have made a meal of it, Camacho was unruffled but the referee hared over and sent Donaghy off. The left-back shook his head in disbelief and headed for the tunnel, leaving 10 men to hold the breach for half an hour. The crowd urged Spain on, ever more hysterically. It was no use. They lacked poise and precision. It was unbearably tense, though Northern Ireland maintained their positional discipline meticulously and threw themselves, sometimes three at a time, to block shots. Yet López Ufarte still had a golden late chance on the left of the box to knock Northern Ireland out but hit his half-volley straight at Jennings. Two minutes into stoppage time, Ortiz put the game out of its misery. Northern Ireland, a nation of 1.5 million, had won the group.

The fans partied hard, chucking themselves into the fountains and eventually congregating at the gates of the Sidi Saler hotel to serenade the team. Bingham told the police to open the gates and invited them in to join the players for a drink. Out came all the old songs. Protestant supped with Catholic. Back home, people celebrated on the streets of Belfast, not mingling, necessarily, but joyous all the same. Little 'Norn Iron' had taken on Spain, its players, crowd and nation, and won. They had suffered to do so, assailed by the heat, the hostility of the home support and brutal, illegal tactics. "To be appalled by Spain's miserable form and the tendency of referees to be scandalously free with their favours to compensate for their inadequacies," wrote Hugh McIlvanney, "is not to belittle the extraordinary deeds of Northern Ireland."

Spain reined it in a little in round two. Stupefied by caution and undone by another Arconada howler, they lost to West Germany and drew with England to finish bottom of the group. Northern Ireland checked into their Madrid hotel and passed Yugoslavia, who had presumptuously taken up residence, in the lobby. They played very well in a 2-2 draw with Austria, a match they should have won, and insist that had O'Neill's 26th-minute 'goal' against France deservedly stood when the match was scoreless, they would not have suffered the 4-1 defeat that sent them home. There was no shame in losing to such a fine side. Bingham, who had played in the 1958 4-0 quarter-final defeat by the same opponents, longed for a different outcome but knew his exhausted players had gone as far as they could.

Hyperbole has contaminated the notion of 'football miracles' now. Bingham oscillated between dispassionately believing that any one-off football match is winnable with shrewd organisation and application, and weeping with a profound sense of pride at their 'unbelievable feat' in beating Spain. When we consider he had only two First Division regulars, two from NASL clubs and a forward line made up of players from Second Division Watford, Third Division Burnley and Manchester United's youth team, his romantic late-night verdict trumps his pre-match practicality.

It would be a delight to write that it had a greater significance, that the messages of congratulation Bingham received from the Taoiseach, Charlie Haughey, and Ian Paisley, or the bringing together of Whiteside's mother from the Shankill and Armstrong's from the Falls to watch the Austria game, had established some broader kinship. While it is true that compared with five sectarian murders in the four weeks before Northern Ireland's first game and 13 in the 28 days after their last, there was one during their participation in the tournament, it would be crass to count that as any kind of accomplishment. Nothing besides football changed. Underdog victories lift underdog nations' collective brows and good, unexpected things sandbag people's morale against all the bad. That is the true measure of Northern Ireland's triumph.

ITALY 1990

8 JULY
GROUP STAGE

CAMEROON
1

ARGENTINA
0

16. Thomas N'Kono	1. Nery Pumpido
17. Victor N'Dip	20. Juan Simón
14. Stephen Tataw (c)	11. Néstor Fabbri
6. Emmanuel Kundé	19. Oscar Ruggeri OFF
4. Benjamin Massing ▮ (89')	*8. Claudio Caniggia ON (46')*
5. Bertin Ebwellé	13. Néstor Lorenzo
8. Emile M'Bouh	17. Roberto Néstor Sensini OFF
2. André Kana-Biyik ▮ (61')	*6. Gabriel Calderón ON (69')*
10. Louis-Paul M'Fédé OFF	4. José Basualdo
15. Thomas Libiih ON (66')	2. Sergio Batista
16. François Omam-Biyik ⊗ (67')	7. Jorge Burruchaga
20. Cyrille Makanaky OFF	3. Abel Balbo
9. Roger Milla ON (81')	10. Diego Maradona (c)

Manager: Valeri Nepomnyashchy

Manager: Carlos Bilardo

San Siro Stadium

Milan, Italy

ATTENDANCE
73,780

REFEREE
Michel Vautrot (France)

SIMON HART

When the 14th World Cup finals opened on
Friday 8 June, 1990, a global television audience
spanning 150 nations had its first sight of a range
of technological innovations.

Courtesy of the Italian broadcaster RAI, there were match
statistics popping up on screen during the action and a full table
— featuring shots, saves, corners, fouls and offsides — displayed
at the end of each half. There were elegant graphics too, notably a
dotted line running neatly down the side of the screen. There was
even a brief glimpse of the players on their walk to the dressing
rooms, courtesy of what might be described as a prototype of
today's tunnel-cam.

The pity for anybody retelling the story of Cameroon's Italia
'90 adventure is that there was no camera following the players
deeper inside the San Siro in the lead-up to their maiden fixture
against Argentina. After all, the private prelude to the biggest
upset any World Cup opening match has ever delivered was an
act of muscle-flexing which hinted at things to come from a bold,
bruising and, at times, brilliant Cameroon team.

With the opening ceremony unfolding outside, down in the
dressing-room area of the San Siro, the two squads of players found
themselves limbering up in the same space. For the Cameroon
players, stepping into close proximity with the reigning world
champions and — specifically — Diego Maradona, the planet's
best footballer, drew strong reactions. Two players, Roger
Feutmba and Alphonse Yombi, had already burst into tears at
their first sight of him. Another, on seeing him juggle a ball,
intoned: "We're dead here."

Their response was to break into song. As forward Eugène Ekéké remembers: "We couldn't carry on like that, so we decided to start making some noise." Which, in Cameroonian football tradition, meant war songs. Jules Onana, one of Cameroon's defenders at Italia '90, continues the story: "We had people in the squad like Benjamin Massing who gave strength to the team by singing. When we went to the warm-up room, the Argentina team were inside. Massing went in there, took off his shirt and showed his big, big muscles. Someone else started to shout and sing and so they went away."

Massing's show of muscle foretold his most memorable contribution to a match which Cameroon ended with two red cards — one of them for the big centre-back himself, following the most cartoonishly brutal foul in World Cup history, inflicted on Argentina substitute Claudio Caniggia.

If Cameroon ended that early-evening encounter with nine men on the field, they had begun it with 16 in another moment which illustrated an endearingly off-the-cuff approach as their five substitutes lined up alongside the 11 starters to sing the national anthem. "Here in Cameroon we used to do that," explains Onana, who today sits on the Cameroon Football Federation (Fecafoot) general assembly. "Everyone wanted to be on the picture. We got fined by Fifa." A tone-setting break from the norm for a contest in which Cameroon, the British bookmakers' 500-1 outsiders to win the trophy, humbled the holders, prevailing through a 67th-minute goal from François Omam-Biyik. Six minutes earlier, his brother André Kana-Biyik had been the first man sent off. As Barry Davies, commentating for the BBC, exclaimed: "One brother is sent off, the other brother scores. Amazing!"

"Historique!" was the exclamation on the front page of the *Cameroon Tribune* newspaper the next morning. The accompanying 14-line report did not mention such key details as the goal or the red cards (or the 28 Cameroon fouls committed to Argentina's nine) but it was right about one thing: "Cameroon and the whole world will always remember this Friday, 8 June,

1990, which saw the striking victory of the Indomitable Lions over Argentina in the opening match of the 14th edition of football's World Cup."

A photograph of Omam-Biyik's goal still hangs on a wall in the National Museum of Cameroon in Yaoundé, the nation's capital, and with good reason. More than 30 years on, this remains the most dramatic World Cup curtain-raiser of all, its impact enhanced by the fact this was the first time a sub-Saharan African side had won a game at the tournament. Cameroon, who had been late submitting their final squad list for the tournament — Fifa receiving three different versions in all — ended up travelling deep into the competition, propelled to the last eight by four goals from their 38-year-old forward Roger Milla, who celebrated each of them with a joyful wiggle of the hips by the corner flag. They were within eight minutes of reaching the semi-finals before succumbing 3-2 to England in a thrilling Naples quarter-final. Fifa responded by awarding an extra qualifying slot to the African nations.

Speaking to me at his home in Yaoundé in 2017, in an interview for my book *World In Motion: The Inside Story of Italia '90*, Roger Milla recalled: "It was pride for the African continent, a real pride, and I think the African continent deserved that because for a long time, Africa had sent out very good players to Europe, but nobody took the African continent seriously."

To measure the contemporary impact of Cameroon's underdog deeds in 1990, it is instructive to revisit Africa's prior performances on the world stage. After Egypt's winless appearance at the 1934 finals, there was no African participation at all until 1970. Indeed, ahead of the 1966 World Cup, the African nations signed up for qualifying withdrew *en masse* in a protest at Fifa's allocation of a single place for three whole continents: Africa, Asia and Oceania. With the African Football Confederation (CAF) awarded its own qualifying place from 1970, Morocco became the second African country to take part, and achieved the continent's first point in the World Cup by drawing 1-1 with Bulgaria.

In 1974, Zaire began by losing 2-0 to Scotland but then disintegrated in a 9-0 drubbing by Yugoslavia. Their players were said to have been warned by the presidential guard of Mobutu Sese Seko, the head of state, that they would not return home if they lost their last game against Brazil by four goals or more. They went down 3-0.

Yet African performances improved thereafter. In 1978, Tunisia overcame Mexico 3-1 and held West Germany to a draw. In 1982 (as retold elsewhere in this book), Algeria earned a 2-1 win over West Germany, the reigning European champions, and then beat Chile 3-2, but missed out on qualification thanks to an infamous 1-0 German win over Austria in Gijón which enabled the European neighbours to advance together at the expense of the north African side.

With the expansion to a 24-team tournament ensuring CAF a second berth, Cameroon made their own World Cup debut in 1982 and, like Algeria, suffered elimination on goal difference after they earned three straight draws with Peru, Poland and Italy. Roger Milla still speaks with sourness of the decision to annul his would-be winning goal against Peru for "an imaginary offside". The team who pipped them to second place by virtue of having scored one goal more, Italy, went on to win the tournament. (Incidentally, in 1982, Cameroon was not yet linked to the international television signal, meaning that it would not be until 1990 that the Cameroonian public could watch the Indomitable Lions' World Cup matches live on TV.)

Africa took another step forward in 1986 when Morocco won their group with draws against Poland and England and a 3-1 victory over Portugal, before a 1-0 loss to West Germany in the round of 16. Progress, but what the World Cup had not seen was a victory by a team from beyond the Maghreb.

The months preceding Cameroon's Italia '90 participation offered no obvious signpost for the exploits ahead. While the Italian embassy in Yaoundé had begun offering language classes to fans travelling to the World Cup the previous November, the team's preparations were less smooth. As defending champions, they performed poorly at the Africa Cup of Nations in March 1990, falling at the group stage after losses to Zambia and Senegal. Argentina coach Carlos Bilardo travelled to that tournament and was quoted as saying: "If that's all they can show us, it wasn't worth the trip."

Then there was the intrigue surrounding Milla. The 1976 African Footballer of the Year, Milla had been living on the Indian Ocean island of Réunion and playing semi-professional football when his return home to play in the testimonial match of an old team-mate, Théophile 'Doctor' Abega, in December 1989 led to probably the 1990 World Cup's most extraordinary plotline. That appearance sparked a campaign to recall him to the national team to which the president of Cameroon, Paul Biya, lent his backing.

Come May, Milla was World Cup-bound. According to Onana, his inclusion did not please the squad's younger players, gathered at the squad's training camp in Yugoslavia. "It was big tension when he came to Yugoslavia. We had established players in the team who thought it was the time for them to shine."

However, Milla soon proved his worth. "When I arrived in Yugoslavia, the next morning they took us out jogging," he recalled. "I'd not jogged for a long time. I felt like my chest was on fire. I did the first run, and the second run, and held my own. The third, the fourth run, I was in front."

"When he did speed tests, only Omam-Biyik would beat him," Eugène Ekéké affirms. A Milla goal in the second of a series of practice matches against club sides, versus Željezničar, showed his scoring touch was still there too.

Overall, it was a Cameroon squad containing only four players based with top-flight European clubs: Bordeaux's Joseph-Antoine Bell, Metz's André Kana-Biyik and the Toulon duo of Cyrille Makanaky and Jacques Songo'o.

Where Milla had played for Saint-Étienne and Montpellier and once scored in a French Cup final for Bastia, Omam-Biyik was playing for Laval in the country's second tier. Goalkeeper Thomas N'Kono arrived having just helped Espanyol win a promotion play-off to Spain's top tier. As for the 11 home-based players, they were officially amateurs, earning around £75 per month. (Consider that 12 years later, when Senegal upset France in the opening match of the 2002 finals, each member of their starting XI was French-based).

The coach tasked with steering Cameroon's squad was Valeri Nepomnyashchy, a 46-year-old Russian who did not speak French — his interpreter was said to have been his chauffeur — and who, the *Cameroon Tribune* lamented, "never smiles".

Yet Ekéké, one of the group's leaders, praised 'Nepo', as he was nicknamed, for his psychologist's touch. "When we prayed, he'd take your hand. When we got in a circle, he was inside it. He observed more, integrated when he had to. When it wasn't necessary, he would leave the group with its dynamic."

Nepomnyashchy had his plans altered by a different kind of dynamic on the eve of the opening game, with the instruction from figures above him in Fecafoot to drop his first-choice goalkeeper, Joseph-Antoine Bell, following an interview with the French media in which he criticised the squad's preparations and predicted a defeat against Argentina.

After the disappointing Africa Cup of Nations campaign, Nepomnyashchy had decided to play a higher defensive line which, in his mind, required Bell as his number one. Now he had to call on Thomas N'Kono. The veteran of Cameroon's España '82 campaign was initially reluctant to play. Summoned to a meeting with Nepomnyashchy at 11am on the day of the opening game, he declared: "I'm not ready." Eventually, after a call from the federation, N'Kono acquiesced, citing the attendance at the match of his country's president, Paul Biya. Bell, for his part, would stay with the group throughout the tournament and, though excluded from training, received his bonuses at the insistence of his team-mates.

If Cameroon had their president in town — along with some 1,000 travelling supporters — so too did Argentina, whose head of state, Carlos Menem, visited the San Siro 24 hours before the opening match to present Diego Maradona with a diplomatic passport as an ambassador for Argentinian sport.

It was Maradona on whom the spotlight dwelled, inevitably, in the lead-up to the opening match. Having returned in March from a problem with his lower back — "Exactly three months and three days before kick-off, I was writhing on the floor," he wrote in *El Diego*, his autobiography — he had inspired Napoli to their second Serie A crown in four seasons. Moreover, to be at his best for Argentina's world title defence, he had begun a rigorous fitness programme and diet, travelling weekly to Rome to the Italian Olympic Committee's Institute of Sports Science and paying $60,000 to install a training machine at Italy's World Cup base in Trigoria, outside Rome.

His "detox work", as he called it, also included a break from his cocaine habit, as his long-serving personal trainer, Fernando Signorini, revealed in the 2019 documentary film, *Diego Maradona*. "Diego got to the World Cup with an insane determination," added Signorini. That said, he had an ingrowing toenail on his right foot — protected by a splint inside his boot — and would struggle anew with the left ankle that, seven years earlier, been shattered by Athletic Bilbao's Andoni Goikoetxea.

Gabriel Calderón, a member of that Argentina team, remembers: "Of all the World Cups he played, he arrived in the worst condition but for us it was important to have him on the pitch however he was, and he always wanted to be in the Argentina team. If you saw his ankle — all swollen and bruised — it wasn't in a good state. No player could play in those conditions but he played all the same."

In the eyes of the San Siro crowd on 8 June, Maradona would be the villain of the piece, having just torn the Serie A title from the grasp of the Milan giants once more — and declared it "the revenge of the south against the racist north". He had already caused a storm when the draw was made and left Argentina in Group B with the Soviet Union, Romania and Cameroon, by saying it was fixed — "Don't talk to me any more about fair

play" — and more thunderclaps would follow. Beginning in the
aftermath of this setback when he said: "The only pleasure I got
this evening was to discover that, thanks to me, the people of
Milan have stopped being racist. Today, for the first time, they
supported the Africans."

To gain a sense of what it was like to be inside the San Siro
that afternoon, Pete Davies is a deft guide. The author of *All
Played Out*, a magnificent account of his World Cup month in
Italy, Davies still remembers a feeling of stepping into the future
when he entered a stadium whose refurbishment for the World
Cup had raised the capacity to 80,000. "They'd put a third tier
on the top and supported it on the spiral walkways that took you
to the top, and it just looked like a spaceship," he says. "That
left a huge impression, compared with what we were used to in
England. It was a brilliant place to have the opening ceremony
and opening match. It was just electric."

For the viewer at home, the aerial shot at kick-off, zooming
out to present a rectangle of green framed by those mighty red
roof girders, offered a wondrous sense of scale. "It was Italy
saying, 'This is what a World Cup should look like'," adds
Davies. "Never mind whether it was going to be ready or not,
the message was, 'Yes, it is ready — now look at this'."

The spectacle of the opening ceremony had included 160 models
wearing designs from four Italian fashion houses and opera
beamed on to the stadium's big screen from La Scala. There were
also two performances of the Giorgio Moroder-produced World
Cup song, starting with the Italian-language version, *Un'estate
italiana*. On a small platform at the side of the pitch, Edoardo
Bennato and Gianna Nannini mimed out of sync as spectators
behind them waved to the cameras. The song's English-language
version, *To Be Number One*, came later, performed by the
Giorgio Moroder Project, whose singer Paul Engemann could
serve as a one-man warning against the fashion excesses of the
time, combining a curly mullet to rival Rene Higuita's, a black
vest and MC Hammer-style white baggy trousers.

For the press inside the stadium, there were more futuristic touches: monitors on their desks and a databank provided by Olivetti, which supplied press clippings from around the world. Pete Davies explains: "It was a kind of pre-internet internet, amassing everything being said by everybody everywhere."

What the watching world could not see was the Cameroon players' reaction to setting eyes on Maradona. As mentioned already, there were actually tears in some eyes, Victor N'Dip recalling "There were some players that were crying in the dressing room at seeing Maradona for the first time." Onana remembers his own first glimpse of Argentina's captain. "I saw four bodyguards — big, big men — and then in the middle of them, I saw this small guy. I thought, 'Wow, this is the guy'. For us, he was the god of football."

Benjamin Massing saw something else when he looked Maradona in the eyes in the tunnel before kick-off. "He combed his hair," he once told me. "It was like somebody going to a night club, sprucing himself up."

Prior to leaving their dressing room shortly before 5pm, the Cameroon players had prayed together, with Eugène Ekéké, the player they called *le Pasteur* (the Pastor), invoking David against Goliath. In the tunnel, they turned to song once more: *Frères camerounais, nous allons gagner.* In English, "Cameroonian brothers, we are going to win". "We were less afraid now," said Ekéké.

On the field, a screech of whistles filled the air when the camera paused on Maradona during Argentina's national anthem. The Cameroonian anthem brought the sight of 16 faces flashing by as the cameraman worked his way up the unusually long line.

If that seems appealingly amateurish to today's viewer, so too would the short video shots of each Cameroon player as the starting XIs appeared on the screen, none of them in their kit but wearing tracksuits of varying colours and styles.

The football itself was a hodgepodge too. Maradona had walked away from the coin toss and flicked the ball up on to his left shoulder and let it bounce four times there. He followed that with some early flickers. Inside the first three minutes, one first-time touch from Argentina's number 10 teed up Abel Balbo inside the D, but the forward — starting ahead of Claudio Caniggia — could not get the ball out from under his feet and shot tamely at N'Kono. Moments later, he crossed for Balbo to flick the ball back for Roberto Sensini to aim another shot at the goalkeeper. Later in the half, a Maradona free-kick gave Oscar Ruggeri a free header that he misdirected wide.

Cameroon's first-half efforts were noteworthy for two things. First, the number of backpasses to Thomas N'Kono, the goalkeeper who had not expected to be playing. This was the last World Cup prior to the rule change forbidding a goalkeeper from handling a backpass and Italia '90, the lowest-scoring of all World Cups (with 2.21 goals per game) would be a catalyst for the change. In the sixth minute, N'Kono picked up the first of 13 first-half back passes.

The other feature was the number of fouls on Maradona, which totalled 12 by the finish. Explaining the Cameroon game plan afterwards, midfielder Émile Mbouh told the media: "The coach told us not to mark Maradona individually." It was a case rather of dealing with him when he entered each player's zone of the pitch. Defender Victor N'Dip explained: "We talked among ourselves — if he was coming in the centre either Massing or I would take charge. If he was going to the left, it was '[full-back Bertin] Ebwellé, you take charge'."

'Taking charge' is one way of describing it. The first yellow card, for Massing after nine minutes, came after he aimed a kick from behind at Maradona's left Achilles. N'Dip was next into the book in the 23rd minute for a considerably worse offence, catching Argentina's captain in the chest with a straight-leg, studs-up challenge. Referee Michel Vautrot, caught by the speed of an Argentine breakaway, saw the offence from behind, rather than sideways on, thus missing its full savagery.

When N'Dip then leant over the stricken Maradona, it was not to ask after his welfare but to warn him against entering his zone again. As Pete Davies recalls: "It didn't take that long to realise they were absolutely going to have a go at them and Argentina looked rattled and bewildered."

In an article for the *i* newspaper to mark the 30th anniversary of this match, Howard Webb, the 2010 World Cup final referee, reviewed this match with me and summed up the Cameroon approach as "honest cynicism", with some challenges more clumsy than malicious. He explained: "What I'd say about Cameroon is I don't think they did anything that was sly. They weren't giving little digs off the ball, they weren't trying to unsettle Argentina by being underhand. It wasn't calculated niggle. Yes, Maradona got fouled but he had the ball a lot and therefore there were opportunities to foul him more and, on top of that, they know he's the dangerman and they have to stop him."

When Emmanuel Kundé did just that in the 32nd minute, raising a leg to block his run and send him to the ground once more, Peter Brackley, the ITV commentator, remarked: "Six fouls already against him."

Maradona would continue to flit in an out of a sluggish first half. Moments after the crowd had jeered one misplaced pass by the Argentina captain, he lofted a wonderful one over the defence for Jorge Burruchaga to break on to. However, a weak touch from the 1986 World Cup final matchwinner allowed the onrushing N'Kono to block.

Cameroon's creative talents shone in patches too with Louis-Paul Mfédé, their number 10, popping up in pockets of space, and Cyrille Makanaky driving forward with energy and purpose. Indeed, the dreadlocked Makanaky had their first scent of goal after 21 minutes when, in a counter from an Argentina corner, N'Kono sent Omam-Biyik away with a long throw and the forward angled a ball towards the penalty spot that Makanaky just failed to get a toe to. José Basualdo, just behind him, did get a touch, diverting the ball towards his own net. Fortunately for Argentina, Néstor Lorenzo rescued his colleague by scrambling the ball clear.

The second half began much as had the first, with Massing clattering Maradona from behind — but escaping a second yellow card. By the 58th minute, an on-screen graphic informed viewers that he had suffered 11 fouls already. By this point, though, Cameroon had found a different target: half-time substitute Claudio Caniggia. When Carlos Bilardo, the Argentina coach, vacillated over selecting the Atalanta forward for his World Cup squad, Maradona — already vexed by the exclusion of Mexico '86 colleague Jorge Valdano — warned him that "if he didn't bring Caniggia, I wouldn't play". Caniggia's bursts of pace — long blond hair trailing behind — soon seized the attention.

His first run took him around N'Dip on the right and ended with the defender bringing him down just before he could enter the box. N'Dip, on a yellow card, got away with it, just as he would in the 76th minute when crudely halting another Caniggia surge down the same flank.

Caniggia featured too in the action that brought the 61st-minute sending-off of André Kana-Biyik. As he ran forward from the halfway line, some 10 yards in from the right flank, the chasing Kana-Biyik caught his heels. There was another Cameroon defender coming across and ground still to cover. Yet Vautrot delivered a theatrical flash of his red card.

As unhappy Cameroonians surrounded the Frenchman, Kana-Biyk departed to cheers from the spectators, blowing three kisses as he stepped off the pitch. "The Argentinians have been getting kicked but you still have got to pick the right one," said an "astounded" Howard Webb when analysing the incident with me.

Cameroon might have had a man less, but within six minutes they also had the lead thanks to Kana-Biyik's brother. Maradona had warned about the "dangerous" François Oman-Biyik when singling him out as his favourite Cameroon player before the match. He had been the first to test Nery Pumpido, late in the first half, with a drive from the edge of the box, and now he profited from an error by the goalkeeper.

The preamble was an Emmanuel Kundé free-kick from the left, driven just over the head of Maradona in the Argentina wall. At the near post, Cyrille Makanaky got a foot to it ahead of Néstor Lorenzo, sending it looping onwards. Omam-Biyik, at the back, got in front of Roberto Sensini and rose high above him. If the leap was formidable, his attempt to direct the header to the far corner was less so, sending the ball straight at Pumpido, yet it squirmed under the goalkeeper's body and into the far corner.

N'Kono, Omam-Biyik's room-mate, had told him the night before that he would score. Omam-Biyik himself had told *France Football* magazine: "I don't believe in miracles". Yet he had now produced one. "François himself said he had never jumped so high before," recalls Onana.

The 10 men had their tails up. One powerful run from Omam-Biyik from inside his own half took him between two defenders, though it ended with him unleashing a wild volley which went out for a throw-in. To a giant cheer from the Milan crowd, Émile Mbouh juggled the ball on his head on a run down the left. Then, two minutes from the end came a moment remembered arguably more than the winning goal as the 10 men became nine.

When a Cameroon attack faltered, Caniggia picked the ball up 10 yards outside his own box and hared forward. He skipped beyond Kundé five yards from halfway then hurdled the high boot of the lunging N'Dip (itself a red-card offence, according to Howard Webb). Striving to stay on his feet, he strode on only for Massing to step across and wipe him out, flying in and planting his right foot on Caniggia's left.

It was a moment that the late Massing recalled when I met him in Cameroon in 2017. He told me he had no choice but to intervene once N'Dip had failed with the hack which left Caniggia wobbling. "When Caniggia hurdles him, I said 'Shit, this is dangerous. I was marking Diego [Maradona] but I left him. I thought, 'If he's got time to get his balance and pass the ball, we're stuffed. That's why I came on him like a truck."

He was not exaggerating. The force of the challenge sent Massing's right boot flying almost as high as Caniggia. The match footage shows Jorge Burrachaga remonstrate with Massing who aims a stockinged foot at him but misses. Vautrot, surrounded by angry Argentina players, gets the order of his cards wrong, showing a red card, then a yellow.

It is fascinating to read the contemporary response to Vautrot's refereeing. Fifa had instructed its referees to take a hard line on professional fouls and warned that those who failed to comply would be sent home. Writing in the following day's *The Times*, David Miller said: "Fifa's reaction to violence on the pitch is 20 years overdue."

There was a very different response in the *Cameroon Tribune* which complained: "Under the pretext of protecting football from violence, in conformance with the wishes of Fifa, Vautrot went too far, clearly showing for Maradona and company a sort of reverential fear."

The paper cited "somersaults, rolls, falls, spectacular pirouettes, broken legs that suddenly healed once Vautrot gave a warning or expulsion" — a harsh assessment compared with today's theatrics. There was even a suggestion that Vautrot might have got the Cameroon players mixed up. Additionally, it produced a cartoon showing N'Kono standing over a sniffling Maradona and telling him: "It's Mr Vulture, er, Vautrot, who got you. A lion is twice as dangerous when it's wounded."

The view from Argentina was understandably different. Gabriel Calderón, a second-half substitute that evening, remarks that "they beat us by kicking us off the pitch with enough fouls to have had half a team sent off". Vautrot, he argues, "didn't want to send off too many players from the underdogs".

That said, Calderón — who has since coached in nine different countries — believes the game provided "a before and after for football. From there, Fifa changed the rules because it was shameful." That summer, the International Football Association Board issued a mandatory instruction that the professional foul, denying a goalscoring opportunity, must be punished by a red card, and it became law the following year. (For Italia '90 it had been a directive prior to the tournament which was put into practice only "by about a third" of the referees, according to Fifa's then general secretary, Sepp Blatter, in his report to their executive committee).

Vautrot himself would tell Roger Milla on the final whistle at the San Siro: "You can thank me because you've gone into legend now for beating the world champions with nine men". Before that last whistle, the nine men could actually have had an extra goal too as Milla, an 81st-minute substitute, showed the first glimpse of his extraordinarily enduring gifts in a stoppage-time counterattack. Breaking from his own half, he slipped between two defenders and fed Émile Mbouh on the right then burst into the box hoping for the return pass, only for Mbouh to strike a wild shot wide. In the corner of the TV screen Milla, nicknamed 'Gaddafi' by his team-mates, could be seen — literally — hopping mad.

Then came the celebrations. Victor N'Dip wept as he saw his country's president, in the stands. It was to Biya that Omam-Biyik dedicated his goal. Back at the team hotel, staff draped a banner with the scoreline across the piano in the foyer.

Onana cites an additional reason for delight. He had been secretary of the group of players who 48 hours earlier had finally succeeded in agreeing potential win bonuses worth three million Cameroonian francs, or £4,000 per match.

"Two days before the opening game there was a challenge between us, the players, and the administrative part of the team. They challenged us to win games in Italy, because it put a lot of money on winning games. When we went to play Argentina, we knew if we wanted to get some money we had to win. When François scored that goal, it was good. Winning the game was so sweet because we won the challenge against the administrative side of the team."

They went on winning too. "We're going to play the Cameroon way" was Nepomnyashchy's promise before the second group fixture against Romania and so it proved: Milla stepped off the bench and hit both goals in a 2-0 victory. With them, he surpassed Sweden's Gunnar Gren as the World Cup's oldest scorer. "A 38-year-old's brain, a 25-year-old's legs," as ITV commentator Brian Moore put it.

Cameroon had a place in the Round of 16 with a game to spare (a game promptly lost to the USSR) and they did not stop there. Next was a brilliant victory over Colombia, best remembered for Milla nicking the ball off an outfoxed René Higuita on one of the goalkeeper's excursions upfield, before rolling in his second goal of a 2-1 triumph. After that success, Biya wrote an open letter to the team thanking them for enhancing "the credibility of our country in general, while working for the affirmation of our creative genius." That same creative genius so nearly took them past England too, in a quarter-final they led 2-1 in the 82nd minute after an Emmanuel Kundé spot-kick and Eugène Ekéké strike had overturned David Platt's header.

According to Onana, one of four players suspended in Naples along with Victor N'Dip, André Kana-Biyik and Émile Mbouh, this was the night their bookings — and they left Italy with more fouls committed, 115, than any other side — caught up with them. "The referees knew we were a rough team, not dirty, but they wanted to make an example," he says. "We were heavily sanctioned."

Writing in his World Cup column for *The Times* that summer, Graham Taylor — soon to replace Bobby Robson as England manager — offered a sympathetic view, arguing: "Cameroon have been criticised for being dirty. I do not believe they are. Many of their fouls have been due to a tendency to tackle on the wrong foot."

Either way, it now meant some significant absentees in their defence. "It's hard to play England minus four important players," says Onana, citing the enforced central defensive pairing of Benjamin Massing, making his first appearance since his opening-game dismissal, and Emmanuel Kundé. After that year's Africa Cup of Nations, coach Valeri Nepomnyashchy had decided the pairing of Kundé and Massing was too slow. "We put N'Dip with Massing and it was better in terms of speed and athleticism. When Massing got the red card, I could play with Victor, we were very fast and athletic and it was good for the equilibrium of the team. If you remember the second penalty-kick, it is a through-ball from [Paul] Gascoigne to [Gary] Lineker between Massing and Kundé. We had no speed."

Two Lineker penalties, one after 83 minutes, another in extra time, ended the adventure and Roger Milla still laments the missed opportunities that night by Thomas Libih and Omam-Biyik, who, at 2-1, tried to back-heel the ball past Peter Shilton when alone against the England goalkeeper. "A team with experience would automatically have won that match," said Milla, who was tripped by Gascoigne for his team's penalty. "The match was won. If they'd continued to play off me so I could keep the ball and win fouls, we'd have won the match."

Ironically, it was Argentina, the fall guys at the San Siro on 8 June, who did make it all the way to the final. After the Cameroon defeat, the daily newspaper *Clarín* had declared that "Even 100 victories in a row could not wipe away the memory of such a humiliation". Coach Carlos Bilardo, meanwhile, displayed his extraordinary attention to detail by ordering the removal of the three white stripes on Argentina's adidas-manufactured black shorts. Argentina had won the previous World Cup in all-black shorts and the fact those were made by Le Coq Sportif did not matter; the adidas stripes had to go.

It was not the only response. Bilardo, as Gabriel Calderón remembers, set his players a startling ultimatum. "He told us we had to qualify or if not the plane would not get home to Argentina — they'd put a bomb in it and it would explode in the air! He also said 'the massages, the pasta, the hot showers', it's all over. From now it's sandwiches and cold water like when you lot started out with nothing, and now you've got to win."

After Nery Pumpido, the goalkeeper at fault for François Omam-Biyik's goal, suffered a double leg fracture in their second group fixture, Sergio Goycochea shone in his place as Argentina squeezed past Brazil in the round of 16, then defeated both Yugoslavia and Italy on penalties to reach a final they lost to West Germany. "We didn't play well but we all left everything out on the field in order to win," continues Calderón. "That was the quality that took us to the final as without playing well, nobody could beat us — and that was without the Maradona we all knew, that player who could score four or five goals. We overcame all the adversities and got to the final and that was down to the side's solidarity and humility."

They fell only to a disputed late penalty in the final — and this after Calderón had had his own spot-kick claim ignored after losing his footing as Lothar Matthäus caught his standing foot. "The referee was two metres away and he didn't want to blow it."

Even before that final, João Havelange, the then Fifa president, had spoken in Rome about proposing a new number of World Cup places for Africa. A third berth would be confirmed by the end of the year. To quote *Jeune Afrique*, the pan-African weekly magazine, Cameroon's feats had proved: "A triumph for Africa".

"We did change perceptions," said Victor N'Dip. "For an African country like Cameroon to reach a quarter-final, nobody in the world expected that." For some of Cameroon's home-based players, their only experience of facing European opposition prior to Italia '90 had come from friendlies against club sides. Within seven months of Italia '90, they were taking on England in a friendly at Wembley. Twelve months after the World Cup, *World Soccer* magazine reported on the "ever-increasing number" of African footballers earning contracts in Europe, counting 267.

The impact on Cameroonian football beyond the short term is a moot point, though. One well-placed source in Yaoundé says that, with the national team's success, "football had showed it could produce money and people came in to loot it". Following Italia '90, there were reports of £400,000 of World Cup profits going missing at Fecafoot. Another example arose with Cameroon's USA

'94 campaign which featured an official fundraising campaign, *Opération Coup de Cœur*, to collect money for team costs. More than $1m was raised but the team still did not get paid until after the second match.

In five World Cup appearances since 1990, Cameroon have won a solitary match — 1-0 against Saudi Arabia during a finals campaign in 2002 that began with a delayed departure from Paris owing to a dispute over money.

When Roger Milla dressed all in white, stepped off the plane at Douala airport on the squad's return from Italy, he declared: "We must now look to the future." Sadly, the most famous Cameroon World Cup goal since 1990 remains his effort against Russia in 1994, which extended his own record as the tournament's oldest scorer to 42 years and 39 days old. Milla has since lamented that "10 or 15 years, we had no youth football".

With the hosting of the Africa Cup of Nations in 2022, Cameroon now has more than 20 new training facilities whose pitches are available for club matches. Yet there is still a scarcity of pitches to train on and the AFCON tournament underlined the country's systemic infrastructural problems. For a start, around 40% of the $5.5bn spent on infrastructure was allegedly stolen. Only a 60km stretch of the planned new 240km expressway linking Yaoundé and Douala was completed. The media facilities at one venue in Limbe were not built in time.

Moreover, there was the tragedy of eight people killed in a crush at the Olembe Stadium before Cameroon's match against Comoros. Onana was Olembe Stadium director for the AFCON and is a member of the Fecafoot general assembly as players' representative. "We thought we were ready," he says, carefully. "To lose people like that ... we don't come to a football game to die. It's very, very, very sad."

On the broader question of football development in his country, he says: "We have good pitches but for 30 years we had no high-standard stadium in Cameroon. The youth development programme was not working. It's difficult because after 1990, and then seven times going to the World Cup, we thought things would be better for the young players but they are not. We're still struggling for the youth development programme, we're still struggling for women's development programmes, we're still struggling with the organisation of clubs. In Cameroon, we're still struggling with governance in the football federation."

His group of players — the group whose defeat by England in Naples led Brazil's *Folha de Sao Paulo* newspaper to lament, "Inventors of football remove joy from the Cup" — know this better than anyone. Just consider what became of the gifts promised to them on their return home from Italia '90. After a tour of Yaoundé in military jeeps — two players per vehicle — they were invited to the presidential palace to receive the nation's second-highest honour, the medal for the Commander of the National Order of Bravery. However, the promise of a villa for each player did not materialise. Roger Milla received his government residence through his position as a roving ambassador for Cameroon. The rest of the squad, though, faced a significant wait.

Onana provides the explanation: "The head of state gave an order and, at the time, His Excellency expected to have a list of 22 players plus a few people around the team — the coaches and medical staff maybe. But the list that came back was very, very, very long, with more than 50 people asking for houses. So they couldn't do anything and put the file away.

"Two years ago, I went to see the new minister of sport, I explained the situation and he wrote a letter to the head of state. One month later, we got a decision to give the houses to 22 players." That was in 2020. Onana gives a chuckle: "Thirty years … a long time, huh?"

USA 1994

18 JUNE
GROUP STAGE

R.IRELAND
1

ITALY
0

1. Packie Bonner	1. Gianluca Pagliuca
2. Denis Irwin	9. Mauro Tassotti
5. Paul McGrath	4. Alessandro Costacurta
14. Phil Babb	6. Franco Baresi (c)
3. Terry Phelan	5. Paolo Maldini
8. Ray Houghton ⊗ (11') OFF	16. Roberto Donadoni
21. Jason McAteer ON (68')	11. Demetrio Albertini
6. Roy Keane	13. Dino Baggio
10. John Sheridan	17. Alberigo Evani OFF
7. Andy Townsend (c)	*19. Daniele Massaro ON (45')*
11. Steve Staunton	10. Roberto Baggio
15. Tommy Coyne OFF	20. Guiseppe Signori OFF
9. John Aldridge ON (90')	*14. Nicola Berti ON (84')*

Manager: Jack Charlton

Manager: Arrigo Sacchi

Giants Stadium

East Rutherford, NY, USA

ATTENDANCE
75,338

REFEREE
Mario van der Ende (Netherlands)

PAUL DOYLE

> At least Michael Collins got to fly through
> space. He also got an eyeful of the moon,
> even if he never touched it, his famous mission
> being to man the Apollo 11 command module while
> Neil Armstrong and Buzz Aldrin boldly strolled
> where no humans had ever strolled before.

Born in Italy, the grandson of an Irish farmer, Collins became an American hero and, in 1994, someone I stopped feeling sorry for.

Because, as I say, at least Collins got as close to the action as it was possible to get without actually doing his thing on the nearest heavenly body. I couldn't help contrasting that with my own sad role in the greatest voyage of ~~discovery~~ debauchery in my lifetime. In the summer of 1994, when it seemed like nearly everyone I knew, including bastards whom I knew for a fact had had little interest in football just a few years previously, was blasting off to New York's John F. Kennedy airport ahead of the Republic of Ireland's lustily anticipated World Cup duel with Italy in New Jersey. And all I could do was wish them well at the start of their journey, and try to flog them a fluffy leprechaun.

I was working in the duty-free shop in Dublin airport, see. In the souvenir department. A job is a job, but this had never been an especially coveted position. Usually, the people to respect were the ones working in the alcohol section, or at the perfume counter. They were in constant demand. And if ever one of their products had to be withdrawn from public sale because a bottle was chipped or packaging was torn, staff might be able to offload it to friends for a pittance or even for free. So it was worth palling up to them. Befriending me, on the other hand, wouldn't have earned you anything but a good deal on a tarnished pewter harp or a sheep plush that was coming apart at the seams. Tourists craved that stuff, apparently, but there was no call for it from folks I knew. Until, that is, the ascent of Jack Charlton and his team, whose services to the Irish thingamajig industry are often overlooked.

That said, Charlton has sometimes been credited with relaunching the entire Irish economy. Siring the Celtic Tiger, no less. That is a bit of a stretch given other obvious factors at play in the country's clamber out of the economic torpor of the seventies and eighties, such as the state's corporation tax policy and the influence of the European Union. But the notion that Charlton helped to release Irish entrepreneurial spirit by qualifying for international tournaments that everyone wanted to attend does have a lingering charm.

After all, from the moment he guided Ireland to their first ever appearance at a major tournament finals — the 1988 European Championships — everyone began to hear tales of people doing exceptional things in order to join the ride. Taking second jobs, selling their cars, starting up businesses — anything from trading ice creams out of deftly-modified vans to importing exotica for resale: fruit, clothes, special interest magazines and more. I knew one lad who got the money to follow the team at the 1990 World Cup by asking for it from his rich landlord father, which goes to show that the most extraordinary stories are not always the most interesting.

There were also, to be fair, occasional portents of Ireland's post-Celtic Tiger collapse, as the zeal for funds to travel in support of the team led to the granting of more than a few sub-prime loans.

Charlton's team sure set a mighty bandwagon in motion, where previously there had been an abandoned shopping trolley with spikes for wheels. In November 1985, the last match under Charlton's predecessor, Eoin Hand, had attracted a smidgin over 15,000 spectators to Lansdowne Road, nearly half of them from Denmark, who swaggered to a 4-1 win as home fans wailed and cursed. But less than three years later, tickets for

Ireland matches were among the most precious commodities in the country. Especially for away matches. There came to be a special glee, a singular pride, in following "the Boys in Green" abroad. Few places on Earth have been untouched by the Irish diaspora but 1988 saw the first massive movement from Ireland of people expecting to return in a week or two. They weren't travelling in search of refuge or employment, they were travelling for kicks. Which meant, in a way, they were travelling to say we have arrived at last. Our country has grown. Behold!

There was, admittedly, trepidation ahead of the first match at Euro '88, a jagged suspicion that fate had contrived for us to finally reach a major tournament only so that we could suffer a humiliating spanking on the international stage at the hands of our first opponents, who were, of all possible adversaries, England. But Bobby Robson's side were toppled 1-0 in Gelsenkirchen thanks to Ray Houghton, a magnificent dynamo whose one major shortcoming was that he didn't score enough goals, even if he netted two of the most glorious in Irish history. The one that secured the victory over England in 1988 signalled, as has since been amply chronicled elsewhere, both a catharsis and a coming of age. Of sorts.

***

Most people like to think of themselves as complex. Deep and interesting, not like others. That's especially true if they live in the shadow of better-known neighbours. Observe how every Canadian slaps a maple leaf on their backpack before venturing overseas, lest anyone fail to distinguish them from Americans. Irish people are no different. Or are we?

Irish people tend to be swift to denounce paddywhackery or to rail against failures to appreciate our diversity and sophistication. But when our team started qualifying for major international tournaments, the first instincts of thousands of my brethren was to converge on foreign cities and go dancing legless in big-buckled hats and shamrock rosettes. When I wasn't selling said wares, I myself ventured into the field to model them. It wasn't actually guerrilla marketing, I was just acting the monkey like my brothers. It was fun.

But it is only proper to place on record one niggling lament from that time. It concerns a stereotype most Irish fans failed to live up to. Much as we may grumble about clichés about our supposed fondness for a drink and a song, we also like to tell ourselves from time to time that we have a special aptitude for the same. Yet most of us used the rise of the national football team to blow up that myth. I saw the best minds of my generation destroyed by shame at being unable to think of anything better to sing at matches than "olé, olé, olé" over and over and over again.

Professional offerings were scarcely more inspired. *Put 'em Under Pressure*, Ireland's official number for the 1990 World Cup, may have been a nod to the old rebel song God Save Ireland but it mostly came across as a dull-witted rip-off of *Ally's Tartan Army*, the musical accompaniment to Scotland's 1978 World Cup fiasco.

Maybe it was fitting that our songs smacked of mimicry, since the Football Association of Ireland's player development strategy consisted mostly of leeching off the efforts of British clubs.

And maybe the lack of lyrical creativity could be explained partly by the fact that there was little common culture of following football in the Republic by the time the country finally reached a tournament. Clubs like Drumcondra and Bohemians had attracted tens of thousands of fans in the fifties and sixties, but the League of Ireland had fallen into relative neglect by the eighties and the best supported local team, Shamrock Rovers, saw their stadium bulldozed for housing in 1987. It so happened that just as the local game began to deteriorate — in the late sixties — British teams with whom Irish people could easily identify, such as Celtic and the George Best-gilded Manchester United, were conquering Europe. Many Irish fans diverted their attention to where the top Irish players played and became passive consumers of televised entertainment.

But none of that accounts for the farce that unfolded on the world stage in 1994.

Remember that a crescendo of sorts was supposed to be reached in New York and New Jersey that June. What better place — we were constantly asked — to demonstrate the unique passion and ingenuity of Irish people than on the east coast of America against Italy? As soon as our opening group fixture was announced, a meta-contest was born to determine which of these huge immigrant communities was the most resourceful. Which country would manage to get the most fans into the Giants Stadium? A-wheedling we went. Strings were pulled, favours called in, wheezes hatched, promises made.

During the Charlton years, the FAI grew so driven by the compulsion to secure as many tickets as possible for Irish fans that the organisation entrusted around £200,000 to an unofficial London-based dealer known as George the Greek. Most tickets never materialised and the treasurer ended up having to pay money back from his own pocket.

Italy were similarly eager to achieve numerical superiority in the stands. The *Azzurri*'s then-manager, Arrigo Sacchi, was more concerned with matters on the pitch, but when he suggested that the country's government try to flex some muscle to get Italy's group games moved from America's east coast to a region where the climate would be more conducive to the style of play he wanted to encourage, Sacchi was told by the prime minister, no less, that shifting the opening match from New Jersey would be a betrayal of Italian emigrants. Maybe Sacchi would have got a different reply if his mentor, Silvio Berlusconi, had taken over his country's politics just a few months earlier. As it happened, Sacchi did not reveal the prime ministerial rebuff until nearly two decades after the event, and he took the opportunity to remind his Italian interviewer that when his team's opening match came around, there were far more Irish fans than Italians in the Giants Stadium. "It seems a lot of our people bought tickets ... and sold them to the Irish," reckoned Sacchi, leaving anything more about betrayals unsaid.

Thus there were buoyant folks in green all over the Giants Stadium — some jazzing up their look with fake ginger beards sold by me — and they were all gagging for a party. Andy Townsend, Ireland's captain on the day, said later that the atmosphere was so giddy and the air so still that when Irish fans opened their mouths to sing the first line of the national anthem, he was almost bowled over by the smell of beer, rolling towards him like an invisible and pungent wave. What Townsend didn't add but probably could have is that he was saved from falling down by the fact that a big chunk of Irish fans stopped singing after the first line. As usual. Our strange secret — the thing that is seldom admitted, especially in front of an international audience even though Charlton's team helped make it obvious — is that most Irish people don't know the words to the country's national anthem.

Abolishing national anthems would be no bad thing. But if they must exist and are to serve a purpose, then it is to rally a people around some shared values or ambition. Leaving aside the fact that Ireland's was written in 1910 as a celebration of centuries of resistance to British villainy — and Irish people of a Unionist bent find that objectionable — the Irish anthem is an embarrassing own goal. What it does is expose a monumental failure of the country's education system and the fallacy at the heart of one of the state's founding myths.

The reason that the song is so poorly known — now as in 1994 and before — is that the version most commonly taught is in Gaelic. That is a language in which most people in Ireland cannot communicate despite undergoing mandatory daily lessons and regular exams from the day they start primary school until the time they leave secondary school at least a decade later. Even now, proficiency in Gaelic is a requirement for civil service jobs in Ireland, and every street sign and official document must appear in both Gaelic and English. The yarn is that Ireland is a bilingual country. But try to converse with an Irish person in Gaelic and, far more often than not, the gift of the gab becomes an alien concept.

Maybe there is another country that persists in promoting a similar delusion, but I don't recall seeing many other World Cup participants look as uncomfortable during their anthems as most Irish players and fans do. What the shams shuffling in awkward silence at the Giants Stadium in June '94 made plain is that two wrongs do not make a right. English colonisers beat Gaelic out of the Irish and, since independence, the Irish government has tried to force it back into us. 'Tis one of the great paradoxes of the freedom struggle.

Granted, it's a cute idea and this ghost dance wouldn't rankle — it might even be more effective — if it were not compulsory. In school I, and every other Irish child, was told it was our duty to learn Gaelic. Supposedly it was our mother tongue even though neither our mothers nor any of our other relations spoke it. It was stated outright, or just insinuated via the sinister glower of a short-tempered teacher, that those of us who resented this mandated identity or thought our time and effort could be spent more interestingly on other things, had no soul or, perhaps worse, a British brain. They tried to make us feel foreign in our own land, saddled a population already bedevilled by Catholic guilt with another sin to feed the shame.

They told us that the anthem was chosen because it was sung by the brave rebels who defied British troops and marched into Dublin's General Post Office to proclaim the Irish Republic in 1916. But they usually omitted to mention that those rebels sang it in English. Liam Ó Rinn did not translate *The Soldier's Song* into *Amhrán na bhFiann* until after the Easter Rising, as he pined for home from a Welsh prison.

It is worth repeating that the success of Charlton's team helped to discredit another myth similar to the language lie: the one that maintained that soccer was an imposter's game and true

Irishmen devoted themselves to Gaelic sports. That dogma was enforced with such bile that, famously, Liam Brady was once expelled for choosing to captain the Republic of Ireland U-15s at soccer rather than play a friendly Gaelic football match for his school. That was in the early 1970s, but the strain of thinking was still prevalent in the eighties. One fearsome teacher/coach at my state school in Dublin warned that anyone treacherous enough to reject call-ups for the school's Gaelic football team would never be allowed to play for the soccer team: he managed both teams to ensure he was in a position to enforce his law. But once cities all over the country — and rural villages in the Gaelic football heartlands — started emptying so that people could follow Charlton's team, it was impossible to uphold the claim that soccer was an undesirable imposition from without.

Anyway, back to singing. The song has not always remained the same. In the early 1920s, after the fug of the civil war and in the absence of any formal ruling, Irish teams used to sing whatever came to mind when invited to perform at international events. Asked to settle on a ceremonial track for the 1924 Olympic Games, the team from the Irish Free State performed to the traditional tune *Let Erin Remember*. That same year a newspaper, the *Dublin Evening Mail*, launched a competition to find "a national hymn to the glory of Ireland". It put up a bumper prize and assembled a distinguished jury, including W.B. Yeats, to pick the winner. Four months later, the paper announced sadly that "having read the poems ... we are all agreed that there is not one amongst them worth fifty guineas or any portion of it." Looking back, you have to suspect that the competition entrants were the very people who begat the people that years later foisted "olés" on each and every social gathering. "Most of the verses submitted to us were imitations of *God Save the King*," continued the disenchanted *Dublin Evening Mail*, who ultimately dropped the competition to avoid any further editorial cringing.

The nation's cringing has continued. Most Irish people still get twitchy when they find themselves in a situation where they are expected to sing the national anthem, even if fortified by 10 pints. After the opening line, which is relatively easy for English speakers to pronounce, folks start mumbling piously, like we all used to do during prayers at Mass, that other weird institution of Irish life. At the Giants Stadium, all that most of the assembled Irish could muster as the band played their anthem was an awkward hum. Of more kind than one, as Townsend reported.

And don't let anyone tell you the band played the anthem wrong that day. Sure, they were confused, but that is only because everything about the national anthem is confusing. The Irish players standing to attention before kickoff appeared bewildered as to why the song went on for so long and George Hamilton, RTE's match commentator and a noted classical music connoisseur, remarked that the American hosts played the tune at a "slower tempo" than was normal. But all that happened was that someone had neglected to tell the band about the Nazi reworking of the anthem.

Ooops, that's another thing that seldom gets mentioned. After independence, the Irish army went looking for a specialist to marshal their band. They found no one suitable in Ireland and didn't want to hire a Brit. In 1923, they ended up luring a distinguished musician from the continent with the promise of a good salary and the rank of colonel. The appointed man had impeccable credentials so it was not just for a giggle that the Irish Army plumped for a German military bandmaster named Fritz Brase.

Brase developed a fondness for adapting traditional Irish reels and jigs into what sounded like booming Prussian marches. He also developed a fondness for Adolf Hitler and, in 1932, joined the Nazi party from Ireland. That didn't please his army employers but Brase had already endeared himself to them by, amongst other things, coming up with a sprucer take on *The Soldier's Song*, honing the chorus while dispensing with the original verses. On one particularly proud occasion, Brase conducted the Irish Army band as they played his adaptation — and *Das Lied der Deutschen* in honour of the visitors — before kickoff when Ireland hosted a swastika-sporting Germany team at Dalymount Park in 1936. Brase's version quickly became the staple in Ireland. But apparently, no one told the band at the Giants Stadium, who solemnly played the verses, too.

Really the Irish national anthem should be wordless, just a jaunty instrumental that everyone could hop around to. That wouldn't alienate anyone and could mask wholesale ineptitude. But if the government persists with a ditty in Gaelic, they should — in the interests of atmosphere and honesty — replace the current lyrics with some of the few lines in that language that everyone educated in Ireland knows. The chorus could go: "An bhfuil cead agam dul go dtí an leithreas más é do thoil é (*"can I go to the toilet please?"*) / Ní thuigim an ceist" (*"I don't understand the question"*.).

* * *

All of which brings us back to Charlton, Ireland's best ever bandleader from abroad, with all due respect to Herr Brase. Here was a quirky and bolshy character with whom we could identify. He had his contradictions, including the fact that he was both a hero and a misfit in his own country, having won the World Cup with England as a player and then been deemed unworthy of even a reply when he later applied to become their manager.

But Charlton also had charisma and, most of all, a pristine clarity of vision. He was the right outsider at the right time for Ireland. Before his arrival, we had gone close to qualifying, only to be thwarted by bad luck, ramshackle preparation or dubious refereeing, all of which fuelled those familiar post-colonial sentiments of inadequacy and resentment.

The first campaign I followed, the qualifiers for the 1982 World Cup, brought these matters to an ugly kind of head. Cast into one of the most difficult qualifying groups in history, Ireland finished above the Netherlands but below Belgium and France — the latter on goal difference — after having goals disallowed in Paris and Brussels under circumstances that stunk more the more they were ventilated.

When Charlton came along with a style of play based on sticking it to the powers-that-be, fairly rigging the game in our favour for once, many Irish felt he was most welcome to give it a go. Let this unashamed and wily contrarian challenge the world's chess masters to a mud wrestle. Of course, it would have been nice to wow the world with searing artistry but, on the other hand, there was a satisfying kind of vengeance in advancing with a system that really annoyed the elite. It's impossible not to laugh at the fact that a highlights video of the most memorable Irish footballing moments under Charlton could double as a blooper reel for bigger nations.

It started with England, who were expected to tear Ireland apart at Euro '88 but were instead transformed into a Charlie Chaplin tribute act. The panic in the English defence that led to Ray Houghton's winning goal was glorious, with Gary Stevens and Mark Wright bumping into each other before Kenny Sansom blootered an attempted clearance into the air, allowing John Aldridge to nod down to Houghton to butt a wobbly header past Peter Shilton.

Soon Ireland turned other slicksters into slapstick artistes. Spain were humbled in Dublin in the qualifiers for the 1990 World Cup when Charlton ordered that the grass be left long at Lansdowne Road and the visiting playmaker, the elegant Real Madrid schemer Michel, got so flustered by the charging Irish around him that he practically fell over himself while turning the ball past his own goalkeeper for the winning goal. And how about Niall Quinn's hilariously primitive goal against the Netherlands at the 1990 World Cup? One bog-standard punt from Packie Bonner, that most wooden of goalkeepers, was enough to provoke a complete loss of coordination from the reigning European champions and grand exponents of total football, leaving Quinn to slide into the six-yard box incongruously, like a magnificent booted diplodocus, and scutter the ball into the net. Even the fact that

Ireland got to the quarter-finals by scoring only two goals and winning no matches brought a mischievous thrill. That's gaming the system for you.

No one pretended this was high-minded. Indeed, it is telling that the one bespoke chant devised during those times was "You'll Never Beat the Irish" rather than the more ambitious "The Irish Will Beat You". But that was the stage of evolution we were at. We knew it wasn't great but it was gratifying, which is why a lot of people simultaneously welcomed the critiques of RTE's resident pundit and aesthete Eamon Dunphy, and bellowed at him to shut the fuck up.

Besides, the campaign during which Charlton's team played their slickest, most critically-acclaimed football ended in nauseating failure, as Ireland finished runners-up to England in qualifying for Euro 92 despite outplaying Graham Taylor's side at Wembley. In that 1-1 draw, Houghton perpetrated a miss that still brings a slew of obscene words to mind despite his previous and subsequent heroics.

Many an obscene word was hollered during the qualifiers for the '94 World Cup but perhaps none angered the Irish team as much as the "bunch of mercenaries" jibe spat by the Northern Ireland manager Billy Bingham before the Republic's fateful trip to Belfast in the last group game. That added extra sporting needle to a contest already taking place around a distressing escalation in sectarian conflict in the North. Jimmy Quinn threatened to shatter the Republic's dream by opening the scoring, but Alan McLoughlin struck a famous equaliser. As the Republic's player celebrated on the pitch afterwards, they did not know that Denmark's match in Spain had not yet concluded: an away goal there would have left Charlton's player looking like prize berks at Windsor Park. That goal never came and the Republic were on their way.

Republic fans have been urged not to travel to Belfast but I and a wide assortment of fellow revellers made sure we were on hand to sing hymns of praise to the team at 1am as they arrived back in Dublin after their triumphant draw. I wasn't working that night. In fact, there didn't seem to be many people working at the airport that night, at least no one who objected to hordes of frolickers improvising a fairground ambiance, using baggage trolleys as bumper cars and, because someone always loses the run of themselves, turning the gents' toilet into a house of horrors.

* * *

Everyone figured the World Cup in the USA would be an epochal event and most weren't thinking farther ahead than the match against Italy. A coming-together of two disparate peoples in a place that each had made a second home. After the summer of 1990, many travelling Irish fans quipped on their return that "I missed the World Cup: I was in Italy at the time", meaning they had only experienced the matches, not the unprecedented outpouring of pride and jubilation that swept across Ireland as the team ground its way to the last eight. In '94, by contrast, everyone knew that New Jersey was the place to be. Which was the main reason that I and so many others were dismayed at not being able to go there. Another reason was that staff in many Dublin pubs chose the night of the Italy match to go on strike, as bar workers showed that Charlton was not the only one who could play hardball.

Ireland went into the tournament in strong form, with an injection of young blood — Roy Keane was blooming ferociously and Gary Kelly, Phil Babb and Jason McAteer were starting to bud — seemingly giving new vigour to an ageing squad. There was a promising swishness to a pair of excellent wins in the build-up, in friendlies away to the Netherlands and Germany. And just how good were Italy, anyway? Like us, they had failed to qualify for Euro 92, an ignominy that convinced them to fire manager Azeglio Vicini and draft in Sacchi. They made it to the USA by topping a tricky qualifying group, a point above Roy Hodgson's Switzerland, who beat them in Bern. But many Italian critics were convinced the manager they had once dubbed "The Prophet of

Fusignano" didn't see so clearly any more, with his system too bland and his personnel changes misguided.

I well remember an Italy-based chum guffawing down the phone as, two months before the World Cup, he read aloud local reactions to Italy's latest warm-up setback: a 2-1 defeat by Pontedera, a fourth-tier outfit from Pisa. Saachi became so agitated in that match that he demanded the linesmen be changed for the second-half, with his assistants, Carlo Ancelotti and Pietro Carmignani, the only ones he now trusted to do the job. They couldn't help avert humiliation, and Sacchi seemed a confused man afterwards when he claimed the caper had been a useful exercise because Pontedera played just like Mexico and Norway. That suggested (a) Saachi thought those two might be bigger threats than Ireland to his team at the World Cup and (b) Italy's manager had a curious way of analysing things, since most observers reckoned Mexico and Norway played extremely different styles.

Still, a lot more evidence was needed to build a compelling 'Italy are there for the taking' case. Not least because Ireland had never so much as taken a point off them. All seven previous meetings between the countries had ended in Irish defeats. And it was Italy who unceremoniously terminated the Irish jamboree in 1990, and they had hinted at their ability to do likewise in the USA by beating us 2-0 in a friendly in Boston in 1992. More pertinently, they went into the World Cup with the reigning world player of the year, Roberto Baggio, and the back four that they selected against Ireland consisted entirely of players from AC Milan, who had just annihilated Barcelona 4-0 in the Champions League final. Franco Baresi was suspended for that match, but was on hand to lead the defence against Ireland, whose strike force, owing to the lack of fitness of Quinn, John Aldridge and Tony Cascarino, consisted of Tommy Coyne who, a couple of years after making his international debut at the age of 31, was about to become the first Motherwell player to grace a World Cup match. Perhaps he would take Baresi & co by surprise?

Actually, Ireland did seem to ambush Italy in a carefully robust first half. Steve Staunton may have looked in danger of being barbecued alive in the sun but he was energetic enough to hurtle forward and fire off the game's first shot after just 11 seconds; it flew wide from 20 yards but the way the chance came about was telling. It originated from a ball into the right-hand channel by Dennis Irwin, who would excel throughout the match, and then Baresi, visibly ill at ease, shanking an attempted clearance to Staunton. Yet again, then, Charlton's team were turning the world's most accomplished players into goofs.

Eleven minutes later came the breakthrough. John Sheridan supplied the long pass into the box, Coyne pestered Alessandro Costacurta into a weak header, Baresi forgot who he was up against and tried to nod the ball gently to Demetrio Albertini at the edge of his own area. Houghton, already on the chase, darted in front of Albertini, nudged the ball sideways and swung his left foot at it from over 20 yards out. It was a strange shot that seemed to have all the propulsion of a paper airplane, but goalkeeper Gianluca Pagliuca had lost his bearings and merely raised his hand and put it back down again, like a man changing his mind about hailing a cab. The ball drifted over him and into the net.

Ireland controlled the rest of the first half thanks to the excellence of their five-man midfield. Italy improved after the break when Daniel Massaro replaced Alberico Evani. He and Dino Baggio began to threaten. But Italy never truly looked like cutting through. In the celebrations afterwards, Irish fans picked their favourite moment from the match: there was the goal, of course, but also Jason McAteer nutmegging Roberto Baggio, Paul McGrath channelling warriors from Irish lore as he fended off invaders with one flick of his mighty thigh or hurled himself in front of spinning boulders. Many proclaimed Charlton the overriding hero: he was the master strategist, he had started Houghton despite the player's lack of form going into the game, and he furiously rebuked local cops for manhandling a jubilant Irish fan to who ran on to the pitch after the final whistle.

All choice snippets. I also liked the moment in the first half when Coyne ran on to a long diagonal pass from Irwin. The prudent thing to do would have been to take it down and wait for support, or maybe try to jink his way past Baresi and Costacurta and drive into the box. He hadn't had much success holding up the ball so far and wasn't much of a dribbler. So he essayed a third option. He tried to send a glancing header into the net from 25 yards for one of the most extraordinary goals in World Cup history. The ball went way wide. A preposterous effort really. But borne of a combination of fatigue, self-awareness and the belief that really committing to something can sometimes spawn lasting memories. Someone should make a pewter souvenir of the effort.

We didn't know it then, but Ireland and Charlton had peaked. Six days later, in the crushing heat of Orlando, they played drably before being pierced twice by a sharp Mexico striker, Luis Garcia. Immediately after the second goal, Charlton's attempt to stimulate a revival was complicated by official bungling, as Coyne and Steve Staunton trudged off but only one substitute — McAteer — was allowed on, leaving the other would-be replacement, Aldridge, in a hot funk on the sidelines. The action off the pitch grew so fractious that it demanded the attention of the TV cameras, which treated global viewers to nearly 60 seconds of Aldridge jabbing fingers and hurling insults at a yellow-capped Fifa mandarin. "You fucking cheat. You twat. You dickhead. You know it too." It was practically a poetry recital, a flame-throated expression of Scouse-Irish fury, with Charlton and assorted Irish officials chipping in some choice words too.

Aldridge reached such a flow that he was in danger of getting himself sent off before even being admitted to the pitch but eventually, after almost four minutes, his to-the-point lobbying paid off. Just before the end, he found the net with what remains the best goal ever scored by Ireland at a World Cup. It was a precise header at the culmination of a swift and skilful move, forcing one to wonder what would have happened if Ireland had played like that, rather than to percentages, from the start.

The goal was not enough to avoid a 2-1 defeat. Nor to persuade Fifa to forget about fining Aldridge, Charlton and the Irish delegation for their "ill-mannered behaviour" before the substitution.

Charlton was even banned from the touchline for the last group game, against Norway. Presumably banning him from watching the match at all would have been deemed too lenient a punishment. After all, under Egil Olsen Norway had risen to their highest ever world ranking — third — by imposing a brutalist style not unlike Charlton's: Ireland and Norway were, therefore, the teams most likely to cancel each other. And lo, they served up one of the worst matches in World Cup history, a 0-0 draw that could have been construed as heinous vengeance on Fifa, an act of sabotage against their attempts to conquer the lucrative US market.

At least Group E produced a quirky finish, as, for the first and still only time in World Cup history, all four teams finished with the same number of points and the same goal difference. Mexico claimed top spot by dint of scoring more goals, while Ireland took second thanks to their superior head-to-head record over Italy, who advanced in third. The bad news for Ireland was that meant not only a second-round showdown with the Netherlands but a return to the Florida furnace. Among fans, optimism was not high, but officials back home were evidently still giddy from the success against Italy and announced that plans were in place for a huge celebration to welcome the team home at the end of their campaign, whenever that may be. "We're not being negative about it," Noel Carr, a spokesman for Dublin's local authority, trumpeted to the media. "We're planning for 19 July when they win the final".

Yes, well, on 4 July Ireland lost 2-0 to the Netherlands, a dispiriting, error-strewn defeat. Charlton and the squad were cajoled into flying back for the homecoming party anyway. After their exploits in 1990, they had been greeted in Dublin by over 500,000 grateful fans, many of whom stuck around to also pay tribute Nelson Mandela, who happened to be in town on the same day to receive the freedom of the city. The South African was acclaimed with happy chants of "Oh aah, Paul McGrath's da", which may sound off now but, at the time, there could hardly of been a higher expression of respect and affection (years later, in an interview for *The Guardian*, I asked McGrath what he thought of that and he said "I'm sure [Mandela] had no idea what was going on but to me, it's just lovely").

The 1994 homecoming was a lamer affair. Around 100,000 turned up and watched besuited players mumble their way through awkward interviews on a big stage. Niall Quinn, on commentary rather than playing duty throughout the tournament because of injury, described the Phoenix Park experience as an "embarrassing" chore for all involved: "everyone cringed and went home".

Meanwhile, Italy had sharpened up and progressed all the way to the final. Roberto Baggio had found his groove. Until he lost it again in the shootout, sending his penalty to the moon to give victory to Brazil. In an office in Pisa, one Luciano Barachini began composing a message. "We wrote a fax to the Brazilian federation to congratulate them and, above all, to invite them to a sort of 'grand final'," revealed the president of Pontedena years later. "They replied and said they would come. But that was the last we heard of them."

Just over two years later, Charlton's glorious decade leading Ireland came to an end with another defeat by the Netherlands, in a playoff for Euro '96. He had shown Ireland what was possible and delivered wonderful memories, but he couldn't lead them to the next stage of their evolution. No one else has yet been able to do that either.

USA 1994

29 JUNE
GROUP STAGE

S.ARABIA
1

BELGIUM
0

S.Arabia	Belgium
1. Mohamed Al-Deayea	1. Michel Preud'homme
4. Abdullah Zubromawi	2. Dirk Medved
5. Ahmad Jamil Madani	14. Michel De Wolf
3. Mohammed Al-Khilaiwi	4. Philippe Albert
13. Mohamed Al-Jawad	5. Rudi Smidts
16. Talal Jebreen	6. Lorenzo Staelens
10. Saeed Al-Owairan 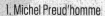 **(5') OFF**	10. Enzo Scifo (c)
2. Abdullah Al-Dosari ON (63')	7. Franky Van der Elst
19. Hamzah Saleh	16. Danny Boffin
20. Hamzah Idris	18. Marc Wilmots OFF
8. Fahad Al-Bishi	*17. Josip Weber ON (53')*
9. Majed Abdullah (c) OFF	9. Marc Degryse OFF
14. Khalid Al-Muwallid ON (46')	*8. Luc Nilis ON (23')*
Manager: Jorge Solari	Manager: Paul Van Himst

RFK Memorial Stadium

Washington DC, USA

ATTENDANCE
52,959

REFEREE
Hellmut Krug (Germany)

JAMES MONTAGUE

> There seems to be little argument against the greatest goal in World Cup history. 22 June, 1986: Estadio Azteca, Mexico City.

A riled up Maradona, fresh from channelling God to beat Peter Shilton minutes before, waltzed through virtually the entire England team and slotted the ball home. The victory had everything; yes, controversy and the greatest player in the world in his pomp. It also had a deep political subtext. The Falklands War had taken place only four years previously and the wounds were still fresh. Maradona had written emotionally in his 2000 autobiography *El Diego* about how the team had played down the significance of the war before the game but how, behind the scenes, him and his teammates were in fact desperate for revenge on the pitch. Argentina, of course, went on to win the 1986 World Cup. I was seven years old and the Hand of God was my first footballing memory (and the first time I had cried watching football, though it certainly wouldn't be the last). But as I got older, I began to wonder whether all was what it seemed.

I can't recall exactly the first time I'd heard the conspiracy theory that Maradona's second goal was in fact a Terry Butcher own goal. It might have been on Baddiel and Skinner's *Fantasy Football League*, and its 'Phoenix From the Flames' segment, but I can't find any trace of it now. Perhaps I'd read it as a joke in *Viz*. Or perhaps it was some form of deep psychological coping mechanism after losing my football innocence at such a young age. Terry Butcher was adamant it was Maradona's goal. "I didn't get a touch," he said in a 1998 interview with the *Daily Mail*. "I'd love to sit here and say that I got a touch and that it wasn't his goal — just to deprive him ... But I couldn't get at the ball. I wish I'd scored the greatest own goal ever but I didn't."

Looking back now, though, the replays *still* appear to be inconclusive. I haven't been able to look at the goal in the same way since. So, I propose a new greatest World Cup goal of all time. 29 June, 1994, the Robert F. Kennedy Memorial Stadium, Washington DC. Belgium vs Saudi Arabia. In the fifth minute, the Saudi midfielder Saeed Al-Owairan collected the ball outside his own penalty box and lurched forward like a spluttering bulldozer. He picked up speed, as the entire bamboozled Belgian back line collapsed around him. At times, it looked like Al-Owairan didn't have control of the ball until he finally penetrated the box and hooked the ball over Belgian goalkeeper Michel Preud'homme, a fraction of a second before two Belgian defenders impotently lunged in. This was most definitely not an own goal.

I remember watching the goal and being mesmerised by the unknown player who scored it. Although England didn't qualify for USA '94, the World Cup left a lasting impression on me. With no England to obsess over, I instead obsessed over then unknown players from faraway lands. The underdogs of Sweden, Romania and Bulgaria. The ginger beard of Alexi Lalas. Letchcov's bald head. Baggio's rat's tail. And Saeed Al-Owairan's wonder goal. I didn't know where Saudi Arabia was. But the story of Al-Owairan's strike was in its own way every bit as fantastical as Maradona's (or Terry Butcher's) wonder goal. It was Saudi Arabia's first ever World Cup finals and the goal secured their passage to the knockout phase, the first time a country from the Middle East had ever managed to get out of the group stage. Qualification for USA '94 had involved navigating one of the most explosive tournaments in football history, with perhaps a little help from US intelligence. And just like Maradona, that World Cup wonder goal brought Saeed Al-Owairan fame and notoriety that nearly destroyed him.

* * *

For Atef Nahass, the rise of Saudi Arabian football begins with one man. Jimmy Hill. "In 1976, the Saudi [football] federation signed a contract with Jimmy Hill. You know Jimmy Hill?" asked Atef, a veteran Saudi sports journalist who has spent 30 years writing about the national team. I had never met Jimmy Hill, but he was a legendary figure in English football. Once gently mocked, there has been something of a reappraisal of his legacy as a reformist renaissance man. And in 1976, he was offered the chance to go to Saudi Arabia and essentially build Saudi football from scratch. The country's FA had only joined Fifa in 1956 and had never even tried to qualify for the World Cup. Hill was brought in as a sort of technical director, paid what was then an astonishing sum of £25 million, to build a new league and a new national team. The boom in oil prices that followed the 1973 OPEC crisis saw Saudi Arabia become exorbitantly wealthy. They had the money to spend and Jimmy Hill seemed as good a person as any to spend it on.

"They finished next to bottom in the last Arab tournament, I think in March. Kuwait won it with only 400,000 people. And Saudi has eight and half million people. So I don't think they liked their neighbours carrying off the trophy!" Hill said when he was interviewed after signing his contract alongside Faisal bin Fahd al Saud, the eldest son of King Fahd, and a minister in the government in charge of promoting sport. The "last Arab tournament" Hill referred to was the 1976 Gulf Cup, and it was indeed a humiliating event. Saudi Arabia in fact finished third from bottom and lost 7-1 to Iraq. Change was needed. "In five years, you can't create a world-class team," Hill answered, when an incredulous English reporter asked what he could realistically do to improve the Saudi team. "What is absolutely certain is that they will play far better than they do at the moment. And what is certain is that a 10-year-old kid who in the past was born in Saudi would have no chance of being a top-class player. Now he will have a chance." For Atef, Hill's three-year period in Saudi Arabia laid the foundations of the success to come. "Jimmy Hill brought over other British coaches and we also sent Saudi people to England to have training courses. That contract with Jimmy Hill was very important for modernising Saudi football."

Under Hill, a new national league was formed in 1976 and Saudi Arabia entered qualifying for the World Cup for the first time, for Argentina '78. They went out in the first round, losing to Iran who would go on to qualify for the finals. But results improved. They won back-to-back Asian Cups in 1984 and 1988, although they kept stubbornly failing to reach the World Cup finals. "We failed in '86. We failed in '90," said Atef. "For USA '94, we said, we must be there." The early 1990s also saw the emergence of a golden generation of Saudi players, alongside perhaps the greatest player Saudi Arabia has ever produced, Majed Abdullah.

Playing for unfashionable Al Shabab in Riyadh, Saeed Al-Owairan was not really considered an outstanding talent until he scored 16 goals in the 1991/92 season, making him the league's top scorer. He went to the 1992 Asian Cup and scored twice, including in the semi-final. "We had a change in the national team in 1988 — most of the old generation retired," said Atef. "Then we had Fahad Al-Harifi, Khaled Massad, Fuad Anwar, [who] all came in by 1992. And Saeed Al-Owairan. He was an attacking midfielder. He was tall, his body was very good and he had shooting power. He had a European style, shooting from everywhere. A good brain and good shot."

Did he remind you of any players today; Messi, Hazard, Ronaldo?

"He wasn't that skillful a player!" Atef laughed. "But he was a dangerous player outside the box. Anytime he could shoot. Majed Abdullah was the most skilful player. But he had setbacks from injuries. In 1994, he was not fit enough."

There was a glimpse of what was to come when Saudi Arabia smashed the USA 3-0 in the 1992 King Fahd Cup, the precursor to Fifa's Confederations Cup. After the failure to reach Mexico '86 and

Italia '90, failure to reach USA '94 would not be tolerated. Eventually, after several sackings, the Saudi federation settled on Brazilian coach Candinho to navigate the final round of Asian World Cup qualification in Qatar. Standing in the way were Japan, Iran and Uday Hussein, and possibly even the American government.

* * *

In October 1993, the final round of Asian World Cup qualification was to take place. It would be a round robin tournament with the continent's six best teams all playing each other in Doha, Qatar, then an unknown footballing backwater. The problem was that it was also, potentially, the most politically charged tournament in football history. Saudi Arabia were there, but so too were Iraq, who had invaded Kuwait and (briefly) Saudi Arabia during the 1991 Gulf War, which had ended just two and a half years earlier. The Iraqi football association was essentially run by Uday Hussein, Saddam's psychopathic and sexually sadistic son, who would often torture athletes if they underperformed. Then there was Iran, returning from a long, self-imposed exile from international football after the 1979 Islamic Revolution and a brutal eight-year war with Iraq that had taken a million lives. North Korea had also made it, as had South Korea. The two had never signed a full peace deal after the Korean War had ended in 1953 and an increasingly bellicose — and nuclear — North Korea had promised to turn Seoul into "a sea of fire". And both countries had long-standing grievances with Japan over its abusive occupations during the Second World War.

Despite never having qualified for a World Cup, both Saudi Arabia, who had won two of the past three Asian Cups, and Japan, the reigning Asian champions, were favourites. The new J-League, started six months before, had been a huge success. Gary Lineker and a host of big-name foreign players had moved to play there too, raising its profile. Only the year before, Japan had won their first ever Asian Cup, beating Saudi Arabia 1-0 in the final. They had their first ever foreign coach, a gruff-voiced Dutchman called Hans Ooft, who would wear a white linen jacket and chain smoke during games. Thousands of Japanese fans, including an incredible 300 Japanese journalists, travelled halfway across the world to be there. They expected qualification.

Three of the teams, Iran, Iraq and North Korea, were still under sanction by the US government. It wasn't certain they would even be allowed into the USA, even if they did qualify. Libya, which was also under US sanction, had recently seen its athletes banned from attending a youth tournament in the States. The tournament had become so politically sensitive that the State Department even sent a representative to Doha to keep an eye on things. So Fifa took special measures as well and flew in Europe's best referees for the occasion. "There were five of us and we were told it was going to be very difficult," said Ion Crăciunescu, one of the referees who was picked. We met in a cafe in his home city of Bucharest back in 2014, so I could ask him about the tournament.

In 1993, Crăciunescu was one of Uefa's elite referees, who would go on to take charge of the 1995 Champions League final. When reality dawned on then-Fifa general secretary Sepp Blatter that the tournament was a potential diplomatic nightmare, his first decision was to put together a crack team of European referees. Crăciunescu was on the list and on his way to Doha. "The amount we received from Fifa was double what we would normally receive," he recalled of his preparations, and his fee, for that tournament. "It was funny when we got there. Blatter was there and he told us that we could expect a horror tournament. That if these countries were at war with each other, you could expect the same on the pitch."

Crăciunescu's first game was North Korea v Saudi Arabia, a relatively uncontroversial match-up that the Saudis won 2-1. But for Iraq vs Iran, he took a tough love approach. "It was a game that was announced to be impossible," he laughed. "The big issue was to try to ensure fair play so that it didn't erupt into war on the pitch as it had outside." So Crăciunescu went in hard. "I gave many yellow cards," he recalled with a guilty smile. "I remember, anyone would do anything, just the smallest thing, I'd give a card." His severity did the trick. The match passed without incident. Iraq won 2-1. "It turned out to be quite peaceful," Crăciunescu said. "There was no problem between the players. I didn't see any political implications. I exaggerated if anything. Because we had been inculcated with the idea that something might happen."

Although the referees had been scrupulous and kept in isolation away from the other teams who, for some reason, had all been placed in the same hotel together, Crăciunescu had an inkling that Iraq's progress was not being appreciated. "There was some sort of a trend ..." he said tentatively, trailing off.

A long pause.

"Some of the teams were not desired there."

Another long pause.

"I could feel something."

Crăciunescu was fidgeting in his seat uncomfortably, reaching for the right words before giving up.

"That's it," he finally offered.

Later, he spoke of how proud he was for being chosen to go, how pleased he was to have been chosen to officiate the toughest games and how happy he had been with his own personal performance. Crăciunescu maintained that no one tried to pressure him into anything, but recalled — in shaky English — a reply from one American official who was not happy about Iran, Iraq or North Korea potentially qualifying for USA '94: "No. Terrorists. In. America."

Saudi Arabia, meanwhile, had arrived in big numbers. Tens of thousands of fans had turned up for their first game against Japan, including Atef. "Everyone came by buses from Al Ahsa region, which borders Qatar. We came in the morning, and stayed in Doha corniche," he recalled. "We were a big crowd. They [the Qataris] said that the fans invaded Doha, that the Saudis invaded our corniche. We were maybe 30,000." It was a rematch of the 1992 Asian Cup final. This time they fought out a 0-0 draw.

By the third round of games, everyone was still in contention. The crucial game for Atef was the game against South Korea. "We equalised in the dying minutes and the crowd invaded the pitch!" he said. Centre-half Ahmed Jamil had snatched a point at the death. "You can see it on TV after the match most of the supporters invaded the pitch and celebrated. The people were very happy. That South Korea match is the most important and the most remembered until now."

The qualification of Iraq, Iran or North Korea was still possible, and a potential nightmare for Alan Rothenberg. A lawyer by trade, he became head of the United States Soccer Federation and was put in charge of organising a tournament revered around the world, but largely ignored in the US. The plan to change all that began with an unmistakable touch of American glamour. The draw for the finals took place in Las Vegas. The late Robin Williams performed stand up. Throughout his performance he referred to Sepp Blatter as "Sepp Bladder".

"The federation was nearly bankrupt. We had to professionalise. We had to organise the World Cup with no one on staff," Rothenberg said of the run-up to the finals when we spoke on the phone. By October 1993, Rothenberg was close to realising his dream. The stadiums were ready. Top celebrities had been drafted in, from the draw in Las Vegas to the opening ceremony. Diana Ross would sing at it (and famously miss a penalty). All was going to plan. But then Rothenberg was told about the final Asian qualification tournament on the other side of the world in Doha.

"We were holding our breath," he said of that month. "Three countries, Iran, Iraq and North Korea, who had no love for the United States, and the feeling was mutual, had a chance to qualify. The security challenge would have been enormous. And they came pretty darn close! The fact that they didn't qualify was a Godsend, quite honestly."

Rothenberg and the USA '94 organising committee kept a close eye on the results in Doha. Years of careful planning would have been thrown into chaos if any of those teams had qualified, let alone two of them. He had to make contingency plans just in case. "We were gearing up for the worst and we had a budget for those teams," he says.

There were talks with State Department officials. They sent a man to Doha who was told that Fifa would insist that those countries would have to be allowed in. In 2014, I managed to track down the State Department official and called his office number. It connected and rang, and he picked up. He was in Afghanistan, he said. I explained why I was calling; that I wanted to find out what interest the State Department had in who qualified for USA '94. "How did you find me?" he asked. But the line disconnected before I could answer. The number never worked after that.

Still, at least one headache was solved, albeit not in Asia. There was a fourth team that Rothenberg prayed would not qualify. England. "It was a time before the Europeans had controlled hooliganism," he says. "The fact that England didn't qualify was a Godsend too." In the end, England's coach Graham Taylor answered Rothenberg's prayers for him.

As the tournament in Doha reached its conclusion, Rothenberg was counting the potential economic and political cost of having two from three of America's greatest and gravest enemies on home soil. "It would have cost millions and millions of dollars, and the government was taking it extremely seriously," he said. Rothenberg kept in constant contact with Blatter on the issue. "I talked to Sepp," he said. "They sent the best referees and line officials and they were prepared for the potential problems. I watched it all like a hawk."

Saudi Arabia drew their next game 1-1 against Iraq, with Saeed Al-Owairan scoring the equaliser. They went into the last game against Iran knowing a victory would be enough to qualify. But, incredibly, Prince Faisal bin Fahad bin Abdulaziz, president of the Saudi Football Federation, decided to sack their Brazilian coach Candinho before the game. There was, according to Atef, an argument with the federation about Candinho sticking by his young goalkeeper Mohamed Al-Deayea who, Atef recalled, had been shaky in the previous two games. South Korea's opening goal in their 1-1 draw with Saudi, for example, saw Shin Hong-gi fire the ball from an impossible angle, at distance, which somehow went through Al-Deayea's legs. "He was young and making mistakes against Korea, against Iraq, but Mister Candinho still had trust in him," he said. "But the authorities said we must give another goalkeeper a chance. I'm not defending anybody but the pressure was so high. From the authorities and from the Saudi people, on the coach, on the players, that we must go to the World Cup. So Mister Candinho said 'I will go, I will not stay. I have my own philosophy,' something like that."

This wasn't that unusual in the Gulf. The Saudi reputation for extreme sackings was legendary. They fired coach Milan Máčala midway through the group stage of the 2000 Asian Cup. And I was in Qatar when they sacked Portuguese coach José Peseiro during the group stage of the 2011 Asian Cup after losing to Syria. I'd been at the airport and seen how Peseiro was literally chased through the departure lounge by a scrum of angry Saudi journalists, as if he'd committed a murder. "You know we have a tradition here, If we fire the coach, the players will respond. You understand?" said Atef. "Most of the Gulf countries think like this. I did not agree with it at the time. But this is how it is."

In the end, it came down to the very last games, which all kicked off at the same time. Saudi Arabia, under caretaker coach Mohammed Al-Kharashy, blew Iran away in their final game and never looked in trouble after Sami Al-Jaber — who would go on to play in four consecutive World Cup finals and, very briefly, for Wolverhampton Wanderers — scored the opening goal. They won 4-3. Al-Kharashy would again be drafted in as caretaker coach at the 1998 World Cup finals, after Carlos Alberto Parreira — who'd won the World Cup with Brazil just four years earlier — was sacked after losing Saudi Arabia's first two games. "I don't feel happy and I don't feel comfortable with the decision taken by the Saudi officials," Parreira said he was fired. "At least they should have let us continue until the end of the World Cup."

In 1993, Atef Nahass was back home in Jeddah when Saudi Arabia qualified for their first ever World Cup, and vividly remembers the outpouring of joy. "You know, dreams come true. It was a historical event for the Saudi people," he said. "I remember in Jeddah there were so many very happy people outside, down the street dancing and raising Saudi flags. Also in Riyadh and Dammam, across the whole kingdom. Until now, I cannot remember seeing that amount of people outside celebrating for the national team. It was a historical thing."

That left one spot up for grabs, and Japan had it going into the 90th minute. But then they conceded a last-second goal to Iraq, the match finished 2-2 and they were eliminated. That day is still known, even today, as the Agony of Doha, a day of national shame for Japan that would hang around the players' necks every bit as heavily as any English penalty shoot-out failure. Remarkably, it remains the last time Japan failed to qualify for a World Cup finals.

In Doha, what was agony for Japan was a miracle for Korea. At the same time across the city, Ion Crăciunescu was taking charge of North versus South in an oddly convivial atmosphere. "Speaking of politics, South Korea's qualification depended on Japan's game and I honestly think that the North Koreans were very kind to the South Koreans," he said. The North Koreans were, he says, kind and very polite. South Korea needed to win and pray that Japan somehow didn't against Iraq. "When the Korea game ended, the Japan result was not known," Crăciunescu recalled. "We had finished the game. The players had shaken hands and South Korea had won 3-0. They [the South Koreans] left the pitch with their heads down."

But, suddenly, the mood changed. News had come through that Iraq had scored. "Then the South Koreans started jumping up and down in unimaginable joy. And I actually saw that the North Koreans were kind of happy for South Korea because they had heard what had happened to Japan." The two nations' players talked, smiled and congratulated each other on the pitch. After all the talk of war, the two groups had found a common ground in the game, their shared heritage and, in Japan, a bogeyman they could agree on. For Crăciunescu, it was a beautiful moment. "It was," he said, "an incredible atmosphere."

In Korea, 28 October, 1993 is known as the Miracle of Doha, the day that victory was snatched from the country's former colonial oppressors while in the jaws of defeat. It would be they and Saudi Arabia who would be going to USA '94.

This was great news for Alan Rothenberg. "It saved a lot of money and saved a lot of headaches," he admitted. "It would have put a different flavour on the tournament. The bad side of international relations would have been there. It was a festive occasion and everyone was there for a good time. The presence of lots of armed forces would have dampened that enthusiasm. There would have been less of a party mood."

Sepp Blatter was happy too. "Sport has this extraordinary power to build bridges in society," Blatter wrote in reply to written questions I sent him about the 1993 tournament in Doha, back in 2014 when he was still president and shortly before his tenure ended in disgrace. "So, I never considered this line-up as 'a politically combustible mix!'" He denied that any specific action had to be taken and, besides, he wasn't worried about the issue of Iran, Iraq or North Korea qualifying. Perhaps it was because he believed he had secured an important 'Get Out of Jail' card. "We had no concerns about any other team qualifying," Blatter wrote, "because we had received assurances from President Bill Clinton that any team would be warmly welcomed."

***

Saudi Arabia now had to prepare for its historic first World Cup as rank outsiders. Their odds of winning the tournament were 500-1. The first problem to solve was finding a coach. The federation decided on Dutch coach Leo Beenhakker, signing him on a big money, one-year deal. And things seemed to be going well. Saeed Al-Owairan prospered, scoring four goals in five warm-up matches. "Anything can happen in football. Remember the opening game in Italia '90?" Beenhakker said, referring to Cameroon's 1-0 victory over holders Argentina. "Every tournament has its surprises. I think Arabia is going to be the surprise of the tournament." But, according to Atef, his Dutch Calvinist methods rubbed both the federation and the players up the wrong way. He was sacked just a few months before the start of the tournament. Which is when the King stepped in.

King Fahd had kept a close eye on the Saudi national team and, fed up with the constant personnel changes, contacted Argentine president Carlos Menem. According to Atef, Menem recommended Jorge Solari. "The late King Fahd had a good relationship with Menem. And he said, 'If the Saudis want a coach, this is your man.'" Solari had played at the 1966 World Cup finals for Argentina and had a strong record as a coach in South America. He lost his first game, a warm up against Greece, 5-1. Although this, according to Atef, might have been a good thing. "That was a big shock for him and maybe after that Solari had to come up with another strategy for those players," he said. "We were good enough, but how to play against the European teams was the biggest problem."

To the outside world, they were complete unknowns. Unless you were one of a few thousand oil workers, it was almost impossible to visit Saudi Arabia. It was an Islamic theocracy, custodian of the two most revered sites in Islam, and a dictatorship. It was one of the most isolated countries on Earth. Saudi players were banned from playing abroad.

Their first World Cup game was against a Netherlands team that featured Bergkamp, Rijkaard and Overmars. "Those matches were early in the morning, 2.30am Saudi time," Atef said of that opening game. "I still remember it. All the houses are open, you can see that people are waiting for it. It's a historical day and nobody wants to miss that match. Nobody is sleeping." And Saudi Arabia went in at half-time 1-0 up, after midfielder Fuad Anwar's early strike. But the Netherlands turned it around in the second half and won 2-1 thanks to a late Gaston Taument goal. "At the end of the match, you can see, as young Saudis and proud Saudis, you can see tears in our eyes that unfortunately we lost. But we are very, very proud of our players and our national team. We were very optimistic we'd beat Morocco." And they did, winning 2-1.

They needed to beat Belgium to make the second round. And five minutes into the match, Saeed Al-Owairan picked the ball up and made history, something no one expected to happen. "Even him!" shouted Atef. "You are watching it and want him to pass the ball. PASS THE BALL! PASS IT! But he's still moving. It's something you can't imagine. PLAY THE BALL! PASS THE BALL! PLAY THE BALL! But Belgium opened all the doors for him."

When the ball hit the net, the entire nation celebrated wildly. But not Saeed, which disappointed Atef somewhat. "For me, his celebration was not good for his goal, he must celebrate with more power because he scored one of the greatest goals in World Cup history. Take your shirt off or something like that, you know? I say to people, the younger generations, every World Cup, every four years, that goal will be remembered. Every four years, you will see Saeed Al-Owairan score against Belgium. And Saeed Al-Owairan is a funny man. He said that nobody will remember any Saudi players, only me!"

Saudi Arabia made it to the second round. Atef hugged his mothers in tears. Although many Saudis thought they could beat Sweden in the next round, it wasn't to be. They lost 3-1 to the team that would finish third but they had achieved more than they thought they ever could. "That goal was a trademark of

Saudi Arabia," Atef said of Al-Owairan's goal. "Everybody was writing about Saudi Arabia, a different side of Saudi Arabia."

***

Saeed Al-Owairan returned home a hero. But not for long. Two years later, it was reported that he had been arrested by Saudi's notorious religious police for drinking and carousing with non-Saudi women during Ramadan. There were various reports that he was jailed for anywhere up to a year in prison and banned from football for a year. Although he was eventually brought back into the squad for France '98 and was asked about the allegations by the *International Herald Tribune.* "It wasn't like a jail, jail," he said. "It was a detention centre, and I was held for questioning for several weeks." He later claimed he was locked up for six months. "The goal against Belgium was a double-edged sword for me," he said. "In some ways, it was great. In other ways, it was awful. Because it put me in the spotlight, everybody was focusing on me."

He retired after France '98 having scored 24 goals in 75 international appearances. But he will forever be known for his wonder goal against Belgium. Today, he is not involved with football at all, and only occasionally pops up on TV talk shows around big tournaments. Atef suspects he will be on TV a lot as the 2022 finals in Qatar approach.

Saudi Arabia is a country in flux. Although there are few civil and political rights, there has been a loosening of some cultural freedoms. Women can drive, even if the women activists that pushed for the policy spent time in jail. Cinemas have reopened. Women can go to football matches. And Saudi football ended its isolationist policy.

Although Sami Al-Jaber was given permission to play briefly for Wolves in 2000, hardly any Saudi players left the country. Former national team captain Yasser Al-Qahtani had a trial with Manchester City in 2008 but he returned to

Al-Hilal despite, he said, being offered a contract. Although legendary former City goalkeeper John Burridge, who was a football analyst on Middle Eastern TV at the time, had a different story. "Al-Qahtani flew into Manchester with a huge entourage. He arrived at the City training ground like a prince and when he took part in his first training session, the members of his entourage lined the length of the touchline cheering his every move," he told the *Daily Mirror.* "When he got the ball, Richard Dunne smacked Al-Qahtani with a good old-fashioned 'welcome' tackle, and he fell to the ground like a bag of chips ... He started rolling around, squealing, and had to be carried off the field. Then he started crying."

But then, in 2018, before the World Cup in Russia, La Liga and the Saudi federation struck a deal. Saudi Arabia's best players young would sign on loan for clubs in Spain in the hope of gaining top-level experience. Learning from the UAE and Qatar, Saudi Arabia is now using football as a tool to reshape its image in the world. The purchase of Newcastle United by the PIF, Saudi Arabia's sovereign wealth fund, will have a similar effect on the public's perception of Saudi Arabia as Manchester City has had on Abu Dhabi, or PSG on Qatar.

But first, there's Qatar's World Cup. Just as in 1993, tens of thousands of Saudis are expected to travel by bus to Doha. It will be another invasion and Atef will travel with them too. This time they will have a team playing as close to home as can be without hosting it themselves, and in Hervé Renard, a world-class coach who has somehow stayed in the job for three years. "It will be a very hard tournament, with Argentina, Poland and Mexico," Atef admitted. "It will all depend on Mister Renard and his coaching philosophy." Only, that is, if he isn't fired in the next few months.

James Montague would like to thank Jonathan Wilson for allowing him to use some quotes and passages from his article "The Agony of Doha" from The Blizzard, Issue 18

S.KOREA & JAPAN
2002

31 MAY
GROUP STAGE

SENEGAL
1

FRANCE
0

SENEGAL	FRANCE
1. Tony Sylva	1. Fabien Barthez
17. Ferdinand Coly	15. Lilian Thuram
13. Lamine Diatta	18. Franck Lebouef
4. Pape Malick Diop	8. Marcel Desailly (c)
2. Omar Daf	3. Bixente Lizarazu
6. Aliou Cissé (c)	4. Patrick Vieira
14. Moussa N'Diaye	17. Emmanuel Petit
19. Papa Bouba Diop ⊗ (30')	11. Sylvain Wilthord OFF
15. Salif Diao	*9. Djibril Cissé ON (81')*
10. Khalilou Fadiga	6. Youri Djorkaeff OFF
11. El-Hadji Diouf	*21. Christophe Dugarry ON (60')*
	12. Thierry Henry
Manager: Bruno Metsu	20. David Trezeguet
	Manager: Roger Lemerre

Seoul World Cup Stadium

Seoul, South Korea

ATTENDANCE
62,561

REFEREE
Ali Bujsaim (UAE)

PHILIPPE AUCLAIR

> Bruno Metsu was laid to rest twice, first on
> 18 October, 2013 in Dunkirk, where several
> hundred people gathered round his coffin in the
> city's Stade des Flandres, then three days later
> in Dakar, where, as was his wish, he was given
> a Muslim funeral.

President of Senegal Macky Sall was in attendance. A number of Senegalese players, El-Hadji Diouf, Khalilou Fadiga and Aliou Cissé among them, were there too, bidding farewell to the man known as *le Sorcier blanc* — 'the White Witch-Doctor', a moniker he detested — in the country which considered him one of its own. The coffin had been draped in the flags of Senegal and of Islam, to which Metsu, raised a Roman Catholic, had converted when he married his Senegalese wife Viviane Rokhaya Dièye two months before the 2002 World Cup.

Many in the crowd of onlookers were wearing '*merci Metsu*' t-shirts or holding posters and placards expressing their gratitude towards the man whom president Sall called "a hero among Senegalese heroes" and "a true Lion' in his eulogy, in reference to the nickname of the national team, *Les Lions de la Teranga*. The grief a whole country felt was commensurate to what Metsu, who'd succumbed to cancer at the age of 59, had achieved, and which nobody thought he could achieve when he was appointed national team manager of Senegal in November 2000. Yes, Metsu was French, and white; but Metsu was also the man who had given his adopted country the greatest moment in its football history, if not its history full stop, as some Senegalese friends told me with only part of their tongue in their cheeks.

On 31 May, 2002, defying all predictions, in front of 62,561 spectators massed in the Seoul World Cup Stadium and hundreds of millions of television viewers throughout the world, Senegal had become the first-ever French-speaking African nation to beat its former colonial power in a full international. Senegal had beaten, and fairly, the reigning world and European champions on the grandest stage of them all, in the opening game of a World Cup. It had to be the greatest shock in the tournament's history since the part-timers of the USA had won 1-0 against England in Belo Horizonte, more than half-a-century previously. Only the country's victory in the 2021 African Cup of Nations, at the 16th time of asking, when one of Metsu's former players, Aliou Cissé, took them to the title, could be compared to the Korean triumph which paved the way for a yet-to-be-repeated run to the quarter-finals of the World Cup.

Metsu made for an improbable miracle-maker. His only previous experience of coaching an African side — Guinea, in 2000 — had turned sour in a matter of months, and he had taken over *les Lions* at a testing time. Unlike their three main rivals in their World Cup qualification group — Algeria, Morocco and Egypt — Senegal had never played in a World Cup finals, and it didn't look as though they would break their duck in 2002. Under Metsu's predecessor, German coach Peter Schnittger, the first two rounds of qualifiers had only brought two points. Their prospects looked bleak; nor was there any convincing reason to believe that the Frenchman with the tousled mane of auburn hair could improve them. There was not much to distinguish Metsu from the cohorts of French coaches who have managed African national teams with varied fortunes since the break-up of the *Empire* at the very beginning of the 1960s.

He'd had an honourable but by no means exceptional career as a player in first and second division French football, enjoying his best years with Valenciennes — where Cameroonian legend Roger Milla was his team-mate for two seasons — in the mid-seventies. His record as a manager was even more modest.

His only taste of managing in the French top division, in 1993, had come to a brutal end when he was sacked by Lille after a run of just five wins in 27 games, after which he looked after Sedan and Valence in France's third tier, with no marked success.

Yet, Metsu proved an inspired choice. His knowledge of French football was his first asset. Unlike Schnittger, he'd seen at first hand the players he could call upon, almost all of whom played in the top two divisions of the French league. In fact, of the 23 Metsu would take to the World Cup, only two played their football outside of France, reserve goalkeepers Omar Diallo and Khalidou Cissokho.

Then there was Metsu's personality: the natural flamboyance in which players like El-Hadji Diouf could recognise themselves, the charm, the open-mindedness. As vice-president of the Senegal FA Bounamar Gueye said — before the World Cup, it should be noted: "Bruno's secret is that he listens to everyone — he listens to players, he listens to the federation and he listens to journalists". He was also smart and brave enough to take some of his most significant (and potentially problematic) decisions almost as soon as he took up his duties, such as recalling a number of players who had been set aside by the previous regime for disciplinary reasons. Metsu was not known for a puritanical outlook on life; as long as the players he trusted gave their all on the training ground and on the field of play, they were free to get on with their lives as they wished, as he did himself.

The group he assembled took very little time to gel. As Diouf put it in an interview with Fifa on the 20th anniversary of Senegal's win over France: "Bruno was a coach who'd come out of nowhere and became the most Senegalese person on earth! What I loved about him — but also about Jules-François Bocandé, who was part of the backroom staff — was that when he spoke, we listened. They were like our parents, or our big brothers. We wanted to play for the jersey, to win, to work together. We loved each other."

The improvement in Senegal's results was immediate. A good draw away to Morocco was followed by impressive wins over

Namibia and Algeria, in which Senegal scored seven goals — six of them through Diouf — and conceded none. Come the last round of the qualifiers, Metsu's team needed as large a victory as possible against already eliminated Namibia to make sure of a place in the World Cup. They scored five, to finish top of their group, equal on points with Morocco, but with a far better goal difference. Senegal would be in the World Cup draw.

Diouf was in Monaco, preparing for a league game with his club, RC Lens, when he found out who Senegal's first opponents in Korea would be. "Our coach Joël Müller had arranged it so that we could all watch the draw live," he recalled. "And who did we get? France, of course. At the time, I played alongside guys like Bruno Rodriguez, Cyril Rool, Daniel Moreira and Guillaume Warmuz. As soon as we saw that France would play Senegal, they all got up and started to make fun of me. That was it, they'd already made up their mind — Senegal stood no chance."

***

Senegal were not just France's first opponents in the defence of their title: they should have been the easiest in what everyone agreed was a comfortable group for the world champions, with Denmark and Uruguay completing the quartet. In the Fifa world rankings, which had been published two weeks before the teams met in Seoul, Senegal, ranked 42nd, were still considered to be the sixth-best African nation despite reaching the AFCON final in February, a long way behind the Danes (20th), the Uruguayans (24th) and, of course, reigning champions France, still on top of the tree despite a less-than-convincing string of results in the six weeks leading up to the tournament: a 0-0 draw against Russia in the Stade de France on 17 April, followed a month later by a 1-2 defeat to Belgium and, finally, a pyrrhic 3-2 win over Korea in Seoul just five days before the opening match of the World Cup, a friendly in which Zinédine Zidane suffered the hamstring injury which would keep him out of the French team for the first two games of the tournament. This didn't trouble the French camp unduly. Zidane would be back soon enough.

Still, *Les Bleus* would face Senegal without two players who had lit up the 2001-02 season for their clubs. Arsenal's Robert Pires, described by his manager Arsène Wenger as "probably the best player in the world in his position at the moment", had ruptured the anterior cruciate ligament in his right knee back in March. And now, *Zizou* too was unavailable, *Zizou* the captain, the talisman, the artist who'd scored one of the greatest goals in Champions League history 11 days earlier, a famous left-footed volley which had given Real Madrid their ninth European title.

As the World Cup had been moved forward by a couple of weeks in order to avoid the worst of the heat and humidity of Japan and Korea's summer, players who'd been involved in the so-called 'business end' of the season should have been given as much time as possible to recuperate before being involved in the competition. Zidane should have remained on the bench in Suwon, just as he'd sat out France's previous warm-up match against Belgium; he had also been at his wife Véronique's bedside when she had given birth to their son Theo on 18 May, hours before the sleep-deprived new father boarded his 19-hour flight to Seoul. The first thing Lemerre asked of him when he turned up at the team's training ground was to run a few laps of the track. Zidane would play, not because it made sense, but because he had to.

First, a win was needed to show that the *faux-pas* against the Belgians was just that, a mere slip in rehearsal. Everything would be fine on First Night. The French press corps — which is just as quick and unforgiving as its British equivalent to seize on any sign of weakness or turmoil within the national team — would have had a splendid target to aim at had France suffered another loss. Had they not been Aimé Jacquet's most severe critics right up to the moment when France qualified for the World Cup final four years previously? There was also some national prestige at stake. France, the holders, must prevail against one of the two hosts of the World Cup, especially since this would be much more than a *match de gala* for the Koreans, in front of their own public; as it happens, one of France's many sponsors happened to be a Korean company, who insisted on having as many of *Les Bleus*' foremost players on the pitch of the Suwon World Cup Stadium on this grand occasion. They got what they asked for.

The laborious nature of France's performances before Lemerre, his squad and a bloated retinue of officials (about 50 suits from the *Fédération Française de Football*) left for the Far East had done little to dent their self-confidence and sense of entitlement as the World Cup drew nearer. When, in April of that year, Marcel Desailly had sat down with the *Fédération* to discuss the bonuses the players would be entitled to for their performances at the World Cup, the possibility that they would not get past the group phase had not even been discussed.

Hubris had swept through the French delegation, from the bag-carriers to the panjandrums, and including, it must be said, some of the players. No team had ever won three global tournaments on the trot, not even Pelé's Brazil or Beckenbauer's West Germany.[1] France would. France were the holders. France, so long a country in search of a centre-forward, could call upon the top goal-scorers in the English, French and Italian leagues: Thierry Henry, Djibril Cissé and David Trézéguet. France were the favourites and had already shown — in Euro 2000 — that they could live with that tag, even thrive on it, as demonstrated by Trezeguet's Golden Goal in the final, when they had been outplayed by the Italians for large parts of the game. France had learnt to be *winners*, you see; but those *winners* were exhausted. Patrick Vieira had played 61 games before landing in Korea. The results of the physical tests run in early May at the altitude performance centre of Tignes in the French Alps were catastrophic. As Youri Djorkaeff put it: "We were carbonised."

[1]   Uruguay won the Olympic Games in 1924 and 1928, as well as the 1930 World Cup, but were runners-up in the 1927 Copa America. Brazil, world champions in 1958 and 1962, lost to Argentina in the final of the 1959 South American Championship.

"Many of the players had had their heads turned by what had followed the World Cup win in '98," Emmanuel Petit told me later. "The sponsors were everywhere, and they wanted their money's worth. We should have focused on our job, but no. There was always a function to attend, a hand to shake, or a photo shoot. We were surrounded by people who kept telling us that we were the best, that we couldn't lose. I lost my head a bit myself. It was a mess."

How much of a mess it was we learnt after the event, when journalists embedded with the national team broke their vow of silence and told the story of what had happened at *Les Bleus*' five-star base in Korea, Seoul's Sheraton Grande Hill Walker Hotel and Towers, a story in which some of them had played more than a walk-on part.

Nothing was too good or too expensive for *Les Bleus* and their numerous support staff. Six tons of equipment were shipped to Korea and Japan, 'equipment' which included 20 cases of Château La Lignane and of Domaine de L'Échevin, two estate-bottled Côtes-du-Rhône which were served at team meals, decent enough, but not in the same league as the £4,000 bottle of Romanée-Conti which the head of the *FFF* Claude Simonet[2] ordered at one particularly lavish dinner held in one of the Sheraton's restaurants — the Sheraton, where a number of the players' agents had booked rooms as well; and representatives of the team's sponsors too, of which there were close to 40 in attendance.

Some French players — almost all of them *coiffeurs*, literally 'hairdressers', a term used for those footballers who were not expected to feature in the first 11 — could not resist the temptations of the Sheraton's nightclub, the Sirocco, and of its troupe of female dancers; they could then retreat incognito to their bedrooms by using a 'secret lift' accessible from one of the karaoke booths.

The lack of focus and discipline of *Les Bleus* was compounded by a growing unease within the dressing room. Senior players,

---

[2] Simonet, who was later found guilty of fraud — he had 'cooked' the books of the FFF in order to hide a deficit of over £10m — ran a personal expense bill of close to £50,000 for the 2002 World Cup.

emboldened by their previous successes, questioned their manager's tactical choices. Lemerre intended to stick with a 4-2-3-1 that Dakar-born Patrick Vieira and his stand-in captain Marcel Desailly, in particular, felt inadequate in the absence of Zidane — who would be replaced by Youri Djorkaeff in the playmaker role — and Pires — for whom Sylvain Wiltord was a not entirely convincing substitute. Lemerre wouldn't budge. When, a week before the game, Metsu confronted the Senegalese journalists who had revealed that their team would adopt a 4-1-4-1 formation against the French, with Aliou Cissé sitting in front of the back four ("You want France to win or what?"), Lemerre's reaction was to say: "I've known how they'd play for a month. But I am not used to building my team according to the opponent".

Then there was the Thierry Henry dilemma. It is as a centre-forward that he'd become one of the Premier League's most prolific goal-scorers; but Lemerre had earmarked Henry's old friend (and rival) David Trézéguet to play at the tip of France's attack, pushing the Arsenal striker back to his former position on the left wing. As Trézéguet had scored 32 goals in 46 appearances for Serie A champions Juventus that season, Lemerre's choice made some sense. Henry, however, didn't see it that way, and said so. He was also frustrated by a mysterious injury which had forced him to play a behind-closed-doors training game against Japanese side Urawa Reds with a bandaged knee. The contrast with the mood in the Senegal camp couldn't have been starker.

***

"I remember us chatting before the match." Diouf recalled. "Bruno Metsu came into the changing room and pulled his hair back, as he had a habit of doing. Then he said: 'What can I possibly say to you today? We've been together for a long time now. I know you all so well. You're a crazy bunch. I know that tonight, after the match is finished, people will be talking about you right across the world. Up you get, and show me what you're capable of.'

It was tremendous. We didn't need to say anything. He looked at us and knew we could go out there and win."

On the eve of the game, Metsu had insisted his players used every second of the hour they'd been allotted to get a feel of the pitch they'd face France on. Not so Lemerre, who cancelled the light training session, as it was "not useful". What was clear from the outset, when a light rain freshened up the warm evening air as soon as the game kicked off, was that this Senegal team was in no way afraid of its opponents. As predicted, France had lined up in Lemerre's favoured 4-2-3-1, whilst Senegal had opted for an apparently more conservative 4-1-4-1. Yet it was the Senegalese who created the first genuine chance of the game, as early as the fifth minute, when Diouf, who perhaps played the game of his life on that night, left Desailly clutching at air to find Fadiga, whose shot was far too close to Barthez to cause him any trouble. This was a scene which would be repeated throughout the evening, with Diouf in the role of tormentor, and Leboeuf and Desailly struggling to keep up with his pace and vivacity, to such an extent that France's full-backs Lilian Thuram and Bixente Lizarazu barely ventured past the halfway line until their team trailed on the scoreboard, checking their natural game in order to compensate for their central defenders' lack of mobility.

Les Bleus had their moments; but luck and *sang-froid* deserted them when it mattered. First, Trézeguet, when one-on-one, was just beaten to a dangerous ball by Tony Sylva, whose superb performance on the night was all the more remarkable given he'd spent the season as Monaco's third-choice keeper behind Flavio Roma and Stéphane Porato; then the same Trézéguet, well served by Henry, curled a shot against the post from just inside the area. Yet, just seven minutes later, as it seemed that France was establishing some kind of dominance, right before the half-hour mark, the unthinkable happened. Djorkaeff was caught in possession just inside the Senegal half; the ball was instantly passed into Diouf's path, Diouf who, in three assured touches and a burst of speed, left Leboeuf for dead on the left wing and sent a low cross which none of the retreating Bleus could deal with. The ball bounced off Petit and Barthez to land in the path of the onrushing Papa Bouba Diop, the sole Senegalese player in a crowd of six panicking French defenders. Diop had slipped to the ground but was still able to hook the ball into the empty net from point-blank range[3]. Lizarazu was still appealing for an imaginary offside when most of the Senegal team gathered next to the right corner flag to dance around Diop's shirt. France were shell-shocked, unable to deal with the constant threat of Diouf, unless it was by fouling him, as Petit did just before the break, earning himself the World Cup's first yellow card.

"At half-time, we went into the changing room with a 1-0 lead and big smiles on our faces", Diouf remembered. "We were giving each other high fives. Bruno came in, and he was annoyed. He proceeded to tear strips off us! He said, 'Lads, it's not done yet! There are still 45 to 50 minutes to play. Nothing's in the bag yet. You can give each other high fives after the match.' It was exactly what we needed."

A reaction had to come from France, but whatever was thrown at the Senegal defence was dealt with admirably by Metsu's back four and Tony Sylva, with Aliou Cissé a one-man wall in front of his box. *Les Bleus* set up camp in the Senegalese half, monopolised possession, and created a handful of chances in the second half, the best being misdirected headers by Henry — never the most efficient of strikers in that exercise — and, again, Trézéguet. It had become clear by then that Senegal, though forced to retreat towards their own goal, were winning the physical contest, just like Metsu had won the tactical battle against Lemerre, not that the two were unrelated.

Much had been made of the experience of the French squad prior to the tournament: these were 'big-game players' who were just as successful with their clubs as they'd been with their national

---

[3] Diop later went on to play for four English teams: Fulham, Portsmouth (with whom he won the FA Cup in 2008), West Ham and Birmingham City. He died, aged just 42, on 29 November 2020, a victim of motor neurone disease.

team over the past four years. Of the players Lemerre put in his starting 11 against Senegal, seven had played in the 1998 World Cup final; but seven were also on the wrong side of 30, and were facing one of the youngest teams in the tournament. Diouf was 21. Only one of Metsu's 23 had entered the third decade of his life, the veteran striker Amara Traoré — and he didn't play a single minute in the five games Senegal were involved in in that World Cup.

France pressed until the very end, but could not find a way to break down Metsu's team. Lemerre's substitutions, Dugarry for Djorkaeff on 60 minutes, Cissé for the ineffectual Wiltord on 81, had no discernible impact (Metsu chose to keep the same XI on the pitch until the final whistle). Perhaps Henry and Leboeuf should have done better when presented with half-decent chances at the death. Perhaps. Henry lobbed the ball against the bar; but Fadiga too hit the woordwork. France's failures were part of a story which, as the minutes ticked away, appeared to have been pre-written, as if the Fates had had punishment in mind all along for the arrogance of the champions. Their failure was the manifestation of failings we should have been aware of but — in the case of the French, not of Senegal — chose to ignore until it was too late to address them. In the stadium, when Emirati referee Ali Bujsaim blew the final whistle to the relief of an exultant Korean crowd which had rooted for the underdog all along, the overwhelming feeling was a mixture of shock and elation. Dakar erupted with joy. Paris ... well, Paris still believed in the heroes of '98 and '00, but not for long. Harder questions would soon be asked. What they were we already knew: Senegal had asked and answered them.

"I dreamed of this match, thought about this match and now it's come true," Metsu said. "We had a tactical game plan. We left Diouf up front on his own and deliberately blocked them in midfield. I said before this tournament that we were not going to be the Jamaica of this World Cup. Today, we proved we are a serious team."

***

It was impossible not to think of this extraordinary win as a form of revenge extracted by the former colony over its former overlord. Yet the exuberant celebrations which greeted it in Senegal — and in the whole of West Africa, and in France too, where it is estimated that 300,000 people of Senegalese heritage lived at the time — did not take the confrontational turn which some may have expected. This reflected the uniquely ambiguous relationship between two worlds which first came into contact with each other as early as the 14th century, where subservience, coercion and exploitation co-existed with respect and even affection. I realise that these words might shock a modern British reader, for whom, as I soon realised when I settled in the United Kingdom, all imperialism must be viewed through the prism of their own imperial experience. I also realise that I speak here from the perspective of a Frenchman whose own family was directly caught up in the contradictions and upheavals of the empire and of its violent creation and dissolution.

Yet the truth is that, of all of France's former colonies, Senegal occupies a place all of its own in French history, which goes some way to explain how Bruno Metsu could become a Senegalese hero — even more than Jack Charlton became an Irish hero — and Dakar-born Patrick Vieira one of the most revered, and loved, players in French football history.

The most powerful illustration of this must be the special, and deeply controversial place that the *tirailleurs sénégalais* ('Senegalese riflemen') occupy in French military mythology, in which they are painted as the bravest of the brave, often in sentimental, maudlin tones. Not all of the *tirailleurs sénégalais* hailed from Senegal. Some came from Mali, Cameroon and other French possessions; the core, however, remained Senegalese, as it had been from the outset, when Louis Faidherbe created their first regiment in 1857. The truth is that many of them were forced to bear arms — and die — on the battlefields of the First

World War, to defend a *République* they'd never set foot on; but many others volunteered too, responding to the call of one of the fathers of modern Senegal, Blaise Diagne, the first black African to sit in the French *Chambre des députés*, in 1914, later to become a minister.[4]

For Diagne, a partisan of African empowerment through integration, enlisting in the French Army was a step towards the acquisition of full citizenship rights: it is during the Great War that the people of *les Quatre Communes*, Dakar, Gorée, Rufisque and Saint-Louis were granted these rights, which made them, at least in the eyes of the law, the equals of the citizens of metropolitan France, which explains why the French Army was the only force to deploy racially-integrated regiments in the Great War. The point here is not to paint the French empire as an enlightened if paternalistic overlord, which it was not: it was at its heart exploitative, racist and brutal. Yet, in some cases, of which Senegal may be the most striking, this empire got caught in its fundamental contradiction (pretending to bring republican values of 'freedom' and 'civilisation' to the colonised, in order to exploit and oppress them) to such an extent that a highly ambiguous relationship developed, of which Diagne — and his son Raoul — were prime symbols. Such is the context in which the epochal victory of 31 May should be seen.

This is where the story turns full circle and takes us back to 2002, as Raoul Diagne was the first black man to play for the French football national team.

The tall, long-limbed, elegant Diagne, whose colour was, in another surprising turn, never mentioned in contemporary press reports, was a mainstay of France's most prestigious club, Racing, and of *Les Bleus* throughout the 1930s, a key member of the team which reached the quarter-finals of the 1938 World Cup, a team which, just like its 1998 incarnation, included a

---

[4] A sign of how Diagne was held in high esteem in his native Senegal (when it could have been thought that his integrationist convictions would resonate badly with following generations) is that Dakar's international airport bears his name to this day.

majority of men hailing from ethnic or national minorities. But the son of Blaise Diagne was far more than a distinguished player, a goal-scoring defender of whom it was said that he could occupy any outfield position with distinction. His playing career over — one he finished with US Gorée, in Senegal — he became a successful coach, winning the North African Championship with Algerian club Gallia Sports in 1951; and when Senegal became independent on 4 April, 1960, following a remarkably trouble-free process, he was the obvious choice to take on the newly-formed national team.

Diagne was no longer in charge — his 1938 World Cup team-mate Jules Vandooren was — when Senegal beat a strong French amateur XI in the semi-finals of the 1963 *Jeux de l'amitié* ('Friendship Games'); but he was among the 20,000 spectators, some of whom had arrived at the stadium nine hours before kick-off, that gathered in Dakar to watch the Lions win 2-0, a victory which prompted scenes which were to be repeated 39 years later. "People exulted and congratulated each other in the streets", wrote *Le Monde*'s journalist Jean Couvreur. "But there was no spirit of revenge or animosity: Senegal is one of these African countries where the Frenchman does not encounter hostility". Couvreur might have sweetened the pill for his French readers; and his article is not exempt from a rather unpleasant undertone of paternalism; but what he wrote was not untrue. That win was to be celebrated for far more than a kind of retribution, and what was true a mere three years after independence would also be true in 2002.

In 2002, a 92-year-old Raoul Diagne, the first black French international, sitting in his flat in Créteil, had the joy of watching Papa Bouba Diop score Senegal's most momentous goal. For him, as for Metsu, as for the whole of Senegal, it was and had always been about pride.

S.KOREA & JAPAN 2002

22 JUNE
QUARTER FINALS

S.KOREA
0

SOUTH KOREA
WIN 5-3 ON PENALTIES

SPAIN
0

S.KOREA	SPAIN
1. Lee Woon-jae	1. Iker Casillas
4. Choi Jin-cheul	5. Carles Puyol
20. Hong Myung-bo (c)	6. Fernando Hierro (c)
7. Kim Tae-young OFF	20. Miguel Ángel Nadal
18. Hwang Sun-hong ON (90')	15. Enrique Romero
22. Song Chong-gug	22. Joaquín
5. Kim Nam-il OFF	4. Iván Helguera OFF
13. Lee Eul-yong ON (32')	*19. Xavi ON (93')*
6. Yoo Sang-chul OFF	17. Juan Carlos Valerón OFF
14. Lee Chun-soo ON (60')	*21. Luis Enrique ON (80')*
10. Lee Young-pyo	8. Rubén Baraja
21. Park Ji-sung	11. Javier de Pedro OFF
19. Ahn Jung-hwan	*16. Gaizka Mendieta ON (70')*
9. Seol Ki-hyeon	9. Fernando Morientes

Manager: Guus Hiddink

Manager: José Antonio Camacho

Gwangju World Cup Stadium

Gwangju, South Korea

ATTENDANCE
42,114

REFEREE
Gamal Al-Ghandour (Egypt)

GUILLEM BALAGUE

> 22 June, 2002. Quarter-final of the 2002
> Korea/Japan World Cup. Spain, one of the
> favourites. A Spain with the likes of Raúl, Hierro,
> Puyol, Morientes, Mendieta, Joaquín in their
> squad against South Korea, one of the joint hosts.
> Ring a bell?

"We scored the goals but they did not give them to us," said the Spain national coach José Antonio Camacho, who had warned his players that something did not smell right having seen how referees favoured Korea against Portugal in the group stage, and Italy in the previous round. "We were kicked out by the referees," Real Madrid's Ivan Helguera said. He had not taken part in the penalty shoot-out against the hosts that knocked Spain out after the game finished 0-0 in regular time.

With the fury of a brush fire in August, Spain united in a sense of outrage and anger, traits that occasionally bring this fragmented nation together against a feeling of injustice. The wrath was seen in headlines across not just the Spanish sporting media, but much of Europe's . "Robbery". "Rotten World Cup". "Hands up. The trio of refs buried the hope of Spain". "This World Cup makes us sick". "Horrible referee decisions that always benefited Korea".

They (the officials, Fifa, a conspiracy) snatched our chance of World Cup glory when we were so close. A clear opportunity to go all the way taken from us, by South Korea for God's sake! One of the officials was from the Caribbean, one from Uganda, while the match referee was from Egypt — their level was poor. It was all that was heard in radio and television shows. Pelé added fuel to the fire. "The problem of this World Cup has been the refereeing," he said.

Over the years, the anger acquired some legitimacy. Since 2015, we have evidence of corruption in Fifa and, in particular, from Jack Warner, a former executive who ended up being arrested by the FBI at the beginning of the corruption allegations and who was kicked out of the organisation for getting his hand caught in the cookie jar. Warner (head of the powerful Concacaf and a big fish in the control of Fifa funding) pressured for the inclusion in that game of the linesman Michael Ragoonath, a Trinidadian like himself, despite Ragoonath never having worked as an assistant of the experienced Egyptian referee Gamal Al-Ghandour.

In May 2015, *Corriere dello Sport* wrote a detailed article suggesting that the World Cup was corrupt. Headlined *"ilotavano i Mondiali!"* ("they 'managed' the World Cups"), the piece listed all the ways in which Jack Warner was corrupt: his undue influence; plus the goings-on during that summer tournament, including the selection of referees and strange unjustified payments to Uganda. It did, though, fall short of providing concrete evidence that the Korea games against Italy and Spain were actually 'bought'.

That proof was not needed in Spain — a country built on a culture of mistrust of authorities, the land of conspiracies. Camacho said: "I asked Villar (President of the Spanish FA) who was going to be the ref, South Korea was getting so much help. There were elections at Fifa and Villar backed (Joseph) Blatter (head of Fifa), who had a terrible relationship with the head of refs (Warner)". In fact, the election was just before the World Cup.

Giving his version of the game, Camacho added, "It wasn't just the disallowed goals, the worst were the offsides … by three or four metres, not just centimetres". The Spain national manager always said that the referees "did not have the level for such a game" and blames Al-Ghandour for hiding the assistants' decisions. He did not mince his words. They were *"tocados"*, literally 'touched', but a euphemism for 'bought'. "I was convinced we would get to the final," he said, which was not a far-fetched possibility in a mediocre World Cup where a half-decent Germany did manage to get to the final, where they lost to the Brazil of

Ronaldo, Ronaldinho, Rivaldo and Roberto Carlos. Spain had enjoyed a spectacular group stage (nine points, nine goals scored against Slovenia, Paraguay and South Africa), although their win on penalties against Ireland should have shown the world that perhaps they were not the force they seemed.

There is more. The former referee and spokesman of the Fifa Referee Committee, Edgardo Codesal, resigned his post after the World Cup and admitted the pressure put on him by Jack Warner with regards to the appointment of linesman Ragoonath. To add to the suspicion, it was reported that, back in Trinidad, he used to earn £37 per game, while Ali Tomusange, the first referee from Uganda to appear in a World Cup, earned just £7 per match.

Every documentary that looks back tells the same story. Witnesses reinforce their view when they talk to each other and reflect on what happened. Fernando Morientes declared "the attitude of the ref was not professional, it was a robbery." Gaizka Mendieta, a peacemaker by nature and one of the mildest men you would ever meet, to this day says he would be tempted to do things to the referee if he ever met him again.

And yet …

Spanish media has interviewed Al-Ghandour, who was refereeing his second World Cup having officiated at five African cups, including a final. But we have decided not to listen to what he says, opting instead to make him the villain of this pantomime. "Tell me what I did bad! The first goal was fairly disallowed, a Spanish player holds a Korean in the box. In the other decisions, it was the linesmen that made the mistakes. I never spoke to them again. It is clear that the Joaquín ball did not go out but I had blown the whistle well before the striker finished. We made a mistake on an offside later on, the linesman again, I have to trust them.

"I was accused by the Spanish of being given a car by the Koreans. I am Muslim, I cannot accept bribery. It was one of my best games. Two days after, in a meeting with Fifa in Japan we agreed that I had taken plenty of right decisions. The referee inspector told me he had given me an 8.7. It was also agreed that my biggest mistake was not to give a red to the Spanish player after his tackle in the first half. Nobody remembers I gave a penalty to Spain against Paraguay in the group stages that at first might not have looked like a penalty." It was converted by Hierro, the definitive 3-1 that qualified Spain for the knockout stages. Al-Ghandour, now a commentator for *BeinSport*, adds, "Spain had chances and missed them, they shouldn't have gone to the penalty shootout."

Ask any Spaniard and they will talk about two disallowed goals and three clear offsides wrongly given against Spain, plus the excessive and continuous use of force by South Korea. But I did not have that same impression at the end of the game. In fact, nobody looked in detail at what South Korea did that day. The football side of things. How they held their own against Spain and Italy. Was it really just refereeing decisions that took them that far? How many of them were really mistakes? And, how was it that Raúl did not play a part? He had a muscle problem, but was he being rested for the semis against Germany by a confident manager?

We remember the result of that game and also the irate reaction in Spain, but when you scratch a little bit, you find that things were not as clear. That is the unsteady nature of history, which relies on objectivity that is impossible to find in football, and much less in the changing waters of memory.

Only if we could really travel in time could we align facts and truth in such a way that doubts could be isolated and ignored, where we could get a better picture of what happened. I was thinking of all that when I discovered a file, buried between thousands, where I kept the notes I wrote during that Korea and Japan World Cup.

Reading them, I confirm a feeling I have had for 20 years. I think I went to a different game to the one watched by the rest of Spain. In fact, I kind of did.

***

I have been in Seoul for around three days ... I think. More or less. I have already lost track of time. My body had to get used to the new timetable, Korea is seven hours ahead of Spain. It required a long sleep on the first day. Or was it the second?

The World Cup had started, and that was good. There was not much more to preview, to predict. All rubbish of course — Senegal go and beat France in the inaugural match and all the predictions go out the window. In any case, who looks at those? I guess there is always an 'Itoldyouso' around.

I'm writing this from the coach that takes me to Seoul airport (heading to Gwangju to see Spain-Slovenia) and it's 10.45am. It's warm and humid, but not as much as Barcelona in June. It doesn't rain, but everybody expects it to start pouring cats, dogs and pigeons from the 15th.

The South Korean capital is a very modern city, built very quickly. It was destroyed during the Korean war in the fifties, so they took the opportunity to try to build a new Manhattan, although what they got looks more like a new Milton Keynes with a few more high-rises. To be fair to the city, I haven't had the chance to explore it much and I don't think I will. But that never stops any traveller going home with a categoric impression of the place.

Food is mostly very Western. I have had hamburgers, fried chicken, salads. I'm off to a smaller city now, so I hope I can taste a bit of the local cuisine, which I believe is spicy and a rather strange mixture of sweet and sour sauces. Sounds like England.

So far, I have spent my time in hotels and in the IMC, the International Media Centre, which is the place journalists work. Or appear to work. The truth is I have never felt so little pressure. When the matches are played, people are waking up at home, so that gives us plenty of time to write our pieces. We all miss that feeling of having just one hour to come up with 2,000 words. At least that gave us an excuse if it came out crap. We might be about to discover that it wasn't the lack of time that made us incomplete writers. Let me make it clear that I am talking about everybody else of course, as I am producing wonderful stuff.

My best piece? It has to be the one I did soon after my arrival when I visited the 38th Parallel that separates the two Koreas, with the US national team. I met up with Kasey Keller, US and Rayo Vallecano goalkeeper, and he was great. "Of course, join us," he told me.

He thought the State department had put them in a difficult position by forcing them to go to see the US forces stationed on the border without really explaining that it was the US and USSR which first divided this country. The players were told how stupid the North Koreans are for not wanting democracy and McDonalds. In so many words. The truth, of course, is that most of the players didn't even know there were two Koreas until that morning.

Claudio Reyna seemed quite impressed by the four South Koreans (not North Americans) who stand next to the line which divides the country, looking towards the enemy. As a US soldier explained, they make themselves a target, so if North Korea wants to start the war, the first thing they will shoot is these four. So they stand there, not moving a single muscle, for hours, waiting for a bullet.

***

In Spain (media, commentators, fans), we used to go to every summer tournament convinced that we were candidates to win it, even if we had never done so and our previous best occurred way back in 1950 when we reached the semi-final. We related the extreme focus and European success of our own domestic competition to an assumption that this would automatically be transferred to the national side. Of course, our players were the best-known and most talked about — we hardly knew of any others. The foreign leagues could not be followed on television and we tended to get to know only rivals from our Champions League matches.

Barcelona had lost in the semi-final of the Champions League against Real Madrid. *Los Galacticos* (Zidane, Figo, Raúl, Roberto Carlos, Hierro, Makélélé, under manager Vicente del Bosque) ended up winning it against Michael Ballack's Bayer Leverkusen with the help of *Zizou*'s stunning volley It was their third win in five years.

The plucky changing room of Rafa Benítez's Valencia (a club that had reached two Champions League finals in the previous two seasons) won La Liga for the fifth time in their history with a hard-working midfield that included David Albelda (injured for the World Cup) and the industrious Rubén Baraja. That season, the runners-up were Deportivo La Coruña, with Real Madrid (nine points back) and Barcelona (11 points) following them in the table.

There seemed to be enough ingredients for a very good summer tournament. Before the final Spain call-ups were confirmed, debates were raging. Raúl had reached 50 games in a pre-World Cup friendly against Holland and was inheriting the authority accumulated by Fernando Hierro and Pep Guardiola in previous years as they neared the end of their international careers. In fact, Pep could not make the squad for Asia because of a problem with his right knee. Some of the media favoured a system like the one used by France in 1998, which would allow Spain to protect Juan Carlos Valerón, a slow but very talented number 10, while others preferred the 4-4-2 with wingers (Joaquín or Vicente) used more often by the popular national manager Camacho. Spain went into the tournament in good spirits having qualified impressively, drawing just two games and winning the rest.

Former Real Madrid player Camacho has a jumbled, slightly hyper way of speaking which sees him jump from idea to idea in a disorderly way and never really complete a sentence. But this is at least coupled with a straight way of talking that makes him charming, uncomplicated and friendly with the media, most of whom felt comfortable with a former Real Madrid figure at the helm. He had proven with Espanyol that he could maximise the potential of a side without a very complex style.

His two very short stays in charge of Real Madrid confirmed that he would never commit to anyone, whoever they might be, if he did not feel he could get along with them, a trait that many envied him for. In 1998, he resigned just 22 days after his appointment at Real Madrid because he did not believe that he would have available to him a side that he could consider to be his, that he could control and that would represent the values he had defended as a player. And although he returned to the bench at the Bernabéu under chairman Florentino Pérez, the *Galáctico* policy — that left little or no room for coaching innovation — meant he would leave his post again just 90 days later. You could have been forgiven for wondering if he was a manager that could cope under pressure.

***

Nobody was meeting my expenses so I booked myself into a cheap hotel, appropriately categorised as a 'love hotel'. It served a purpose because it was located just 30 kilometres from Ulsan, one of the six big cities in South Korea, where I was going to get my first look at the pre-tournament favourites Brazil against Turkey. It would have been nice to have been a little closer to the city, but being in a 'love' hotel did allow me to learn some things about myself. For those of you who don't know of these establishments, they are hotels that you can rent for a few hours at a time. "Are you staying until morning?" was the first question I was asked, followed swiftly by, "Are you sure?" It's the sort of place that you would take a 'friend'. A room with thin walls and plenty of thick towels, and a VHS player with two different tapes. Every day, the tape left at the bottom gets replaced by another one, similar to the one at the top, and in no time, the cleaner (or VHS changer) gets to know all your mental machinations. I did not watch any, I must add. Promise.

***

The final squad was announced on 13 May. Goalkeepers: Cañizares, Casillas and Ricardo. Defence: Curro Torres, Puyol, Nadal, Hierro, Helguera, Romero and Juanfran. Midfielders: Baraja, Xavi, Albelda, Valerón, Mendieta, Joaquín, Sergio, Luis Enrique and De Pedro. Forwards: Raúl, Tristán, Morientes and Luque. Just five players left from the disappointing France World Cup, where Spain were knocked out at the group stage, and six from the Euro 2000 campaign when they were beaten by World Cup winners and eventual champions France in the quarter-final.

Camacho, whose natural instinct was to ask the team to send the ball wide and cross, was uncertain whether to play that way or use a 4-4-2 system with Valerón but without real wingers. His main worry was whether or not the five European and four league champions, together with the rest of his squad had enough nous and were streetwise enough to be able to win. Raúl was one of the few that were leaders in their teams, mostly organised around talented foreign imports. Camacho needed to know if they were capable of defending and attacking set pieces well, and whether they could manage games to a degree that would mean they would not be susceptible to football's fickle finger of fate, which had so often in the past marked Spain's destiny. A mature team should not be affected by things that they cannot control.

In goal was the 21-year-old Iker Casillas, at the time fighting for the number one shirt with Valencia's goalkeeper Cañizares, and also number two at Real Madrid, where César was preferred by Vicente del Bosque. Sometimes in football, your career advancement can come about as a direct result of someone else's misfortune. The story has it that prior to the World Cup when stepping out of the shower, Cañizares dropped a bottle of cologne and in trying to stop it, stepped on it, cutting a tendon in the process. He would play just 10 more times for his country, while Casillas would go on to earn 167 caps and become the second-most capped player in Spain's football history.

***

There is still more than three weeks before I return home. I have plenty to do. I have to visit a volcano if I can, get an oriental massage (which is free for journos in the Media Centres) and I am also planning to visit a Sumo wrestlers' residence while in Japan. I will be kept busy by a Spain that has left no doubt in their credentials as a seeded nation by cruising through their group stage matches. Our first victory was against Slovenia (3-1), the first time since 1950 that we had won the opening game of the tournament and then despite conceding the first goal against Paraguay, we turned it around with a 3-1 victory (including a penalty converted by Hierro) that took us to the next round — the first time (again since 1950) that we had won the first two games. With the B side, we beat South Africa too.

There was a rumour doing the rounds yesterday. Not sure it could be noticed on the telly, but the crowd noise in the France-Senegal game and others, sounded more like a computer game. When excited they did a strange sort of an increasing 'uuuuh', a bit like a kettle about to boil up, which started and finished always at the same time, without warning. An Italian journo told me the organisers, unsure about the response of the neutral Korean fans, had connected a special effects CD to the speakers whose volume went up or down depending on the danger of the move.

It is a strange World Cup. In the Japanese streets it does not seem like anything particular is happening and you hardly see any foreign fans, probably because it is so expensive to get here. Korea is a bit different.

I needed to get some local Korean cash and I had brought American Express cheques to change. I walked from my 'Ulsan' hotel that was actually nowhere near Ulsan, to the nearest town. I say 'town' but it was in fact a village that I came across around an hour later consisting of one main street and a row of bungalows. I asked a young lady where I could find a bank. I then asked an older man. Then two teenagers. I couldn't make myself understood.

But young or old, male or female, the one common denominator was all of them mentioned the World Cup. Football, or better said, the event that was taking place, was in every conversation after the national team had picked up seven points from their opening three games. If someone started talking about it, others walking past would stop to share the moment with whoever was discussing it. The traditional restrictive Korean relational networks seemed to have loosened. The nation was mobilised around a common interest that transcended age, class, locality.

The nationalistic fervour saw the novelty phenomenon of the flag used as a fashion item, and could be seen in cars and windows. It moved from being a holy and sacred object, to something that was as popular as it was secular.

I expertly mimed the word 'bank' only for everyone to point to the grocery store. "No ... no money, coins, exchange ...". A middle-aged woman took me by the hand and led me to the store. A man was sitting at the back behind an old table next to where they kept the vegetables. "Bank," she said. Ah.

I was invited to sit. I got my cheques out. The man looked at them and waited for my instructions. "I give you this and you give me money". That did not register with the man who smiled patiently while still holding onto the cheques. All of a sudden it hit me; the absurdity of the social agreement that makes us exchange pieces of paper for other pieces of paper. "No, no," he kept saying. "Yes, yes," I insisted. We both laughed.

Extra help was required. He decided to make a phone call. There is always someone you can call to sort out those minor pitfalls we encounter as we limp through life. Not this time, however. In broken English, which I thanked him for, he told me someone had found a solution. "I keep these. You come in three days. I give you money." No, no, that is not how it goes, I told him. Another three calls were made, an agreement was reached and the final exchange made at long last, bringing me handfuls of the local currency I would be needing.

Sensing I was now on a roll, I asked him for advice. "Anywhere to eat?" The smile across his face grew visibly bigger. Standing up he deposited all the paperwork into a drawer and beckoned me to follow him. The bank was closing for the day. It must have been around four in the afternoon. What, I wondered, would be open in a small little village at this time of the day? Nothing, as it turned out. But he asked the owner of the only restaurant in town to open for me. I was welcomed in straight away and pointed towards one of those tables at knee level where you sit on the floor. The bank man sat in front of me and the food started arriving. My companion did not want to eat, he just wanted to accompany me. Delicious meat and vegetables in little plates were consumed in between my constant smiling at my hosts. Our English did not go any further. Although there is always football talk.

I congratulated them on their victory against Italy and then attempted to chat about the controversial extra-time, with the sending off of Totti for diving in the Korean box despite there being clear contact; the unfairly-disallowed Tomassi goal for an offside that wasn't. I mentioned a possible conspiracy, refereeing mistakes, how they had been helped by the officials. That way of thinking was so alien to them that I might as well have been talking about organising a bike trip to Mars. They jumped again remembering the golden goal that took them to the quarters. The restaurant owner, still standing by us, offered more tea and food.

I tried to explain that Spain, having struggled, but finally beaten Ireland on penalties, were going to meet Korea without Raúl, our best player, who was injured. They did not seem that bothered that we were favourites or by who was going to win. They were just so terribly happy about having visitors and above all were looking forward with great anticipation and excitement for what they felt was one of their nation's biggest-ever days.

I was not allowed to pay. I then needed to get a bus to save myself the hour-long walk back to my hotel. My 'bank manager' took me to the stop, embraced me warmly before handing the driver a note. The driver in turn smiled at me, nodding wisely, as if in confirmation that he was aware of his instructions, before finally telling me when I had reached my destination.

***

The Spanish players watched the Italy-Korea game too and discussed two ideas: the Koreans are physically very strong and consistent, plus referees clearly help them. The group were told they had to prepare for things not to go their way. Camacho allowed the idea of unfair influence of referees to fester in the head of everyone in the group. He had talked to the head of the FA about it and made it part of the pre-game chat: be careful, he warned them more than a few times.

Training the day before the match was eventful. The facility, where Korea had just been working, was closed. When it finally opened for the Spanish team, there was neither hot water nor electricity. Showers were cold and in the dark. Camacho and the players started accumulating reasons as to how and why the organisers were conspiring against them.

Raúl was told his injury had not healed sufficiently. Despite his absence, a splendid generation of Spanish players, unbeaten that summer and most of whom were in their prime stood just one game away from Spain's first World Cup semi-final for 52 years.

To witness it, I had to make my way from Japan to Korea to get to that quarter-final. In an international tournament jointly organised by two nations, what could possibly go wrong?

***

"Ah, no, sorry, impossible." That is no way, one would think, to start planning a trip that was going to take me from Shizuoka, the stadium in Japan where Brazil would play England, to the Korean city of Gwangju where the following day I would see Spain beat Korea. I knew it was going to be complicated — I had 22 hours between the end of one game and the start of the other and the two cities are separated by a sea and over a thousand kilometres — but I assumed that World Cup would have in place a plan. "Ah, no, totally impossible," insisted the woman from the travel agency.

My plan was certainly one filled with potential pitfalls. Flights between the two cities had been full for weeks and I had no intention of crossing the Sea of Japan by ferry — it takes three days. I returned to the travel agency the next day unable to process just why I could not make the trip to a place that on the map lay just three fingers width away to the west of Shizouka.

The woman, seeing me again, welcomed me with traditional Japanese politeness. The message, however, was the same. "I told you it's impossible." What she did not know was that I had come prepared. A colleague had discovered that Gwangju could be reached via Fukuoka, an airport in southern Japan that would take me to Seoul and then two coaches would get me to my destination, a bit like going from London to Manchester, via Edinburgh. But, if everything went on time, it would get me to the match with just five minutes to spare before kick off. But get me there it would.

The whole trip had its perils. It needed the Brazil-England game not to go to penalties so I could catch the last train combination, with two transfers, to Fukuoka, and then a taxi that would take me to the hotel in which I would spend the night near the airport. I had then to catch an early plane to Seoul from where I would make my way, via two coaches, to the stadium, 250 kilometres away.

If all went to plan, 22 hours after setting off from Shizuoka I would be entering the Gwangju stadium as the two teams made their way onto the field. Spain were poised to make history; it was all worth it.

After convincing the woman at the travel agency of my cunning intentions, I asked her to book the corresponding planes, train and taxi that I would be requiring. Unfortunately, the agency did not specialise in trains or coaches, neither in taxis, and there was the added problem that I could not pay for my plane ticket with Visa, which was a little inconvenient bearing in mind that I didn't have any Japanese yen. I could do it all by phone, the woman told me. Ah, makes sense, of course!

Undaunted, I made the necessary arrangements by phone from my hotel. "No!" I barked down the phone, "I want to go from Shizuoka to Fukuoka, at no time have I mentioned Ibaraki or Miyagi!"

The following day, the Brazil v England match finished in normal time, with the South Americans crushing European dreams after a set-piece goal from 30 metres or so from Ronaldinho. I set off on my journey.

It began well. I got to Fukuoka without any problems and I even managed to snatch about five hours of much-needed sleep. The travelling between countries and on my own was catching up with me. The next morning though, the plane landed late in Seoul. There then followed a number of security checks, the fourth of which took longer than usual, perhaps because I was a foreigner, maybe because I had had my passport stamped in some of the world's more 'suspicious' places (Jordan, Cuba, Israel, China ... Canada?). I was openly wearing my World Cup press pass as we had been told it would help "speed up" any such procedures. Nope.

In order to get to the stadium, I had to take two buses from Seoul airport. I had not much time to think, time was running out. Feeling tired and restless, I opted to take a taxi from the airport to Gwangju. It would cost me the proverbial arm and leg, but at that point money was the least of my worries.

Surprisingly, the taxi driver confused a nervous gesture from me as an invitation to drink the iced tea I had bought for myself for the upcoming three-hour trip. I still wonder what gave him the impression I was inviting him to it. His English was limited and he double-checked my destination. I insisted, that yes, I did want to go to Gwangju. He kept looking at me amazed and I shrugged my shoulders. He must be the only South Korean not to know what is happening today.

Traffic was horrendous but at least it did allow me to ponder briefly what advantages there might be to listening to the game on Korean radio. Absolutely none, I calculated. I fell asleep just as the traffic started to move more fluidly.

I woke up almost three hours later. The game was about to start but we were arriving. The conspicuous lack of atmosphere as we made our way to the stadium made me suspicious. There was the occasional Korean, wearing his country's red shirt but not much more around. A very thin, irregular line of people seemed to be queuing by the ground.

The taxi driver was overjoyed as he opened the door for me having made it to the stadium at the scheduled time ... five minutes before kick off. Then he pointed out the ground. "Wonju stadium," he said. The Wonju stadium has only got one tier, so it didn't take me too long to do the maths. And the phonetics.

There is a subtle sound difference between Gwangju and Wonju. The more observant amongst you will realise that Wonju is lacking a 'G' as well as being the owner of an 'O' not present in Gwangju. I was not where I needed to be. Wonju is 600 kilometres from the stadium in which the game was about to kick off.

As I handed over 250 dollars for my semi-comatose trip to a part of South Korea I had not intended to visit, my initial anger was swiftly replaced by hysterical laughter at the absurdity of it all.

I positioned myself strategically in the centre of the Wonju pitch, surrounded by 15,000 hysterical Koreans, mostly girls under the age of 15 who seemed to make up the bulk of the Korean crowd at every World Cup match, but also plenty of older people. Grounds like these had been filled in every town in the country at that time.

The two screens positioned at each corner of the ground were not big enough to see details of the game and the crowd only became very noisy when the camera did a close up of their heroes, or when Hiddink joked with the referee, which happened once or twice.

I was looking forward to hearing their silence as Spain knocked South Korea out of the World Cup.

***

When the Spanish national side arrived at the Gwangju stadium, the security men asked first Camacho and then the rest to show their credentials. "What?" the manager shouted, clearly distressed. "We are, you know, the other team." The humidity was considerable and his shirt started to show wet patches under his jacket.

He saw the vice-president of the Korean federation and owner of a big Korean automobile firm start to walk around the pitch and talk to the referees. He saw it as a sign of things to come, and shared that thought — "What is he doing here?"

Spain replaced the injured Raúl with Joaquín and reinforced the wings, as well as adding a physical midfield. They starting line up was Casillas; Puyol, Hierro, Nadal, Romero; Baraja, Helguera; Joaquín, Valerón, De Pedro; and Morientes.

In recent years, South Korean football had been growing, with forward Ahn having signed for Perugia and Seol playing for Anderlecht. After that tournament, Park and Chun Soon, who started on the bench, would move to Europe. In their fifth consecutive World Cup, coach Guus Hiddink had been working with a very risky 3-4-3 system that imposed a high defensive line, plus adding pressure in all parts of the pitch, controlling the ball and using a lot of calculated movements into space to surprise their rivals.

Al-Ghandour had been given the chance to referee Spain for the second time in this tournament.

Somehow, after 90 minutes neither team had managed to score.

***

From a distance, and without the interference of commentators or colleagues interpreting the action, it is easier to notice on the TV screen the pattern of the teams. You might miss the detail of a dribble or what exactly Camacho is telling the linesman (you just get that he is being aggressive), but a picture was becoming clear — the team in white (South Korea) always had two or three players near the ball when Spain had it. And they stretched wide and at length when they had it themselves.

Spain were struggling to create a consolidated way of attacking: they did not keep the ball for long enough, played long too often, the full-backs did not get forward, they could not find Valerón or other players that could offer an opening. And they were not adapting to what was happening, in an alarming lack of collective ideas. The ball to the winger Joaquín was the most common tactic, and he was sharp and willing and more than ready to immerse himself totally in all aspects of the game, even diving for a couple of fouls that ended up being well defended by the hosts.

Korea were brilliantly coordinated, one- and two-touch football that only lacked precision in the last decision. They reduced spaces constantly, their lines were close together and the pressure was asphyxiating in the geometrical spider web they created and maintained. They needed the linesmen to be alert because they were playing offsides to stop Spain finding space in behind.

The only influence on my analysis was the youthful cheers of the Korean fans, still enthusiastic and hopeful, shouting with relief when the soft shooting of Spain was easily gathered by the goalkeeper Lee Woon-jae. They kept looking at each other in amazement that this was happening to them. They also looked at me wondering what I was doing there. I exchanged a lot of smiles with a lot of people during that match.

Spain were lucky to keep 11 men on the pitch when the full back Enrique Romero stepped on Nam-il who had to leave the pitch injured minutes later. Frustrated as they were not growing on the pitch, the Spaniards (Baraja, Helguera from behind, Morientes) were not afraid to tackle hard. The Koreans made life uncomfortable but were not overtly aggressive. Romero was in a clear offside position and the ref had blown his whistle when Morientes scored before half-time.

In the 50th minute, Al-Ghandour disallowed a Korea own goal after a Spain free kick. There were normal clashes when the ball arrived in the box, but the referee understood the scorer, Kim Tae-young, had been pushed by Helguera's elbow.

The movement of the Koreans, who enjoyed going forward with short elaborate passing and then looking for runs in behind, was constant for the first hour of the game with and without the ball, with some successful changes of player positions to correct their weaknesses. The first big chance of the game fell to Park who shot from the corner of the six yard box and needed a strong hand and a big save from Casillas. The tiredness of a humid and hot afternoon and the fear of losing meant not much happened in the minutes before extra time.

Even while Spain were resting and preparing, Camacho kept protesting to the Trinidadian linesman and even got hold of his arm to take him away from the Spanish bench area. There was no collective chat, whereas Hiddink was gathering his side calmly to give them instructions.

Just two minutes into extra time, Joaquín left Lee Young-pyo for dead, crossing the ball before it had gone out of play. Linesman Ragoonath begged to differ, raising his flag immediately. Accepting the linesman's decision, the referee immediately blew his whistle and what happened next was directly influenced by that decision. The goalkeeper jumped but did not stretch his arms, the defender didn't defend, the striker (Morientes) cushioned the contact, in fact everyone acted in the full knowledge that what they were doing at that precise moment in time was not going to be counted. While there had certainly been an earlier mistake from the officials, this was not a 'disallowed goal'.

Spain could only try to find a tired Joaquín, who ended up stretching and playing as a centre-forward, unable to run any more, and used counterattacking as their only weapon. Twice very tight offsides were given by a matter of centimetres, this time by Tomusange, one of which would have left Luis Enrique on his own and the other not a clear goal chance, but one that would have created the opportunity of a cross.

Morientes hit the post and Mendieta kicked the ball high in the follow up in what was Spain's best chance of the whole game. Hwang fluffed his lines on the edge of the six-yard box in what was Korea's best moment of extra time.

And then finally, with penalties looming, Spain won a corner, only for the referee to blow for full time before they could take it. The game went to penalties and the explosive frustration felt by all the Spanish players either on the pitch or on the bench was palpable. For two minutes the only thing that any of them could think of was that they had been robbed.

***

Casillas did not stop any of the five superbly hit penalties taken by the Korean players, who had been practicing them the day before and a few times during the summer. Joaquín, the youngest player in the squad and, as he admitted then, not "a penalty specialist", missed his, and Myung-bo scored the winning one. Korea went to the semi-final of the World Cup.

The Spanish players ran towards the linesmen and Al-Ghandour while the whole of Korea exploded with pleasure and shock. Morientes cried, Xavi consoled him. Luque shouted at Ragoonath. Juanfran too. Helguera had to be stopped a few times as he wanted to sort it there and then with the assistants. Al-Ghandour first and then Camacho, who shielded the officials, stopped the Spanish players. The referee seemed to wear a half-smile, bewildered by the fury of the Spaniards, but that incensed them even more. Camacho decided to take the Egyptian away from the scene and towards the tunnel. Hierro told the referee it was the linesmen they were against. Every Spaniard left thinking both of them had been bought in order to benefit the home team.

Later on, once everyone had cooled down, Spanish players exchanged their views with the media. Not Raúl. He left the stadium without speaking. His forced smile said a lot. He was on the way to fight for a *Ballon d'Or*, the first Spanish player close to winning it since Luis Suárez did so in 1960. Why had he, on the way to becoming the man of the tournament after scoring three goals and having transferred his great partnership with Morientes from Real Madrid to the national side, not played a single minute against Korea? Camacho said he was injured and there was a potential semi-final with Germany to keep an eye on. Raúl, after a few double sessions of physiotherapy, wanted to take part in the game, and said as much to the doctor, Genaro Borrás. He knew the risks of making his tiny muscle tear worse, but was happy to take them. Too late now.

***

Nobody ever proved the bias of the linesmen, but things were done incorrectly and Fifa admitted as much when they modified their criteria for the selection of officials — from then on, all would be from the same country to ensure better communication and performance.

I was lucky to see the game where I did. Mauricio Pochettino says football is a context of emotions. I separate them — it is context and emotions. They can both add to our understanding and reading of a match, and they can both bring different conclusions. Despite initial concerns in South Korea, hosting the event became a pivotal event that brought both economic benefits and national revitalisation in the years after. Winning helped of course. When I walked away from the ground, following the masses, unaware of the narrative that was going to take hold in my country, I felt a sense of being part of a group that had found momentary happiness, that thought they were special, that they had helped create a world where industry and organisation was rewarded. The fact that a nation had become richer and more complex through a football event lessened my pain of the defeat.

Emotions last longer, especially rage, and they are still very high when witnesses look back at that quarter-final today. What took place, in the Spanish eye, was daylight robbery. End of! But ... when everyone sees a football game the same way, despite the millions of contexts and emotions, be suspicious. There are always other ways of looking at things. Were Cristiano Ronaldo and Lionel Messi really close in terms of influencing a game? Was Spain an offensive team when they eventually did win the World Cup, even though they won all their games by just a goal's difference? Why has cheating always been part of English football but never admitted? Was it raw talent that made the Brazilians the best footballers and the most admired all over the world or was it science? Is 2-0 really a more dangerous lead to have than 1-0, and is there really a problem with scoring too early? We will not all agree in our answers to these questions and a thousand more besides. And that is how it should be.

So what game was played that day in Gwangju? The one for which Korea deserves the plaudits or the one where Spain discovered, again, that luck was not on their side?

When Paul McCartney is asked about the diverse versions of even the smallest of details of the Beatle's biography, he tends to say the following: "In an earthquake, you get many different versions of what happened by all the people that saw it."

"And they're all true."